SWIMMING TO FREEDOM

SWIMMING

TO

FREEDOM

MY ESCAPE FROM

CHINA AND THE

CULTURAL REVOLUTION

AN UNTOLD STORY

~

KENT WONG

ABRAMS PRESS, NEW YORK

Library of Congress Control Number: 2020944982

ISBN: 978-1-4197-5150-9
eISBN: 978-1-64700-186-5

Printed and bound in the United States
10 9 8 7 6 5 4 3 2 1

Abrams books are available at special discounts when purchased in quantity
for premiums and promotions as well as fundraising or educational use. Special
editions can also be created to specification. For details, contact specialsales@
abramsbooks.com or the address below.

Abrams Press® is a registered trademark of Harry N. Abrams, Inc.

ABRAMS The Art of Books
195 Broadway, New York, NY 10007
abramsbooks.com

DEDICATION

This memoir tells a story of the heroic freedom swimmers, a by-product of the political upheaval in China during a bygone era. But my heart in writing this memoir is for my mother.

Every friend of my family called my mother "Mommy," just like I did. Some were even older than her! Mommy was caring, and she was witty. She made us laugh with her smooth voice and calm bearing. Her presence was one of those unique elements that make a dwelling a home one treasures for life.

Mommy was apolitical. Her heart was solely with her children. During the twenty-seven years she lived in Communist China, from 1951 to 1978, the world around her was against her—depriving her of peace and joy, burdening her with worries and threats, punishing her with separation from her husband and then three of her children, torturing her with the knowledge that her children were enduring harsh labor in a poor village without hope; and frightening her with the loss of her children as they escaped to Hong Kong while she remained behind, defenseless. All she could do was to pray to Heaven—alone, in the dead of the night, crying and clutching burning sticks of incense—to open Its eyes.

For her, Heaven did open Its eyes. Her children survived and succeeded, and she was allowed to leave China in 1978, becoming a proud U.S. citizen and living in America for thirty-three years, until she passed away peacefully in 2011. But there were mothers whom Heaven ignored, or still ignores . . .

This is for Mommy and for all mothers like her.

CONTENTS

"IT'S YOUR TIME TO FLY AWAY"

I LEARNED EARLY ON THAT some lives end abruptly, but I didn't know why. The elementary school I attended was across the street from a funeral home. The sound of blaring trumpets and popping firecrackers from the funeral services punctuated our classroom lessons. I was reminded of death almost daily. Would it happen to me? Who decided when a life should end? Soon, death became a routine part of my school life, no different from standing up straight to greet the teacher when she walked into the classroom.

One day, I saw a weeping mother standing outside the funeral home holding in her trembling hands a picture of a beautiful little girl. The girl's innocent eyes and cheerful face lingered in my head that night as I stared at the dusty lightbulb shining dimly from our concrete ceiling.

"What's eating you?" Nothing could escape the eyes of my mother, whom I called Mommy, as she tucked the mosquito netting under my mattress. She did it every night. Several mosquitoes had been buzzing outside it, looking for a way to get in to suck my blood.

Mommy and I in Hong Kong, 1949.

"Mommy, what will happen to me when I die?"

"You're too young to ask this question."

"I want to know."

"Is the funeral home bothering you? That's the only issue I have with your school."

"Today it was a little girl, Mommy."

"Death comes to all ages."

"Who decides when a person should die?"

Mommy paused, "Who else? Heaven. Heaven decides."

"When will it happen to me?"

"Now you're scaring me." Mommy loosened the taut netting and sat on the edge of my bed. "You've said something like this before."

"What did I say?"

"I was carrying your youngest sister. One night, you told me, 'Mommy, I'll die if I have a brother.'"

"Did I say that? No, I didn't." I couldn't believe it.

"Yes, you did. You were serious, and I couldn't sleep that night."

"Was I being bad?" I didn't want to be bad. Mommy always told others that I was a good boy.

"No. You just surprised me. I thought it might be Heaven talking to me."

"How can Heaven talk to you? It's in the sky."

"By dreams, or maybe by way of your mouth."

"By Buddha, too?"

"I've never heard it said that way. But why not? Heaven has Buddha to tell the Chinese what to do, and God to tell the foreigners."

"But Buddha doesn't talk. See? I tricked you." I chuckled.

"Then by a fortune-teller." Mommy was getting impatient.

"Can I ask a fortune-teller?"

"No, you can't. You talk to Mommy."

"I want to tell the fortune-teller that Heaven isn't fair."

"The world isn't fair. But Heaven will watch over you and protect you."

"I want It to protect you too, Mommy."

Mommy smiled. "Yes, It has. It has also given me a good boy. A good boy who needs a good night's sleep."

Fortunately, no more little girls or little boys passed through the funeral home that I was aware of, but the sounds of screeching trumpets and popping firecrackers remained throughout my elementary school days.

Mommy was right. Heaven must have been watching over me, for I had another sister, four in all, and no brother.

I was not bothered again by the thought of my own death until fourteen years later, when I reached the lowest point in my life and when I was pushed—by Heaven, I wanted to believe—to set aside my fear of dying and join the hundreds of thousands of men and women from my generation to escape our home in China in a desperate grasp at freedom in Hong Kong. After a tortuous path that tested my will to succeed, Heaven gave me Its blessing through the mouth of a fortune-teller, a friend of my family.

"It's your time to fly away," Mommy told me through tears on the eve of my first escape attempt. "Heaven will bless you."

Heaven did bless me by keeping me alive, but It didn't bless me with success. It took me two years of struggle and two failures. All the while, I wondered why Heaven had closed Its eyes to me. I wondered if I had to be pushed to the edge early in life in order to achieve a bigger goal in the New World. "Before Heaven grants a man great responsibility, It must frustrate his spirit and will, put his flesh and bones through toil, deprive him of food and wealth, ruin his actions and efforts." This ancient Chinese poem rings true for me.

For several decades, my American friends have encouraged me to write a book recounting my story of growing up in China and my multiple attempts to flee the Maoist regime. I hesitated. I am not trained as a writer. I'm a scientist, trained in medicine. So, I waited, believing that some other freedom swimmers would tell a story that mirrored mine. More than forty years have passed, and I am still waiting.

Hundreds of thousands of Chinese freedom swimmers escaped to Hong Kong during the "Ten-Year Calamity," the official verdict of the Cultural Revolution rendered by the Communist Party of China after Mao's death in 1976. Why were they all silent? Were they afraid of being punished by the Communist Party? I asked a few freedom swimmers.

"Today's China is so good," they replied. "Why put dirt on her face?"

Papa taught me that being nationalistic was essential to being a "true" Chinese, as was saving face. Papa buried his painful past and loved and defended China until his last breath. But in my heart, I am an American who believes in the grand ideal of "life, liberty, and the pursuit of happiness." I do not value blind love for China simply because I was born in China.

Many freedom swimmers who dreamed of a decent life—the same dream as mine—died on their journey. One of them was a dear friend. He was with me in our first, failed attempt at escape. During his second attempt, he died in the sea. Does his life mean nothing? Should he be forgotten? My heart keeps telling me no.

Ten years ago, I woke up in the middle of the night with the thought: *What if some molecules that once belonged to him are still floating in the sea? Should I try to touch at least one of them, to let him know I still remember him?*

In 2010, thirty-seven years after my friend's death, I flew to Hong Kong. After a long ferry ride, I set foot, for the first time, on the "Beach of Bean Curd Rocks," a unique feature of the island of Tung Ping Chau, in Mirs Bay. Freedom swimmers used to write on a large boulder there to mark their successful flight to freedom, but I found that the Hong Kong UNESCO Geopark now resided where the boulder once stood. Across the bay was a dark, jagged mountain range. I couldn't discern which peak we traversed before descending to the coast where the People's Liberation Army soldiers caught us during that first attempt, but I felt a chill run down my spine at the memory.

I followed the Bean Curd Rocks to the edge of the sea and splashed my hand in the water. I felt at peace as I dreamed of a molecule that had once belonged to my friend dancing around my fingers and palm. I heard my friend begging me, "Please remember me." I mumbled, "I will."

From Hong Kong, I flew to Canton City to meet up with friends. "You know what we call our generation?" my high school classmate said when we met up for dinner. "The 'Lost Generation of Chinese baby boomers.'" She was well-off and living a happy, comfortable life now.

"The Lost Generation?" I was shocked. I googled "the Lost Generation." It normally refers to the generation who reached maturity during and just after World War I, whose survivors were confused and aimless. Was the generation of Chinese baby boomers lost? Wandering? Directionless?

I don't believe so. A "silent" generation we may be, but not lost.

Unlike textbook baby boomers, Chinese baby boomers endured two of the greatest acts of human destruction during peacetime: the Great Famine, the result of the "Great Leap Forward," and the "Ten-Year Calamity" of the Cultural Revolution, during which hundreds of thousands in Guangdong Province risked their lives to escape to Hong Kong. Since the death of Chairman Mao forty-five years ago, those who remained in China have enjoyed a much better material life, but limited freedom. In public, most Chinese baby boomers remain silent about their painful past. Why? Are they just like my Papa, who refused to put dirt on the face of the Motherland? Or are they afraid of their likely incarceration for speaking out? For the freedom swimmers, is the rebel spirit that once drove us to attempt escape now dead? Should I keep silent just like the rest?

I hear Mommy from Heaven telling me no.

And I feel a rush just as I did when I undertook those escapes. I feel the animal spirit of rebellion come back to me. And just as I did back in China almost a half century ago, I'm determined to grab it and let it guide me through this journey into my past, to expose the wounds created by the utter destruction of humanity, wounds that I hope future generations will finally heal.

CHAPTER I

HONG KONG IS NOT CHINA, AND WE ARE CHINESE

I WAS BORN IN 1948 in a small, peaceful Chinese coastal town whose name in English is "North Sea"—that is, north of the South China Sea. The Chinese Civil War between Chairman Mao's Communist insurgent forces and General Chiang Kai-shek's National Revolutionary Army was in its final stages. Three years before I came into being, the Nazis were defeated and the Japanese imperialists surrendered. I was blessed, for North Sea had no military significance in the Chinese Civil War.

Three years before the Japanese invasion in 1937, Chiang drove Mao's guerrilla forces on their "Long March" to a remote area of northwest China, far from the reach of the Japanese invaders. By the time I was born, Mao had perfected his "Protracted War" against the Japanese and turned it into a full-scale attack on Chiang. Chiang's army had been badly depleted by the Japanese invaders, and Chiang's ally, the United States, was exhausted after its brutal fight with the Nazis in Europe and the Japanese imperial

Family photo in Canton City, 1951.

forces over the Pacific. And Mao was winning. The Yankees would not want to fight another war to help Chiang. "The globe is round and it turns full circle"—so goes a Chinese saying. Mao was destined to rule China.

A month after I was born, Papa and Mommy held a celebration for my having come into the world. Back then, Chinese did not celebrate life when it started. They waited a month to see if that life was still vibrant. Why waste money and excitement when many babies didn't live past a month? The Chinese were practical people.

I was the second child. Mommy brought five of us into the world, and we all passed the first-month test. She got the job done in good order, over eight years, at two-year intervals. So, I can always figure out how old the others are, unless I forget how old I am.

Mommy said I brought good fortune to the family. A few days after my "birthday" party, Papa and all the other officers working for the customs agency of Chiang's government were told to relocate to Hong Kong. Papa and his colleagues knew Chiang was losing the war and planning to flee to Taiwan Island. Back then, Hong Kong was a British colony, and Chiang's government had a much bigger customs agency there. Papa was not happy to go to Hong Kong, but Mommy was elated. "North Sea is too small for raising children anyway," she declared. "Hong Kong is the place!" Mommy liked to link the size of a city to how good its schools were. "It's true, always. No sound-minded teacher prefers to teach in a small town." To the Chinese, nothing is more important than a good school with good teachers.

"But Hong Kong is not China!" Papa said, annoyed. "It's a British colony, and we are Chinese."

"You aren't working for the British." Mommy reminded Papa, "You're an employee of Chiang's government."

Papa raised his voice: "Chiang's government is corrupt, and you know I hate it."

Mommy was calm: "How do you know Mao will be better than Chiang? You're not corrupt; you don't take bribes. That's good enough for me."

Papa loved China. He had a deep loyalty to it. But there was no work available there that would pay as much as his job in the customs agency. Or maybe it's more accurate to say that there was no job available anywhere. China was a mess. There was blood everywhere. The violence had spread from the battlefields to every liberated village. Mao's army was shooting landlords, taking their land away, and redistributing it to poor peasants.

When the day came, reluctant Papa and joyous Mommy dragged the family's luggage and my older sister, Jing, who could walk by then, and carried me onto a ship to Hong Kong. We settled in an apartment in Causeway Bay on Hong Kong Island. We would be safe there, even if Mao invaded the Hong Kong peninsula. The peninsular part had two districts, Kowloon and the New Territories. Mao's army could march over the peninsula, but it could not reach the island of Hong Kong, just as it could not reach the island of Taiwan: It didn't have warships! The mighty Pacific Fleet of American warships was roaming the Taiwan Strait to protect Chiang. It would take no time at all for them to sail to Hong Kong to help out their British pals.

Although Mommy was thrilled to move to Hong Kong, the move did not come without its difficulties. I became sick with a cough for days, and on the recommendation of a neighbor, Mommy took me to the British Hospital. "There were many kids there like you, coughing and crying," Mommy told me years later. "The doctor said you needed to stay in the hospital in order not to spread germs to others. I left you there, but when I got home, I felt something wasn't right. I went back and found you and many other kids crying inside a room full of brownish fumes."

I got excited: "Did the doctor burn opium in the room?" I asked. I had just learned about the Opium Wars, when the British Royal Navy beat the Qing Dynasty army so the Englishmen could keep trading their opium for our Chinese tea.

"Of course not! What a silly question. I took you away and swore not to go there ever again." The British Hospital frightened me to death with the way they treated the sick kids. There should be a sign in front of it reading, "CHINESE AND DOGS ARE NOT ALLOWED." In those days, many parks had such signs by the entrance.

To be fair, the Chinese way of dealing with the sick was not much better. All we used were bitter-tasting soups made from dried plants most people couldn't name and ugly-looking insects. I'd seen sick people drink sake from a bottle in which centipedes and venomous snakes had been placed while still alive and kept for years, the longer the better. People also rubbed the sake onto their skin to soothe pain. But the worst were the cooked bugs sold in stores. They looked just like cockroaches except they were black! Parents would force their kids to eat them if they couldn't control their bladders while they slept. Thank Heaven I was able to wake up when the need to pee arose.

The Chinese had peculiar ways to deal with the human body. For them, being sick meant that some invisible element inside the body was out of whack. For example, pimples were a sign that the body was too hot. So, logically, one must drink "cool tea"—but illogically, one must drink it while it was still hot, to counter the "hotness" inside the body. No kid liked "cool tea." It was very bitter. When I had pimples, I was instructed to bite off a little bit of an extremely salty and sour dried plum with every sip of hot "cool tea"—to distract my taste buds from the bitterness. The skin of my forehead would tighten until it tugged at my eyebrows.

Mommy laughed. "Look at you! You're suffering terribly, aren't you?"

"How can you laugh, Mommy? You try it!"

"Mommy has no pimples."

Cantonese still drink "cool tea" in today's China. Some smart guy added a whole bunch of sugar to our Cantonese "cool tea," refrigerated it, and sold it in cans all over China, calling it "Chinese Coca-Cola." Adults, without pimples, drink it ice cold while eating—to get fat, I guess.

Mommy liked to say that moving to Hong Kong was a blessing from Heaven. It gave us peace when Mao's army was approaching the area north of Hong Kong to wipe out the remnants of Chiang's government, so Mao could declare, on October 1, 1949, on the Gate of Heavenly Peace in Tiananmen Square in Beijing, the birth of the People's Republic of China. I was too young to remember living in Hong Kong, but in the photos from those years, I feel the calm and ease and I see the joy in our faces. Mommy took a lot of pictures of me alone, me with her and me with her and Jing. Papa seldom showed up in the photos. "He was always busy at work," Mommy explained.

A happy person takes pictures to remember happy moments. Many happy moments left behind many pictures. Of the many pictures of our family, quite a few show my fat cheeks and curious eyes. The one that always made me laugh features ice cream. I stuffed my mouth with too much of it, causing it to spill out and drip onto my shirt.

"Mommy, how come I don't like ice cream anymore?" I asked years later, when we were back in China.

"China has no ice cream. It has ice chips."

For all that Mommy loved Hong Kong, Papa did not. His heart was always with China. "Hong Kong is not China," he'd say, "and we are Chinese. We must go back to China!" He never went deeper to explain why he liked China so much, so I asked Mommy. She explained that all Papa's brothers and sisters were in China, and besides, he was stubborn. Once he decided on something, it was hard to change his mind.

"Is stubborn good?" I asked.

"No, it's not good. You don't want to be stubborn."

"What's 'stubborn' mean?"

"When Mommy asks you to do something in the right way and you keep doing it your way."

"But what if my way is the right way?"

"Then Mommy is stubborn."

"Oh, Mommy can be stubborn, too?"

"Everybody can be stubborn."

"Who is not stubborn?"

"Nobody. But your Papa is more stubborn than all of us combined."

But Papa didn't need to be stubborn to bring us back to China. For two thousand-some years, Confucius's teaching had become part of the Chinese "cultural DNA," which dictated that the Chinese act as family units, not individuals, and that the authority of a family rested on the husband, not the wife. That was great for Papa. It also dictated that a woman's greatest duty was to produce a son, not a daughter. Being a woman, Mommy faced insurmountable odds in keeping the family in Hong Kong.

Before Mao, Chinese emperors had relied on Confucius's teaching because it had taught the Chinese to respect and obey authority. Then, in 1966, when Mao was seventy-three, he decided to launch the Cultural Revolution to achieve his political and cultural goals. He replaced all -isms (except, of course, socialism and communism) with Maoism. Mao wanted all Chinese people to worship only him—not Confucius, not Buddha, and especially not the Christian God. After Mao died in 1976, Confucianism made a miraculous reappearance and has been strong ever since. The new leaders of the Communist Party of China appreciate the beauty of this Chinese cultural DNA—conformity and obedience. Capitalizing on the Western intellectuals' admiration of Confucian teaching, the Chinese government has opened hundreds of "Confucius Institutes" in the democratic world to serve its global ambition. I wonder how the Western world can reconcile its advocacy for independent thinking and women's rights with its endorsement of this Chinese cultural DNA.

In 1951, two years after the founding of Communist China, Papa joined an insurrection in the customs agency to bring the family back to China. Jing was five, I was three, and our baby sister, Lily, was one. Lily was born in Hong Kong, and therefore given a British first name, just like "Mommy," one she was proud of. But when she grew up, Lily complained often that Mommy had lost her British birth certificate. Back then, Cantonese loved all things British.

Papa's insurrection ended our happy, peaceful life in Hong Kong. At that time, Papa was young and handsome, ambitious and hardworking. While many of his colleagues worked hard out in the field hustling bribes, he worked diligently in the office on his way up the career ladder. Neither he nor Mommy could have foreseen that working for Mao's enemy in Hong Kong would turn out to be perilous for Papa and our family later on in China.

When I was old enough to understand the meaning of the word *insurrection*, I was disappointed. Mommy told me there was no gunfire or bloodshed involved in Papa's insurrection. Papa and some of his colleagues simply walked out of the office and declared, "We quit! We're returning to the Motherland!" The customs office didn't stop this patriotic bunch. There were many qualified people waiting in line to fill the vacancies. And the British governor of Hong Kong didn't give a damn. Their insurrection didn't affect the money flowing back home to the Queen.

Why Mao did not take over Kowloon or the New Territories on the peninsula during the liberation—together, these two places comprised more land than the island of Hong Kong—was a mystery to me for years. If Mao had taken over the peninsula, Papa would have been working for the new China from the get-go, as his office was on the peninsula. And I'm sure Papa would have joined Mao's forces and become a revolutionary comrade instead of one of Chiang's former officers—Papa had complained that Chiang's government was no good because it was corrupt. But Jing said that

Papa could be shot dead by the People's Liberation Army for having been an enemy of Mao. Politics was bloody in China.

Why Mao did not take over Kowloon Peninsula remained an aching question for me. But it was hard to find out the truth in China. Not a single book I found said a word about the Yankees' Pacific War, which destroyed the Japanese navy; or about the American atomic bombs that brought the Japanese invaders to their knees; or about the evil Chiang's government representative standing beside the leaders of the Allied powers to accept the surrender of Imperial Japan on the deck of the mighty USS *Missouri*.

In the end, Papa had a simple answer for me: "China needs Hong Kong to trade with the world. It needs a stable Hong Kong as a whole, so it honors the Qing Dynasty's leases and lets the British run the island. The trade gives me my job. That's what I'm doing every day."

So, I learned that things happen for a reason. That I could not find the reason did not mean there was none. Yet, in China, we were not taught such reasons in school. And when no reason was found, gossip took over.

"Don't tell anyone what I've just told you," Papa warned me.

"Why?" I asked. "Isn't it true?"

"Of course it is; Papa doesn't lie. But it's not good for China's image. If someone hears it, it'll spread like wildfire. Twisting and spinning gossip a few times will get me in trouble."

"What trouble?" I was curious.

"Trouble is trouble," Papa said. "I don't know what it would do to me."

Mommy wasn't excited about Papa's insurrection, but China was. The insurrection brought us to Canton City (now known as Guangzhou). Upon our arrival, we were greeted by people beating drums. Banners on the train station platform bore the words INSURRECTION HEROES in bold characters. By participating in the insurrection, Papa was seen as officially rising up against Chiang's government; he was a hero. It earned him a good job: as the head of the import/export department of the provincial government in the province of Guangdong.

As the family of one of the heroes of the insurrection, we were driven around Canton City, the largest city in Guangdong Province, by a young comrade, to view various apartments. We were jammed together in the car like sardines in a can. Papa sat in front, and Mommy, holding crying Lily, sat in the back between Jing and me, to separate us—even though we were too tired to bother each other.

"It was exhausting," Mommy recalled. "There weren't many differences among the apartments." She was right. I had been in some of my classmates' homes, in old concrete buildings. Most had electricity and water, but no heating or air-conditioning. (I didn't even know there were such things, as I had been too young to appreciate them in Hong Kong.)

We were given two rooms on the ground floor of an old four-story building. The bigger room had space for a square dining table, a large bed with a steel frame for mosquito netting, a dresser, and a desk under a window covered in rusty bars. The bed was for Mommy and Papa and my youngest sister. (That sister would later be Bun, the last of Mommy's five babies.) I slept in the smaller room, in a small bed with a circular mosquito netting, the worst kind because it allowed my forearms and legs to touch more of the net's surface, giving the mosquitoes a better chance to suck my blood. My bed was about one foot from a larger bed that took up almost half the room. The larger bed was for Jing, Lily, and Ning—Ning would be born one year later, but she would not share the bed with my other sisters until Bun was born.

Isn't it complicated? Allocating a small living space and a limited number of beds for family members was always complicated in China. To make it more complicated, in 1950, a year after Mao founded the new China, he called upon women to make more babies. In fact, the government gave material rewards to the "Hero Mother" who gave birth to many babies. Mommy told me once that she was praised by a member of the Street Committee when she was carrying Ning. Then, in 1980, four years after Mao's death and thirty years after the "Hero Mother" campaign, China adopted its One-Child Policy, which upset many inside and outside China. Confucius had taught the Chinese that a woman's most important duty was to give birth to a *son*. During implementation of the One-Child Policy, this culture was deadly to the female fetuses who were aborted many times more than male fetuses, and more female newborns were killed or left somewhere to die.

Westerners say China is complex and full of contradictions, but it isn't. China, being an authoritarian country, is rather straightforward. "Hero Mother" and the One-Child Policy each served national interests at a specific moment in time. The unborn could be either members of China's future labor force, and therefore welcomed even in vivo, or a burden on China's economy, and killed, also in vivo.

I can hardly remember much from my early days in Canton City, but I remember the kitchen and toilet we shared with our neighbor. The kitchen served two functions: as a place to cook and as a place to wash our bodies using a bucket of tap water. In the winter we would mix the tap water with a pot of hot water. A bathtub or a showerhead was unheard of. The kitchen had a concrete floor with a small open ditch in the corner to drain wastewater. That ditch also served as a passage for rats and cockroaches. This was not to be confused with the toilet, which was a hole in the concrete floor that one had to squat over to use.

Our neighborhood was a cluster of buildings of various designs having no discernable order or layout. Small dwellings made of brick, wood panels, and sheet metal were juxtaposed at odd angles to our four-story concrete building. A wide alley off a busy street broke through the mess to reach our building. Off the alley, small lanes twisted their way through the clusters of small dwellings. Compared to these makeshift shacks, we lived in Heaven. Those shacks had no running water and no toilets. Their inhabitants had to use the public toilets. Life in those places was particularly difficult for kids. They had to lug large buckets of water every day from the public faucet to their homes, which were usually filled with the adults' heavy cigarette smoke. And when they needed to use the public toilet, which was also always filled with smoke, the nastier adults—and there were many—would harass them to hurry up.

"You have small butt! It should take you no time to get it done!"

Canton City, just like Hong Kong, was very hot and humid. Starting in spring, it became so humid that it was hard to breathe. Inside our home, the moisture in the air condensed on the cold concrete walls into droplets that ran into one another to form tiny streams. Using my fingers to guide those streams to merge into bigger ones was something I'd do for fun. The moisture in the air trapped the odor of dead and decaying rats in the house, and the stench perpetually lingered. We could never get rid of it, not even by keeping the windows and door open.

Canton City challenged us with two enemies I could attack: rats and cockroaches. I hated mosquitoes, too, but there were too many to catch, and killing them provided no fun. As for the rats, one rat was so huge it scared our neighbor's cat when it emerged suddenly from the kitchen drain. I hated that rat and the way it chased our neighbor's cat through our rooms. So, I cut down a forked branch from a banyan tree, attached a rubber band to it to make a slingshot, and picked up several sharp-edged rocks to use as "bullets." I wanted to kill that big rat! Patiently, I sat on a stepstool facing the drain hole with my slingshot ready to go. Finally, the rat emerged, and I fired the slingshot—and hit it! The rat screeched and ran back into the drain—and that was it. It didn't come back again. It was smart.

Though there were many rats in people's homes, Mommy was against having a cat. "A cat is useless. It couldn't face up to that big rat. Worse, it might drop any rat it kills in a place we may not see, and a rotten rat can spread germs that'll make us sick."

"But I hate the little rats pooping in our rice container. Their germs in their poop will make us sick," I argued.

"Then you should find time to pick their waste out of the rice. You know I'm too busy taking care of the five of you."

By then, Ning and Bun had been born. They were born in the Year of the Dragon and Tiger, respectively. I, much to my dismay, had been born in the Year of the Rat, which I complained about often, for I was the only Rat baby in the family. Mommy always said, "It's not for me to choose. Heaven chose it for you, and Buddha loves creatures of all kinds."

I didn't want to pick rat feces out of the rice. It would be a big waste of time. The rice came to us already dirty because it had been stored in a warehouse for years, where it collected waste of all kinds, including cockroach poop, which I hated the most. We city dwellers were not allowed to eat the new rice of the harvest. We had to eat the oldest rice first, to make room in the warehouse for the freshly harvested rice. China had stored rice for several years in preparation for wars with foreign enemies. Mao called it the "Protracted People's War," and us Chinese, patriots. Eating dirty, age-old rice was the least we could do for the Motherland!

Mommy used to say, "Heaven is fair. City folks can't have all the good things. You can dismiss the harsh life in the village, but the harsh village life comes with fresh, shining white rice."

China always had enemies. Mao would tell us from time to time who the enemy was, and we trusted his judgment, and his fighting skills. The easiest enemies to recognize, and also the most hated, were the Yankees and their running dog Chiang of Taiwan. They were our perpetual enemies. When I was old enough to go to school, I learned that Mao could beat any enemy.

The party secretary of the school declared, "Don't be frightened by the American imperialists. Chairman Mao teaches us they are paper tigers!" As a kid, I didn't know what a paper tiger looked like, but I knew I could burn anything made of paper. "Our weapon is Chairman Mao's protracted guerrilla warfare," the party leader said. "Be prepared!" He liked to conclude his speech with "Be prepared," and we heeded that.

Like our neighbors, we raised several chickens for their meat and eggs, as both were always in short supply at the markets. Papa and I built a cage for the chickens and put it in the hallway. Among the chickens was one hen. Other hens sooner or later went into our stomachs, but that one hen remained. She was a consistent egg producer. We all loved her for that. Every time I got close to her cage, she'd stare at me with her big eyes.

"Mommy, the hen knows me."

"That's natural. You feed her."

"I like her."

"Then feed her well so she gives us more eggs."

I tried to catch grasshoppers to feed her, but they were difficult to come by—there wasn't much grass around for them to hop in. Cockroaches, however, were everywhere. They were filthy, but chickens loved to eat these disgusting creatures. I didn't want to catch them by hand, so I made a trap using bamboo strips and put rice inside it as bait. I'd place the trap by the kitchen drain in the evening, and in the morning I'd find many cockroaches inside it.

I was torn. I hated the cockroach's poop in our rice, but I wanted to keep them around so I could watch them be chased, caught, and eaten by my hen. "Nothing strange about that," Mommy said. "No needle is sharp at both ends."

ooooo

PAPA WAS HAPPY IN HIS new job as head of the import/export department. He was content, and it showed. Several days before New Year's Eve, he'd start to hum the classical tune Toselli's "Serenade, op. 6/1." For some reason, that tune always made me sad, but Papa hummed it in good spirits. His head moved to the beat, and his right foot tapped the floor as he hummed.

"Papa, why do you like that song?" I asked. "It makes me sad."

Papa said, "It's not a sad song. It reminds me of when I was your age. We always sang it in church at Christmas."

"We don't go to church, Papa."

"But I went to church when I was about your age. The pastor of the Seventh-day Adventist Church was a good friend of your grandpa. He said your grandpa was his best helping hand."

"Who are the Seventh-day Adventists?"

"It's a denomination of Christians. The pastor was sent to us by his church in America."

"From America?" I was shocked. "The imperialists!"

"Christians are not imperialists!" Papa was annoyed. "Without that priest, I wouldn't know how to read English, and I wouldn't have a good job to afford to raise you and the family."

"The church had a school?" I couldn't believe it. Canton had a few churches I knew of. One neighborhood boy I knew, Curly, went to one. But his church didn't have a school. Curly was a nice kid, and smart, but he was picked on all the time by nasty boys for his wavy hair. Almost all Chinese hair was thick, black, and *straight*. Anyone who looked different was picked on.

"Papa, was the pastor a white man?" Curly had told me that his priest was a Chinese man appointed by someone in Rome. I assumed that if someone was from the United States, what else could he be other than white?

"Of course, he was." Papa said. He was in a good mood. "He gave me a job working in the church after school because we were poor."

"I want to work after school like you."

"No, you don't. You need to study. Remember, knowledge is gold. It's my job to take care of the family."

"Where are Grandpa and Grandma? You've never told me about them."

"They died young, way before you were born," Papa said in a sad voice.

Unlike Mommy, Papa did not want to talk about his parents and sisters and brothers, other than to say that he was the eldest of seven siblings. Mommy told me Papa was from a very poor family. "Your papa won't talk about them because he does not want to lose face," she explained.

"Being poor has nothing to do with losing face," I argued.

"But your father thinks so, and you can't change him."

That ended our conversation. When, during the Cultural Revolution, I finally got a chance to visit Papa's sister, I learned of the gut-wrenchingly distressing suffering that took place on Papa's side of the family. Only then did I find the answer to my aching question: Why would Papa want to return to China, why would he never let go of his bond with it?

I didn't tell anybody about the pastor and the church school. I knew, by instinct, that if the story leaked out, it would become gossip that could do harm to Papa and the family.

∞∞∞

NOBODY EVER SAID ALL CHILDREN were created equal in China. Papa told me that as the only male child, I would be master of the family when he died. I didn't like to hear it. I didn't want to be the master of my sisters.

I liked things wild and adventurous. I played cops and robbers with boys in the neighborhood, and one of my favorite photos shows me standing up straight, carrying a toy rifle and wearing a red scarf of the Young Pioneers.

As for my sisters, they liked chitchat. They laughed over little things and played dolls together. They never helped me fight the big rat or catch the cockroaches for our hen. They didn't even know how many chickens we had! But I didn't mind. My sisters and I lived a "perfect" but detached coexistence with one another. Still, as the only son in the family, I always had Mommy and Papa's attention, but my sisters, especially the younger ones, didn't.

Chinese society had unwritten rules and expectations for what a boy should do around the house compared to what a girl should do. The houses in our neighborhood were close, and when someone broke a social rule, such as arguing with his siblings, the neighbors would inevitably learn about it—and sure enough, it would spread throughout the neighborhood, causing the kid's parents to lose face. For Mommy, as for all Chinese of sound mind, saving face in public was of upmost importance. I learned this the hard way, when I was eight.

Mommy had brought me to visit my grandparents, aunties, uncles, and cousins, all of whom lived in a small city called Liuzhou, in the neighboring province. Liuzhou is ninety-five miles southwest of Guilin, which was known to the world as having strikingly gorgeous clusters of limestone peaks and caves along the translucent green Li River. Yet, despite their beauty, for some reason, no one paid much attention to the mountains in Liuzhou or to the Liujiang River, even though they were just as pretty as Guilin's. Liuzhou had only itself to blame: It was famous for producing great coffins. But who wanted to be reminded of death when they were having a good time enjoying life? Also, travel and sightseeing were rare for most families. Still, Guilin made a point of boasting about having the "Best Mountains and Water Under the Sky."

Our visit took place in the summer, and every day was hot and steamy. "Coming from a big city, you have to look different," Mommy said while putting new leather shoes on my feet. "I want you to look sharp and presentable so no one will look down on Mommy."

But I didn't want to look different from my cousins, so I hid my shoes under the bed.

"Why is it so difficult for you to put on something new?" Mommy asked. "Don't you want to look good in front of the others?"

"No," I said. "I don't want the others to feel bad because they don't have what I have."

"What if your friends wear new clothes and yours have rips here and there fixed with stitches?"

"It won't bother me, but I hate smelly clothes."

"Everybody does, but everybody loves new clothes and new shoes." Mommy shook her head. "You'll change when you grow up."

"I won't."

"Promise?"

"Promise!"

"Too bad your sisters aren't like you," Mommy said, trying to hide her smile.

When I grew older, I understood what Mommy meant. Envy was often part of being human. Thank Heaven I was not given a heavy dose of it when I was born. If someone in my class at school did better than me on a test, I just wanted to beat him the next time.

Wearing nothing but shorts made me feel wild and adventurous while I chased after my barefoot cousins Big Fluffy and Little Fluffy. I liked their mother, my auntie. She was funny and artistic and creative. Perhaps she gave both her boys the name "Fluffy" when they were born because she saw them as lovely as little white rabbits worthy of her tender touching and petting. But they were definitely not cute or lovely when I met them. They were rough and tough, and their skin was darkly suntanned and filmed with sweat that was sticky to the touch.

Big Fluffy and Little Fluffy told me they'd learned to swim in the swift Liujiang River, which ran straight through the city. Auntie would wrap a long rope around each boy's waist and tie the other end to a long bamboo pole. Holding the pole, she'd sit in

the shade of a big tree on the high riverbank to read her books—
Auntie didn't finish high school, but she read a lot of books—and
bite her fingernails, while the miserable Fluffys struggled against the
strong current, flapping and kicking and choking, but not drowning.
When the exhausted Fluffys inevitably got pushed downstream,
Auntie would simply pull them back, then resume her reading and
nail biting. Half her fingernails were gone, but there was no blood!

"Does it hurt, Auntie?" I asked.

"Does what hurt?" Auntie asked.

"Your fingers."

"No, why?"

One hot day, as the two Fluffys and I aimlessly walked along
the street looking for shade, a pedicab (a motorized three-wheeler)
passed by us carrying Mommy and Auntie. Mommy was holding a
small parasol to block the sun—"tanned skin makes one look old
and ugly" was what she and most Chinese believed—and Auntie
was cooling her face with a small sandalwood fan.

The Fluffys and I chased the cab, shouting, "Give us money
to buy ice pops!"

When they saw us, Mommy's and Auntie's faces were stern.
Auntie yelled at us as if we were street urchins, someone else's children: "Go away! Go ask your mothers for money!"

That evening after dinner, Mommy and Auntie gave us a
warning. "Stand up straight, look at me, and listen," Mommy said.
"We two sisters are reputable ladies. We can't lose face because of
you! Dirty faces, bare chests, and muddy feet!"

Seeing that her words had shaken us, Mommy laughed.

"Sister! Stop laughing," Auntie said. "This is a serious matter." She turned to us and put it bluntly: "We cannot have beggars
as children!"

I was at a loss. Me? A beggar? Nobody had ever called me that. Then Mommy and Auntie laughed. I was relieved, and Little Fluffy asked, "Can we have a ghost story now?"

"Why not?" Mommy said, in a good mood.

Mommy was a much better storyteller than Auntie. Like our Cantonese cuisine, Mommy's voice was smooth and textured, and her words were never rushed, so I had time to digest them. As for Auntie, her talks were like northern cuisine: pungent, spicy, sour, and salty. But nobody could beat her at singing and dancing. Once, she performed for us a scene from *Liu the Third Sister*, China's first movie musical. I loved watching her stretch her arms out, fingers extended, circling the air, but I wished she had longer fingernails.

Like an angry father, the sun was finally exhausted from punishing the earth and went into hiding. The moon, mother of the earth, arrived, bringing with it a gentle breeze to sweep clean the dust of the fields outside the Fluffys' small house, revealing fussy layers of gray. The moon also woke up hidden creatures who played like an orchestra of deaf musicians without a conductor. We had thrown open the front door and all the windows, hoping to bring in cross ventilation to drive out the heat that had built up during the day. Each of us oscillating a palm leaf fan back and forth, three punished boys awaited a good ghost story to end a not-that-good day.

Mommy loved to read and tell ghost stories. She had read *Liaozhai Zhiyi* (*Strange Tales from a Chinese Studio*). That night, she stopped at the scene that would reveal the ghost and stared blankly at the open front door. We all turned our eyes to the door and held our breaths. Calmly, Mommy said, "I should have warned you not to sit with your backs to the door. The ghost always comes in through the door." Swiftly, we moved our stools and sat close together facing the door. My heart was pounding.

"Go close the door!" Big Fluffy ordered Little Fluffy.

Mommy and Auntie laughed, then I followed, and then both Fluffys laughed.

∞∞∞

ALTHOUGH I ENJOYED ROAMING FREE with my cousins, I spent most of my time when home behind the desk, studying and reading novels. When I was bored, I watched the clouds through the iron-barred window. I was perplexed by their shapes, which never seemed to repeat themselves. I had no interest in going outside for the sake of going out.

One day, Mommy called me to come out to the alley.

"Why?" I asked.

"Our neighbor wants to see you. She doesn't know who my son is."

In those days, kids had very few toys. Just like other families, our family had a bicycle, and that was my ultimate "toy." I was too short to reach the pedals and still stay seated, so I set my left foot on the left pedal and slid my right foot through the triangular frame to reach the right pedal. Then I'd stand on the two pedals, instead of sitting on the saddle, but I had to tilt my body slightly to the right to balance the bike. It was much tougher to learn to ride it that way, but I didn't give up. It wasn't any fun having abrasions on my palms, elbows, and knees from my repeated falls, but when I mastered it, you couldn't imagine how happy and proud I was! The greatest joy came when I was tall enough to sit on the seat properly.

Any chance I got, I'd ride that bike. I'd volunteer to ride to the farmers' market to buy meat, fish, or whatever Mommy needed when we had friends over for dinner. Mommy loved to entertain friends. And to entertain was to eat together. "For the common people, food is Heaven"—so goes the advice a scholar gave the Han dynasty emperor about two thousand years ago; it has been a common belief among Chinese ever since.

Mommy was more than happy to send me out, for I was "useless" and an "eyesore" in the kitchen.

Cycling on the county road and tasting the dust kicked up by the passing dirty trucks, I felt free to chase the clouds in the wide sky.

CHAPTER 2

CHASING SPARROWS

GOING TO SCHOOL WAS FREE, and mandatory for kids once they turned seven. Many kids started school earlier. Jing started at five, but I started at seven. Mommy never told me why I didn't start earlier, even though I was supposedly mature enough at five. It would have been a big deal if I had gone at age five, for I wouldn't have this story to tell—I would have been at a university before the Cultural Revolution and therefore would not have become a "sent-down student," that is, sent to the country to work as a peasant, and I would not have become a freedom swimmer and escaped to Hong Kong. *Was my starting school at seven years old a blessing or a curse?*

The elementary school and junior high accepted anyone who met the age requirement. Admission to the senior high and university, though, required the passing of an entrance exam and, most important, a political evaluation. School started at eight A.M., and we didn't return home until five in the afternoon. We went to school six days a week, with Saturday afternoon devoted to cleaning our classroom and the school.

Future communist successor. In elementary school in Canton City.

If a member of the "Street Committee" spotted a school-age kid wandering around during school hours, he or she would intervene and tell the kid's parents. Scolding and spankings inevitably followed. I never heard of a girl skipping school; the troublemaker was always a boy. I myself never experienced physical punishment by Papa or Mommy, because I was always a nice kid—if not the nicest—in school.

Living under the watchful eye of the Street Committee was a part of life. The committee was run by several retired Communist Party loyalists who cared about an orderly and well-functioning socialist neighborhood. The committee was the mouthpiece of the party and the ear of the police. It helped the police keep track of every household in the neighborhood by way of a "Household Register." The register listed the personal information of every member of each family. Even we kids knew how important the Household Register was. Without it, our family would not have been allowed to stay in the city and we wouldn't have been issued the ration coupons we needed to buy rice, pork, cooking oil, sugar, and other foods.

On a bright red concrete wall in my elementary school were large golden characters spelling out CULTIVATE COMMUNIST SUCCESSORS! We kids didn't really know what communism looked like. Our teachers wouldn't give us the details, wouldn't tell us what it meant to live in a communist society, other than that we would have so much of everything that no money would be needed and we would have whatever we needed whenever we wanted it. This confused us even more. How could we live a "normal" life without using money? Of course, we would like to live a life without ration coupons. But without *money*?

So, we let the grown-ups decide how they would turn us into Communists. Our job was to "obey the teachers!" And we did. But no parent told us how to deal with the school principal or the party secretary. We figured the principal was the head of the school, so he had to be obeyed, but what about the party secretary? He seemed unhappy all the time, and every teacher listened to him, so we assumed he was like an unhappy father at home: Mother listened to him, and the children were scared of him.

As students in China, we had been so disciplined and "pure" that during my early years in the States, the American TV sitcom *Welcome Back, Kotter* fascinated me. The only "disruptions" to my class in China had been from a few boys who made up stupid questions just to get the attention of a young, pretty teacher. (The Chinese word for "stupid" is very commonly used in China in all sorts of conversations by native speakers—between parent and child, friend and friend, and even teacher and student. Chinese seems to lack the equivalent of the synonyms dumb, naïve, idiotic, and so on. So, for the sake of authenticity, I use *stupid* in this book when I am speaking to a Chinese native or to myself. Many Chinese immigrants in America have learned the hard way about using the word *stupid* here in the States, including me. But they should be understood, shouldn't they?)

I studied hard to have my name listed at the top of the score sheet the teacher posted on the wall after an exam. Once, I cried over missing two points on a test, but I didn't want to admit it. The Chinese said, "A real man sheds blood, not tears," and it was what I believed. I wanted to be a real man.

My teachers chose me to be the head of the class every year through junior high. There was not much for the head of the class to do. The most important task was to call out, "Stand up!" when the teacher first walked into the room. Only one teacher was meticulous about this routine; he wouldn't nod his head until everyone was quiet and standing up straight. Finally, he'd nod, and I'd call out, "Sit down!" Some teachers were impatient with the routine and nodded their heads as soon as they walked into the room. Everybody liked those teachers.

To keep order in class, the teacher would pair a boy and a girl to share a desk—given that the troublemaker was always a boy, letting two boys share a desk would have been asking for trouble. We had more than fifty students, and fortunately, the ratio of boys to girls was about fifty-fifty. All the desks were old and made of wood, and all had a groove, carved with a pocketknife by the boys who'd preceded us, to divide the desktop into two halves. When a crossing of the line happened, a nasty boy could "legally" hit the "invader's" elbow with his fist or throw her cross-border things to the floor. Fortunately, our class had no such nasty boys, so as class head, I didn't need to deal with it. Otherwise, I had to report it to the head teacher and make myself an "enemy" of the boy in question. As for the girls, they were always nice. They never enforced the "no crossing" rule; they simply didn't care. The only "bad" thing about the girls was that they loved to perform in the annual school show, and we boys didn't, but we had to do what the girls told us to: dance. If we didn't obey, they might use their ultimate weapon: crying. At which point, we boys quickly surrendered.

Even without the need to carve boundary lines, boys still brought their pocketknives to school, to find and kill bedbugs. There were a lot of bedbugs hidden deep in the desks and chairs. When a bedbug attacked, it attacked fast and then ran away fast, leaving a large flat welt that itched for hours. It took a great effort to dig out the little buggers. Unfortunately, years of digging at the desks and chairs to fight bedbugs only created more hiding places for them. When a bedbug was found and killed, it was a victory worthy of being announced to the class, and we'd all cheer.

There were other disruptions. A boy might fight another boy by wrestling him, but they seldom used fists. As class head, it was my responsibility to stop the fighting. Using a pocketknife to fight was unimaginable, absolutely unheard of. As for the girls, they never fought among themselves or with boys.

Once we were in elementary school, we automatically became Young Pioneers, with no application or selection process needed. Being a Young Pioneer was the first step toward becoming a "Communist successor." Young Pioneers wore a red scarf tied around their necks. The red scarf was emblematic of the blood of our revolutionary martyrs. The party secretary of the school ran the Young Pioneer battalion. I was chosen to be the leader of the battalion, the highest rank under party secretary, a role recognizable by a badge of three red stripes, which I wore pinned to my shirt below my left shoulder. As the leader of both my class and the Young Pioneer battalion, I believed I was—how could I not be?—a shoo-in to be a Communist successor.

Before an assembly, I would lead the battalion to shout out, "To struggle for the cause of communism: Be prepared!" and all the others would shout back, "Always be prepared!" The grand purpose of the Young Pioneers was to make sure we believed that communism was our common goal. This was superfluous, however, for we didn't know any future other than communism.

Next to our school was a public market where peasants sold produce hauled in on horse carts from the suburbs. One day during a class break, I saw several boys surrounding an unattended horse there. They were waving their red scarves in front of its eyes and shouting, "Longer! Touch the ground!" The horse was stamping and kicking. I went closer and was shocked to see the horse's penis extending almost to the ground. The boys' scarves, the color of the blood of our revolutionary martyrs, were stimulating the horse! The peasant whose horse it was returned, saw what was happening, and shouted obscenities at us. We ran as fast as we could back to school, thinking the peasant would chase after us.

I started to worry. What if the peasant complained to the party secretary? If he did, I'd have to go to the party secretary to explain what had happened. And he'd ask, no doubt with an angry face and a harsh voice, why I hadn't stopped it. I couldn't tell him the truth: that I'd been amused by it. He would ask what the red scarf stood for, and without waiting for my answer, he'd raise his voice and say that I had disgraced our great revolutionary martyrs. I didn't mind losing my leadership position in the Young Pioneers if he kept it to himself, but I was sure he wouldn't. I just didn't want him to tell Papa about it and break his heart. I was sure Papa would spank me for the first time. Mommy would come to my defense because she was not an uptight person. But then she and Papa would argue because of me.

Above all, I was concerned because my mischief had had something to do with "sex"—a horse's sex organ, to be precise—and sex was taboo in China; it ranked as the highest, most egregious form of gossip. What a bloody mess I had just made! I was bothered by it for the remainder of the day. Heaven must have cast Its blessings on me that day, though, because the peasant never did come to school to make a fuss about it.

Still, life would have been dull, leaving no memory to recall, if it hadn't had some sparks. One of those sparks was Auntie's visit. At the time, Auntie was going through a nasty divorce and needed a place to stay. She was fighting for custody of her four children: the Fluffys and their younger brother and sister. Back then, obtaining a divorce was a long, hard process. The couple had to have the approval of their workplaces and of the local government, and if either of them was a member of the party, his or her workplace party secretary had to approve, too. Auntie's husband was a party member. The worst part about a divorce was the swirling gossip among coworkers and in the neighborhood. Fortunately, Auntie had a strong mind and a sharp tongue. But even she needed a break.

I was happy to see her, but she was indifferent as she glanced at my Young Pioneer leader badge. "Huuh! We've got a little Communist here," she said.

"He is doing very well in school." Mommy was proud.

"Listen, both of you, don't waste your time. Communism will never happen!" Auntie was emphatic.

"Stop poisoning my son," Mommy scolded. "I don't want him to get in trouble." Mommy warned me, "Don't listen to your auntie. Listen to your teacher."

Auntie turned to Mommy, "Sister! Your son is a good boy. I'll make him a smart boy." Then she turned to me: "You know why communism won't work?"

"No." I didn't think the teachers would lie to me, so I had never doubted that it would.

"Communism produces lazy ghosts. Worse yet, if things are free, the world will be buried under the throwaways."

"What throwaways, Auntie?" I was confused.

"Everything. A dress I try once but don't like anymore. The pork I don't like after my first bite. I'll throw everything away, even if I like it, without blinking an eye. We save everything because we don't have money. But we could easily go the other way if we didn't have to pay for it." Auntie saw I was getting her point. "And you, the dearest son of my beloved sister, will turn into a lazy ghost, just like Big Fluffy."

"No, I won't." I couldn't see myself being lazy anywhere—in the house, at school, or in the neighborhood.

"Of course you will. Everyone will except your papa," she said, chuckling. "He doesn't know how to relax."

Although our teachers were vague about what communism would look like, they did tell us that the idea of communism came from a European named Karl Marx. "What you must do," they said, "is exactly what our great leader Chairman Mao says." So, we had no need to learn more about communism. What we needed to do was focus our limited attention on what our teachers said and let them deal with the party secretary, who would in turn deal with Mao. Still, I had to keep what Auntie had said a secret, my intuition was telling me.

∞∞∞

IN THE MAKING OF A Communist state, we were never short of things to do. Mao had an active mind and would not let us be idle. In one of his poems, he told us, "Ten thousand years are too long. / We must seize the day!" Over a twenty-year period from the founding of the People's Republic of China in 1949 until his death in 1976—excluding the seven years between 1959 and 1966 when Mao was forced to yield his presidency to his comrade-in-arms Liu Shaoqi—Mao unleashed nine major political campaigns. He seized the day all right, but who paid the price?

Except for historians, it is hard even for the Chinese who lived through those years to keep track of Mao's various campaigns. So, I will divide these years into three periods and call each period an "Act of Mao."

Mao's Act I from 1949 to 1955 secured Mao and the Chinese Community Party's absolute control of China. Mao succeeded by executing four major political campaigns. The people who drew the shortest straw from these campaigns were the landlords and so-called counterrevolutionaries of all stripes.

Mao's Act II (1956–1959) sought to secure the economic power of China. But its four political and economic campaigns brought about the Great Famine (1959–1961), costing Mao his presidency. In my family, Papa was punished as a capitalist rightist. But the people who drew the shortest straw were the rural peasants. Tens of millions of them died from starvation.

Mao's Act III was from 1966 to his final year, 1976. The people who drew the shortest straw then were high school students, including Lily, Ning, and me, who were still in high school in 1966. Many of us were misled into brutally purging Mao's political enemies, who were innocent, and indiscriminately destroying Chinese culture. After Mao had achieved his goals, in 1968, he sent all high school students to the countryside to be reeducated by the peasants. In Guangdong Province, hundreds of thousands of students risked their lives to swim to Hong Kong. They were the Freedom Swimmers, and Ning and I were among them.

ooooo

IN 1951, IN THE MIDDLE of Act I, our family moved from Hong Kong to Canton City. We lived through this period without being harmed because Papa was basking in the glow enjoyed by all patriotic insurrection heroes. I was too young to know what Mao did during those six years, but later, when I was in high school, I learned a little about the four political campaigns launched during this period. They frightened me, with their arrests, labor camps, and executions of landlords, counterrevolutionaries, and the other usual suspects: supporters of Chiang who'd remained in China after the liberation and "bad" capitalists, businessmen, and intellectuals.

Mao's Act II aimed at economic development. During these four years, Mao carried out the Hundred Flowers Campaign, the Anti-Rightist Campaign, the Four Pests Campaign, and the Great Leap Forward. Papa was purged during the Hundred Flowers Campaign. This started the downward spiral for our family. How did that happen?

In 1956, Mao declared that "criticism of the bureaucracy will push the government to be better." Because he was dealing with intellectuals, and being a poet himself, he quoted a beautiful line: "Let a hundred flowers bloom and a hundred schools of thoughts contend." I believe Mao was thinking about workplace efficiency and effectiveness, but could he himself take criticism? There was no precedent for this among the emperors of the past. Motivated by Mao's words, intellectuals like Papa opened their mouths to criticize bureaucracy in the workplace. In a moment of passion, Papa spoke his mind too freely. He criticized the poor management of his department and upset the department party secretary, the real boss. Papa never told Mommy exactly what he'd said—now you can see why I detest the Chinese desire to save face—but the criticism from him and other patriotic intellectuals was too much for Mao. After one year, he changed his mind. In 1957, he replaced the Hundred Flowers Campaign with the Anti-Rightist Campaign and accused 5 percent of those who had opened their mouths of being capitalist rightists who had used the campaign to attack the leadership of the Chinese Communist Party. Over two years (1957–59), that 5 percent were forced to confess, humiliated in public, and finally sent to labor camps for reform. Papa was the last one in his department to fill the 5 percent quota. He was under a cloud for months, waiting to be punished. Finally, in 1959, he was sent to a labor camp. The Chinese Communist Party did not cut him any slack for having been an insurrection hero eight years earlier. Indeed, like Papa, almost all his fellow insurrectionists were declared "capitalist rightists."

"Tell your man, my sister," Auntie said after Mommy told her about the 5 percent, "there's no difference between being the first or the last to go to a labor camp. He'll carry a black wok for life." In China, a person who "carries a black wok" never gets rid of the black stain on his body, even if he jumps into the Yellow River to wash. Auntie often said things just to wound, but what she had said was true. Like castrated animals, Papa and his capitalist rightist insurrection colleagues became obedient and downtrodden for many years to come.

"Socialism needs bribery," Auntie said. She liked to make shocking statements out of nowhere, to get people's attention. "Tell your Papa he can't work hard to get ahead or even to save himself."

"Being lazy keeps you safe?" I asked. I was puzzled.

"No. Everybody is lazy. You need to be lazy just to make sure the people around you know you're one of them. But your Papa won't do that."

"What about bribery? Why does socialism need bribery?" I really wanted to know.

"Stop listening," Mommy said abruptly, raising her voice to warn me.

"Don't shout, my sister. I'm teaching your son here." Auntie faced me. "Only the person above you can punish you. I'll bet your dad already works too hard to make those above him uncomfortable."

"How do you know?"

"Human nature." Auntie continued: "He should praise the management instead."

"You mean lie?" I asked.

"What's wrong with that? To lie is to survive." Auntie added: "Or he should work less and spend more time at home."

Mommy cut in: "I don't need him around the house."

"See, this is the problem." Auntie said, laughing.

"How does one bribe?" I pressed, still curious.

Mommy was very firm: "You, go out and play. Your auntie has run into a ghost again." The Chinese say that if you run into a ghost, the ghost takes over your speech. But I actually enjoyed Auntie's ghost talks.

As I grew older, I realized that no matter how much Papa loved China and no matter how hard he worked, he couldn't survive there. Even if he hadn't criticized the inefficiency of his department, he lacked the skills to bribe—and in China, bribery was a must-have skill; it ensured the "survival of the fittest" and enabled one to become a "man above other men." Bribery was needed when

China was poor, and it was needed even more when China was developed—the richer China gets, the bigger the bribe is called for. Papa, with his antipathy to Chiang's corruption, had been a poor fit for China. Mommy was right all along: We should have stayed in Hong Kong.

∞∞∞

WHEN 1958 CAME, I WAS in the third grade. Papa was increasingly depressed as he waited to be punished. In the meantime, Mao had turned his attention to the "pests." He'd identified "Four Pests" China had to rid itself of in order to pursue his grandiose economic development: rats, flies, mosquitoes, and sparrows. Flies and mosquitoes were ubiquitous—tiny, in the air most of the time, and more important, too hard to catch, and thus no fun for us boys. I was all for killing rats, but why those cute sparrows? Mao said that sparrows ate too many grains and fruits before we could harvest them. He called them the "capitalist public enemies."

Our teachers allowed us to skip school for the Four Pests Campaign, which made the hunt for sparrows even more alluring. We used slingshots to shoot anything that flew above our heads or hid in trees. We searched anywhere and everywhere—sparrows were shrewd and hid in places no one could even guess. Throughout the day and deep into the night, we banged drums, woks, pans, and hollow metal containers of all kinds to keep the sparrows from sleeping. Exhausted and disoriented, they dropped from the sky like hailstones. Jubilant kids shouted and laughed as they stomped on the birds, smashing them into a bloody mess while yelling, "Down with capitalism!" and "Down with the counterrevolutionary!" I skipped the bloody mess part. It would have been too much for me.

In the end, nature beat Mao. Without sparrows to eat them, locusts and other insects swarmed the skies the following spring, eating the grain and fruit at will before we could harvest them. Quietly, Mao replaced sparrows in the Four Pests Campaign with cockroaches. But by then, the campaign had lost its charm.

"Lifting up a rock only to drop it on your foot," Auntie concluded.

Mommy was annoyed again: "If you keep saying nonsense to my son, he'll repeat it to others. Then the police will come take him away from me."

"Your son is smarter than you think, my sister. Don't worry. I'm making him smarter than most, including you!" Auntie laughed, I laughed, and Mommy laughed.

That same year, while the Four Pests Campaign was going on, Mao came up with the Great Leap Forward. He gave us a grandiose vision to "surpass Great Britain in fifteen years and catch up with the United States." He didn't tell us how many years it would take us to catch up with the United States, but that didn't bother us. We already knew the Yankees were a "paper tiger," as Mao put it, and that we had beaten them thoroughly and kicked them out of North Korea.

Auntie was unmoved: "Do you know anything about the British or the Americans?" she asked me.

"No, not really," I answered.

"Be smart now. How can you chase someone if you don't know where he is?"

"But Chairman Mao knows."

"How does he know? The only place he's gone outside China is Moscow."

∞∞∞

WHAT WE IN THE CITY didn't know was what the changes in the countryside meant to the peasants. Eighty percent of China's population was peasants. During the formation of the People's Republic, Mao took the land from the landlords and assigned it to the peasants. The peasants really loved that. Then Mao's Great Leap Forward brought collectivization of that land. The peasants' assigned land was taken away and given to the newly formed people's communes. Each commune comprised thousands of families, who were divided into several production brigades, and each brigade comprised several production teams. The people's communes owned and managed the land. The goal of this structural land reform was to "go all out, aim high, and build socialism with greater, faster, better, and more economic results."

In the commune, everything was shared. Communal kitchens were set up, and private kitchens were no longer allowed. Peasants' private livestock, such as chickens and pigs, and their grain were confiscated by the communal kitchens. The kitchens then prepared the food, the "Big-Wok Meal," for the peasants for free.

Before the Great Leap Forward, the peasants meticulously managed the land assigned to them, working hard so that they would have some of the fruits of their labor left over after meeting their quota. The forming of communes took away their incentive to work hard. The free Big-Wok Meals resulted in the same disincentive because the meals were not distributed according to how hard one worked or how productive one was. This dealt a double blow to productivity.

Peasants worked at the tasks assigned to them by their production team leader. The leaders of the production teams, brigades, and communes made things worse by falsifying the records, reporting larger and larger quantities of grain produced per unit of land since collectivization. (To be fair, some of those leaders were not born liars, but if they didn't make up this larger harvest, they would lose their jobs.) And the newspapers kept reporting this false information to warm the hearts of every Chinese. At the time, I believed that China's socialism was turning into the longed-for communism, as did my countrymen.

Where were the voices of the cool-headed, the ones using common sense? There were none. They had either been purged as capitalist rightists like Papa or scared by the Anti-Rightist Campaign that had begun a year earlier.

Naturally, when the food in the city started to run out, Auntie finally felt that her prediction about communism had been proven right. She had come to stay with us again; Mommy said she'd lost her custody battle with her husband.

"People's communes produce lazy ghosts!" Auntie said.

"No, Auntie. You said *communism* made lazy ghosts." I needed to set the record straight.

Auntie shook her head. "I see no difference. 'Three monks living together have no water to drink.'" She was quoting a Chinese folktale that speaks of a monk living alone self-sufficiently in a temple. One day, two monks come to join him. The next day, nobody fetches the water, each hoping one of the others will do it. The three monks wait, and suffer together.

"What did you learn from the monks?" Auntie asked me.

I gave it some thought and then said, "'Every man is out for himself. Otherwise, Heaven and Earth will destroy him.'" I quoted the meanest, most brutally honest Chinese wisdom I could think of. I wanted to show Auntie I could see deep and far.

Auntie smiled. "That's street smarts! But I was expecting you to say 'Big-Wok Meals, people's communes, socialism, and communism all make lazy ghosts.'"

I don't know why Auntie hated lazy ghosts as much as she did when she always looked down on Papa for working so hard.

∞∞∞

STILL, THE GREAT LEAP FORWARD gave us kids one fun thing to do. In school, we were kept busy collecting scrap metal so China could produce more steel. The teachers would give us the afternoon off and we'd run around digging for bits of iron and copper. The teachers had built a furnace to melt the scraps we collected. Also, Street Committee members knocked on the doors of every home to collect anything made of metal. Enthusiastic neighbors contributed their utensils, pots, and pans, the very tools they'd earlier banged together to scare those poor sparrows.

A boy one year ahead of me, Wood Win, named after his carpenter father's vocation, became my friend during this time. Wood Win and I were both fast swimmers and could hold our breaths the longest while swimming in the Pearl River. The river ran through Canton City and collected many tributaries before reaching the Zhujiang River Estuary. On one side of the estuary was Hong Kong, to the east, and on the other, Macau, a Portuguese colony to the west.

People drank the water from the river but also dumped things in it, including garbage. Back then, there wasn't much garbage in it because there wasn't much food. But there was construction waste. When Wood Win and I bumped into some while swimming, we knew we'd found a gold mine to contribute to the Great Leap Forward.

"Can I join you?" Curly asked us one day as we were about to set off to mine our newfound "gold."

"No, you cannot!" Wood Win said.

"I won't tell anybody, I promise." Curly looked sad.

"You can come," I said. I didn't like to see anybody cry. "But you can't dive."

That day, we collected so many scraps that the teachers cast an admiring eye on us as we proudly piled them up by the furnace.

Word of our triumph reached Mommy. She was happy for me, but Auntie said sarcastically, "Sister, your son has contributed more than your family's share of scrap, so you deserve to dream your revolutionary dreams on your steel frame bed."

By extending our scrap metal search to the river, Wood Win and I made a "great leap forward" in our ability to hold our breaths underwater. (There wasn't much improvement in Curly's swimming, but he didn't seem to care.) Our scores were almost even. Curly was a serious judge and did his best to count out the seconds we were able to stay under—"One, two, three"—but Wood Win said Curly favored me by counting fast when it was my turn. To settle the issue, Wood Win and I dove under side by side.

∞∞∞

AT HOME, PAPA HAD CHANGED. He spoke very little. He didn't ask me about my homework as he used to. When Christmas came, he didn't hum Toselli's "Serenade." It was the first time he neglected to do so. Strangely, without hearing that piece, I was sadder. But I hated to feel sad. I would rather have been angry. At least I could deal with my feelings by kicking a wall; the resulting pain in my foot would lessen my anger. And Mommy would say, "Why don't you go find a steel pole to kick?" Strangely, that would calm me down. But for sadness? Physical pain wouldn't do it. And there wasn't any happiness around.

One day, out of the blue, Auntie said to me, "'The chick who thrusts its head above the nest gets its head blown away.'"

"I don't want to hear!" I shouted. I'd had enough of Chinese wisecracks.

"But you must! It's for your own good." Auntie really raised her voice this time.

I was shocked. Auntie wasn't one to win an argument by raising her voice. I walked out, throwing the door open so forcefully that it slammed into the wall.

"Sister, your son has a big temper!" I heard Auntie say. "He's become a man. No man should be kicked around like a smooth river rock."

I am a man? I thought. *Not yet.* But I walked away feeling better.

CHAPTER 3

HUNGER

THE YEAR 1959 MARKED THE beginning of a prolonged period of sorrow and hardship for my family. I was eleven years old and in the fifth grade. That was the year Papa was finally sent to a labor camp and his salary was cut by one-third. It was also the year Mommy started to borrow money from friends to make ends meet and singlehandedly raise the five of us because Papa was no longer living at home.

That year also gave a lot of pain to the Yankees. The American president had to send sixteen thousand "advisors" to Vietnam to bolster the United States in its fight against its three enemies: the North Vietnamese, China, and the Soviet Union. That year saw North Vietnam formally authorize the Viet Cong to undertake military action against South Vietnam's forces, which were backed by the United States. And it was the year North Vietnam finished the construction of the Ho Chi Minh Trail through which military supplies from China and the Soviet Union poured into the hands of the Viet Cong.

The year also saw China and the Soviet Union begin jostling to lay claim to the title of leader of the world Communist

In front of the multi-level building (my home was on the ground floor)
in Canton City during our family visit, 1993.

movement—the guerrilla leader Mao of China versus the proletarian
leader Khrushchev of the Soviet Union. Mao won the title, and his
protracted guerrilla warfare would light fire in many corners of the
Third World. It was also the beginning of Maoism's struggle against
Soviet revisionism, a struggle that would incite Sino-Soviet border
conflicts starting in 1969 and bring about Richard Nixon's historic
visit to China in 1972.

The most shocking event of 1959 had to be the beginning of the Great Famine in China. Within three years (1959–62), tens of millions of Chinese would be wiped out by starvation. In anticipation of such a catastrophe, the Communist Party installed Liu Shaoqi in place of Mao as president of China. The loss of the presidency ended Mao's Act II and planted the seeds of his comeback seven years later, to carry out his third and final act.

The true number of deaths from the Great Famine will forever be kept secret for reasons of national interest. At first, China's official verdict was "Three Years of Natural Disasters." When nobody bought that, this was changed to "Three Years of Difficulty." When I was in China, I didn't hear the teachers using "the Great Famine."

∞∞∞

CHINA STARTED TO FALL APART. Overnight, the great production news disappeared from all newspapers. For a year, the front page of every daily newspaper had warmed our hearts with claims of escalating grain harvests. Perhaps the best was the photo of several young peasants smiling while standing on *top* of a dense wheat field. The accompanying headline claimed that the wheat stalks were so thick that they could support the weight of several adults. Yet, if you looked closely, you could see glimpses of a wooden bench behind the stalks; it was that bench the peasants stood atop for the shoot. But nobody looked closely, and those who did kept their mouths shut.

By reporting elevated quantities of grain harvested per unit of land, the communes had then had to send more grain to the state—the required amount of grain due to the government being a fixed percentage of the reported harvest. No leader of a people's commune would have dared admit to falsifying his reports. So, to make up the difference, the leaders confiscated part of the peasants' share by force. With resulting unrest, militiamen were sent in to serve the dual role of keeping the peace and preventing the peasants from leaving the village to beg for food. So, the peasants starved to death in their own villages, and cannibalism took place. In his book *Tombstone*, Chinese journalist Yang Jisheng estimates that 36 million Chinese died from starvation during the Great Famine. As a comparison, the Holocaust killed 6 million Jews. Every educated person in the world knows about the Holocaust. How many in the world have heard of China's Great Famine?

With the Great Famine, the public kitchens of the people's communes were gone. The scraps we melted into iron chunks in our school furnace were rejected by the steel mill for containing too much dirt and debris. Rumors that North China had run out of food and people were starving to death shocked the Cantonese. Their survival instincts drove them to line up in front of stores before they opened, in order to buy their rations. This caused the supplies to sell out very quickly. When their ration coupons were no longer honored, panic set in. In the end, we Chinese were forever sorry for having chased the British only to be rewarded with three years of Great Famine.

The newspapers started to blame the bad weather for the food shortages. The weather in Canton hadn't changed, but because the Chinese seldom traveled, nobody dared to think the newspapers were lying about the weather in the north.

The newspapers didn't blame Mao's policy of taking away land that had been assigned to the peasants and forming the people's communes.

The newspapers didn't blame the people's communes, which had lied about the large quantities of grain produced.

The newspapers didn't blame the Anti-Rightist Campaign started in 1957, which had suppressed the intellectuals, preventing them from telling the truth and giving good advice.

There were rumors that our rice was being sent to help the North Vietnamese fight the Yankees, but the sarcastic Cantonese brushed these off: "Vietnam is too small to need that much rice!"

At school, the teachers told us that the Big White Pigs had demanded that China pay back monies the Soviet Union had loaned it through the 1950 Sino-Soviet Treaty of Friendship, Alliance, and Mutual Assistance, and that China had had to pay it back in rice and pork. We kids found it all too complicated to understand: loans and treaties, and rice being used as money! But we understood enough that we started to hate the Soviet Union. The teachers also told us that the Soviets had betrayed Marxism-Leninism and become revisionists. To be honest, even as the head of the school's Young Pioneers, I had no idea what revisionism was. I doubted my classmates did, either. So, we just put the Big White Pigs on our enemy list along with the Paper Tiger.

Things were different at school now. Gone was the chasing and shoving in the schoolyard. As our growing hunger depleted our energies, the teachers ruled that no sport of any kind was to be allowed at school. To keep us "healthy," we learned to practice tai chi.

"Tai chi is for the old people, not us!" the boys shouted.

The exercise was slow moving and required concentration, something we were never very good at. But we had to be serious because the teachers were serious, and because the party secretary said it was "for the revolution." He devised a punishment: Anyone caught running in school would be fined the equivalent of a little under two U.S. cents for each violation. Back then, an average starting salary in China was five U.S. dollars *per month*.

The rule was effective. No kid wanted to be spanked by his parents for wasting money for some stupid running. And anyway, by then we were so weak that even if the teacher had offered us a dollar to run, we couldn't have done it! We barely had enough energy to move in tai chi!

We started to see puffy faces on some of our classmates. Our teachers didn't explain to us that the swelling was due to malnutrition. The good thing was it didn't hurt. It just made the kids look strange. Looking strange for a boy was no big deal, but the same could not be said for the girls. Some cried. The teacher told them, "Revolution needs sacrifice, and having a puffy face is your sacrifice for all of us."

Newspapers started to publish stories of how people were dealing with hunger. Mommy tried one of the examples given: cooking rice and then adding water to cook it again. This was called, logically, "double-cooked rice." The idea was that the double-cooked rice would have more volume and would better fill our bellies. But the idea's promoters hid the truth that the swollen rice would also pass through our stomachs faster. Mommy said the trick was not to add too much water for the second cooking; too much could turn the rice into porridge. Each grain of Mommy's double-cooked rice was puffy like the puffy faces of some of my classmates. I hated the double-cooked rice. Not only did I have the same degree of hunger as before, but I also had to pee more often.

"Sister, you cheated yourself and wasted coal cooking the rice twice. Coal is not free." Auntie continued: "I prefer a sip of water following each bite of the 'skinny' rice." This time I didn't laugh.

The newspapers continued cranking out revolutionary ideas with which to cheat our bellies. Most of the ideas were so ridiculous that even us kids couldn't get excited, such as the recipe for "braised pork": chunks of winter melon cooked in dark soy sauce.

I was waiting for my puffy face to show up, but it never did. My sisters' faces didn't get puffy, either. Neither did Mommy's or Auntie's. Only quiet Papa's face became swollen.

"Does it hurt, Papa?" I asked.

"Does what hurt?" He was puzzled.

"Your face," I said.

"It doesn't hurt. Don't worry. You want to see?" He pressed his index finger into his fat cheek and then lifted it. "See my 'dimple'? See it going away?" It did, and I was amazed.

"Let me do it! Let me!" my little sister Bun yelled.

"No!" I was firm. I usually didn't boss my younger sisters around, but when I did, they listened. In truth, I didn't boss any of my sisters, and they didn't bother me. We were always in a state of peaceful coexistence.

The school had its own way of dealing with hunger. The party secretary announced that we would begin raising algae. "There are a lot of nutrients in algae," he declared. Nobody was excited. Who'd want to eat that yucky, slimy stuff? Our teachers guided us in building a brick pond on the flat concrete rooftop of a small, one-story concrete building, the offices of our classical Chinese literature instructor, Teacher Lee, and two other teachers.

It was hard work hauling bricks up a ladder to the rooftop, and even harder lifting the buckets of water to fill the pond. (The party secretary was always impatient for the pond to be built, but he wouldn't dirty his hands helping us.) After several days, the pond was finally completed, and we were told to take a break. We all sat down in the shade of the trees in the school yard, about fifty feet from the pond building. No one had energy left to speak.

Suddenly, Teacher Lee ran out of his office shouting, "Water is coming down!" Then the other two teachers also dashed out of the building, yelling, "The ceiling is falling!" The three teachers stood frozen in front of the building, staring up at the roof as the event unfolded.

In front of our eyes, the brick walls we had built to surround the pond started to crack and water started to leak out. Then the wall broke into pieces. Suddenly, the flat roof of the small one-story building buckled and collapsed.

"Teacher Lee! Run!" I shouted, and the others joined me.

Teacher Lee stumbled farther away from the building. We rushed to him, and he let us hold his hand as we ran. He used his other hand to hold his thick glasses in place.

The collapse of the algae pond ended the school's plan to produce alternative sources of food. But as Mao had taught us, "A bad thing can turn into a good thing": Wasting our hard work building the pond was a bad thing, but avoiding eating the mucky algae was definitely a good thing.

Many Canton City residents had relatives in Hong Kong who came to visit often. Mommy said they brought with them Hong Kong money that our government could use to buy things from the countries that wouldn't take Chinese currency. We were fortunate to live next to the East Train Station, where every day, Hong Kong visitors came through. Wood Win told me they carried suitcases full of food. Unlike me, Wood Win was a street-smart kid and spent most of his time wandering the neighborhood. He told me that a large bag of sweet potatoes from Hong Kong could be exchanged for a new bicycle of the highest quality.

He left the best for last: "Hong Kong people are nice. They hand out cookies to the hungry kids on the street."

"Why are you telling me this?" I asked.

"Come with me," Wood Win said. "We can get cookies from them. You won't have a puffy face like your dad."

I followed him to the crowded train station.

"You watch how I do it, then do as I do," he said.

A line of pedicabs was waiting at the curbside. A newly arrived visitor from Hong Kong approached the curb, and Wood Win sidled up to her and helped her lift her luggage onto a pedicab. He then pushed the cab from behind to help get it rolling. Before it picked up speed, he reached his hand out to the passenger. Without saying a word, she handed him a cookie, as if she already knew what he wanted. Wood Win turned and waved the cookie at me.

That was easy, I said to myself.

I was a quick learner, and soon I was as effective at begging as Wood Win. Unlike him, though, I always smiled back at the passenger after I was given the treat. Wood Win shared his cookies with me, and I shared mine with him. They smelled so good, and the taste was even better. I would never have believed the world had such beautiful food!

It hurt me to think our family could have eaten cookies like these every day if Papa had simply stayed in Hong Kong. I started to hate the insurrection. Without the damn insurrection, Papa would never have gotten a puffy face or been punished by the stupid Hundred Flowers Campaign!

That day at the station, a lady approached pulling a large wheeled suitcase and grasping the hand of a little girl. I rushed over to help her lift her suitcase onto the pedicab, and then I lifted the little girl up onto the seat. As the pedicab started to move, the lady handed me a bun, big and soft. Then, before I could smile, the little girl thrust a magazine in my face. The lady said, "You can have it. I'm done reading it."

I waved the magazine at Wood Win. But he didn't seem interested. He was shouting, "Watch your back!"

I turned around. A policeman was walking toward me. Quickly, I disappeared into the crowd, as Wood Win had done. We were small and could hide easily in crowds. The policeman gave up.

We ran at least a block away and stopped by a large banyan tree on the roadside. I shared the bun with Wood Win. It was not as sweet as the cookie, but it was so soft.

"How could people make a bun so white and so soft?" I asked.

"I don't know," Wood Win said.

"I'm going to save it for Mommy."

"I don't care; it's yours. I prefer the cookies."

The magazine was full of writing and pictures of people in nice dresses and of girls with most of their bodies exposed, except the parts Wood Win and I didn't dare mention. Even the girls were better looking in Hong Kong than in Canton.

"It's because of the color of their lips." Wood Win was sure of it.

"It's the color of their clothes," I said. In China, everybody's clothes were white, dark blue, gray, or black.

A big, colorful picture jam-packed with tall, white, shining buildings behind blue water caught our eyes.

"Hong Kong even has a better-looking river. See! The blue is prettier." Wood Win's dirty finger was touching the page.

I pulled the magazine away and corrected him: "That's not a river. It's the sea."

"How do you know?"

"We lived there."

"Lying!"

"Go ask my Mommy."

"How can they make buildings with pointed angles?" Wood Win said.

"If we had beautiful buns and cookies, we could do the same," I said.

Wood Win was at a loss. "They are two different things."

Later, at home, I offered Mommy the rest of the bun. At first, she was reluctant to eat it. "Begging for food is bad," she said. Then she took a bite, and her eyes turned red.

"Mommy, are you crying?"

"Mommy is not crying. Mommy is thinking." How could thinking turn Mommy's eyes red?

"This time it's fine for you to beg for food, because I cannot help you," she said. She handed me the remaining bun. "You finish it. You need it. We're lucky to live near Hong Kong. People in the north are dying from hunger."

"Dying? I don't believe it." The sounds of the trumpet and firecrackers from the funeral home came back to me.

"Have I ever lied to you?" Mommy asked me calmly. "In one village, starving people first ate the dogs—after the chickens, pigs, and horses were all eaten. Then they ate the grasses and the bark. And finally, the still-living ate the dead."

"Stop it, Mommy! I don't want to hear."

How could people eat dead people? I wished it was just one of those blown-up rumors we heard once in a while. But Mommy had never lied to me before. Unlike Auntie, she lacked the imagination for exaggeration. And I had not been to the north. How could I know? I was sure nobody in Canton or its province would eat a dead person. Cantonese would never resort to that. Heaven had blessed us by letting us live in Canton City. Heaven had blessed our family all along, and if Papa had listened to Mommy, we would be in Hong Kong and he would not have a puffy face.

Unlike in the north, our subtropical climate made everything grow, and grow fast. We had water everywhere, in the sea and the rivers. Cantonese ate everything that moved in the fields, in the water, or in the air, as long as it wouldn't harm them. When a Cantonese spotted something that moved, his first thought was *Can it be eaten?* If it wouldn't kill him, he would try it. If it tasted good, many others would follow suit. If it enhanced health, everybody would fight to get it. If it healed an illness, it would end up in a bitter-tasting soup or soaking whole inside a bottle of sorghum liquor. I once saw a pale, sick-looking man suck blood directly from the tail end of a poisonous snake while it was still moving, its head stuck firmly to a wooden bench with a knife blade. The snake turned pale and stopped moving. The owner had intentionally set up this show on the sidewalk outside his snake soup shop to advertise the healing power of the snake's venom and blood, but the blood sucker's bony face, sunken eyes, and paper-white complexion scared me away from the snake soup shop.

If worst came to worst, people from Guangdong Province would say good-bye to their families and get on a ship to run away. After the abolition of slavery a century earlier, merchant ships from England and other countries frequently sailed to Hong Kong for cheap Chinese contract laborers. The cheap laborers from Guangdong Province were called "coolies," most of them from the Taishan area south of Canton City. Some coolies landed as far as America, to dig gold and build the First Transcontinental Railroad, and many more settled closer to home, in small countries in Southeast Asia such as Indonesia and Malaysia. The coolie trade was a thing of the past, but migrating to other countries to make a living was ingrained in the Cantonese mind.

Since the liberation, Mao had closed the border, so the Cantonese were stuck in their homeland this time around. Rumor had it that Mao had said, "It is better to let half the people die so the other half can eat their fill." But the governor and the party secretary of our province were not as zealous about the Great Leap Forward as many provincial leaders in the north. Before 1959 came to an end, and at the height of the starvation, our governor secretly ordered the train station to sell a limited number of tickets without the required travel permits to people who wanted to go to Hong Kong. Within hours, thousands of people had come to the station to buy tickets. The governor realized he had done something stupid and ordered the ticket sales to stop. People were angry. Our home was right next to the train station's maintenance shop. We could hear shouting deep into the night. One of our neighbors went out to check and came back to tell us that people had turned violent. They were flipping police cars, and many were arrested when the army arrived.

The next day, on my way to school, I walked by the temporary checkpoint set up by the soldiers overnight. Many sandbags were stacked together, and standing behind them was a soldier with his finger on the trigger of a machine gun. Several others had sparkling bayonets attached to their rifles. Soldiers checked every grown-up wanting to get through, and no one who was not a local was allowed. Children could pass the checkpoint freely, but they were scolded if they tried to hang around.

The train station was heavily patrolled by soldiers all day long. Our neighborhood was located outside the station's long brick wall and encircled by a stream. The soldiers were smart. Instead of setting up checkpoints on the many streets, alleys, and lanes leading to the station, they set them up on the few bridges crossing the stream. From there, they could spot anybody trying to cross. The stream was narrow but deep, and it eventually ran into the Pearl River.

No kid cared for that stream. It was always dark and stinky and full of garbage, but it served the adjacent houses well as a dumping ground. Once, I saw a dead cat floating in it.

There was really no need for the soldiers to set up any checkpoint. The mere fact that no tickets to Hong Kong were being sold would deter any Cantonese from coming to the station. The presence of the soldiers turned our neighborhood into a ghost town at night. Kids no longer hung around outdoors, and gone was the familiar sight of old men playing chess under the streetlights.

"People are scared, let me tell you," Auntie said with a shrug, "but I won't even get a chance to be scared."

"What are you talking about, Auntie?" I was puzzled.

"Ask your mother. It's all her fault."

"What has she done?"

"She should have stopped your dad from moving back to China." Auntie raised her voice so it would reach Mommy in the other room. "Even if the government gave me a ticket, I wouldn't go. I know nobody in Hong Kong."

Mommy heard this and walked into the room. "How do you know I'd invite you to visit me?" She laughed. Then Auntie laughed, and I did, too.

"Mommy, where did we live in Hong Kong?" I asked.

"I told you before: Causeway Bay."

"I mean where in Causeway Bay?" I asked.

"What's the matter with you? You can't go there anyway." Mommy was annoyed, "Near Happy Valley."

"What is Happy Valley?" I really wanted to know now. I liked the sound of it.

"Sister, your son is a curious boy. You need to explain as much as your small brain can." We laughed again.

I learned from Mommy that Happy Valley was the name of the racetrack. From our apartment in Causeway Bay, we used to be able to hear the sound of the trumpet at the start of each race. Happy Valley was always full of people coming in with hope but leaving in frustration and anger, and they let their feeling be known by throwing their losing tickets in the street. Some even slammed their cheap little radios to the ground, smashing them. The place was a mess after each race.

"Why did they need a radio?" I asked Mommy. "Couldn't they see the race?"

"They wanted to hear the announcer and his colorful comments. But you must never gamble!" Mommy warned me. "Your Papa doesn't gamble."

"But I want to watch the horses racing," I said.

"Not much to see," Mommy said. "You see one race, you've seen them all."

"Sister, you should tell your son that people in Hong Kong don't do communism or Hundred Flowers Campaigns."

"What purpose would that serve?" Mommy said. "Hong Kong people are different. Nobody cared who the governor was."

After about a week, the soldiers were gone, leaving behind no trace of their checkpoints. Slowly, the neighborhood's normal night scene returned. People again walked freely across the bridges and again noticed the bad odor of the dark stream beneath. The newspapers didn't say a word about what had happened that night. It seemed no one cared how many people were jailed or executed for expressing their anger and frustration at losing the opportunity to buy a train ticket to Hong Kong.

ooooo

ONE DAY, I CAME HOME and found three strangers there. The youngest one stood at Papa's side holding Papa's head down. The man's fingers were stained brown from smoking. The other two were searching our drawers.

Mommy stood in the corner with red eyes. "Go play outside," she told me.

"No. What are they doing?"

One of the men searching our things stared at me, but he didn't say a word. Papa raised his head as if wanting to speak to me, but the brown fingers pushed his head back down.

The men were rude. They threw our papers, even my homework, to the floor. The third man picked up a photo from the Danish cookie tin we used to store pictures and handed it to the older man. That's when I saw his hand. He had an extra little finger!

He asked the older man, "What about this?"

The older man took a look.

Mommy said, "We took those pictures in Hong Kong, before we joined the insurrection to come to China." Mommy accentuated the word *insurrection*. The older man stared at her, then told Extra Finger, "Drop it."

I went to pick it up. It was the picture of Mommy holding me while sitting on a stone wall in the Tiger Balm Garden, a well-known attraction in Hong Kong.

I looked up and, just then, saw tears fall from Papa's eyes and onto his glasses. I took out my handkerchief, soiled with dirt, and handed it to him. But my hand was slapped away by Brown Fingers; his slap also knocked Papa's glasses to the floor. Before I could pick them up, Brown Fingers kicked them away.

In the end, the men found nothing, it seemed, but they dragged Papa out the door anyway. The older man told Mommy, "He won't come home tonight. We need to interrogate him."

"Interrogate him for what?!" I asked Mommy, but she didn't know.

Papa didn't come home that night. He didn't come home the next night, either, or the night after that or the night after that. He didn't come home for a whole year.

When he was finally allowed to come home, Mommy said to him, "See what they've done to you." Although their eyes were red, neither of them cried, and they didn't hug. Papa and Mommy never showed affection to each other in front of their children. (Chinese couples seldom did.)

Papa didn't say a word. I was hoping he'd admit he'd made a mistake by coming back to China.

We learned that while he was away, Papa had been kept in the "Cowshed," a guarded section of an office building set up by revolutionary employees to "jail" counterrevolutionary employees during a political campaign. Many of his insurrection colleagues had ended up in the Cowshed, too. Every day, they were made to write confessions of their "crimes" and were interrogated by their revolutionary colleagues. What did Papa confess to? He never said a word about it.

"Mommy, what did Papa do wrong?"

"Why do you ask?"

"I've got it all figured out," Auntie interrupted. "The party doesn't need your Papa's English anymore. They've trained their young people to take over."

"Not because Papa didn't bribe someone?" I challenged Auntie.

"Your papa wouldn't need to bribe anyone *if* his English were still needed."

"Dismantling the bridge after crossing the river, that's betrayal!" I shouted. I always hated betrayal. I loved to read novels of heroes, friendship, and loyalty, such as the old Chinese classic *Outlaws of the Marsh.*

"No loyalty in politics," Auntie said. "But you should blame your Mommy, too."

"What does this have to do with me?" Mommy was not in a good mood.

"You should have knitted your honey a bright red sweater with a zippered pocket on the right side to thrust his right hand inside every time he went to a meeting. That way, the only hand he could have raised would have been his left."

It took me a few seconds to get what she meant. In China, politics was a game of identity. Even we kids knew that the evil ones were the "rightists," in black, and the revolutionaries were "leftists," in red. The red sweater that would allow Papa to raise only his left hand would have reminded him to vote only with the leftists, no matter what. I thought this was funny, and I laughed.

But Mommy was not amused. She told Auntie, "I'm not interested in your ghost talk."

While Papa was in the Cowshed, Mommy visited him, bringing him clothes, a toothbrush, and a razor. After a few weeks, Papa was sent-down to labor on a chicken farm on the outskirts of the city. The man with the extra finger came by to pick up his clothes. He told us the chicken farm would decide how often Papa could come home for a break.

The farm allowed him one week once a year. Papa came home during the New Year. It felt strange at first to see him, after I had not seen him for so long. He asked me, "How's school?" and I said, "Fine." But I didn't want to talk about school.

That night after dinner, Papa hummed his usual song, but it was not Christmas Eve. Strangely, the song made me happy, but Papa had tears in his eyes.

"Papa, can I talk to you?" I paused, trying to find the right words.

"What is it?" He looked tired. The labor camp had taken a toll on him.

I got straight to the point: "Papa, coming to China was 'a single misstep that brings eternal regret' to our family," I said, quoting a well-known Chinese proverb by a not-so-well-known poet of hundreds of years ago.

Papa didn't like to hear this. His face turned red. "What did your mother tell you?"

"Mommy didn't say a thing," I said. "It's what China gave you in return."

"It wasn't a mistake," he said firmly. "I did the right thing. Chiang Kai-shek was no good for China! He was corrupt!" Papa walked away. This ended the conversation, and I didn't have the guts to say what I wanted to: "Looking back, your whole life has slipped away." I knew it would make him sad. Papa needed a peaceful time while home.

When Mommy learned about our exchange, she was not surprised. "Your papa can't lose face."

"Tell Papa I want to raise the chickens for him." I wasn't joking. "I'd be better suited to raise those damn chickens. I know how to catch cockroaches for them to chase, and I know how to examine the hens for their coming eggs."

Mommy hugged me and started to cry, but I didn't know why.

Papa was fortunate. Many of his insurrection colleagues had been sent to remote regions to do harsh labor, harsher than raising chickens. But in public, just like Papa, they wouldn't talk about life in a labor camp. Were they scared to talk? Or did they simply not want to lose face in front of their families? Papa wouldn't be scared, I was sure, and I didn't want him to be scared. I wanted to believe he couldn't lose face in front of us.

After Papa's downfall, our family lost many friends. Mommy said they regarded us as lepers. She didn't hold a grudge against them, though. "They're scared," she told me. But I saw it as a betrayal.

Uncle Bian was an exception. He wasn't our real uncle, but our neighbor. The Chinese tradition is to call friends "uncle" or "grandfather" or "auntie" or "grandmother," instead of "Mr." or "Mrs." This is to show affection and respect. Uncle Bian saw things clearly with his heart, even though he didn't say a word. He was a truck driver and had been born in North China. We Cantonese saw northerners as honest, but lacking in sophistication.

Uncle Bian didn't like to talk much and would never have gotten into trouble like Papa. He came from a very poor family, and joined Mao's revolutionary army at an early age. He learned to drive a truck while in the army. We Cantonese described such a person as being purplish-red, meaning he would always be secure politically unless he committed murder or arson.

Papa's salary had been cut by one third, and Mommy was always running out of money. Uncle Bian would bring us vegetables he'd bought in remote places along his truck route, where they were much cheaper. Mommy insisted on paying him for the food.

"Mommy, Uncle Bian is a good man," I said.

"I know," Mommy said. "He told me I raised well-behaved children."

"His kids are too young to play with."

"Someday, when they grow older."

"Then I'll play with them and help them with their homework. I promise." I was already thinking what to teach the young kids.

One day, Uncle Bian told me he could bring me to see Papa. He needed to deliver goods to a place close to the chicken farm. I was excited. It would be my first time riding in a truck. The ride on the country road was bumpy and noisy. After more than an hour, Uncle Bian stopped the truck.

"We're here." He looked at me. "Go tell your Papa not to worry. I'll do what I can to help your family."

I nodded, but I didn't know what he meant by "not to worry."

"It's hard for your mother to care for five of you by herself. She's a tough woman all right." Uncle Bian chuckled.

"What are you saying, Uncle Bian?"

"I saw her fight with the people from your Papa's work unit."

"What fight?" I asked. "When was that?"

"You were in school. I saw them leaving your house. Your mother went after them and shouted that she'd kill herself if they relocated the family with your papa!"

"Relocate? Is Papa not coming home?" I asked.

"Probably not. That's how things are done. Don't worry. Your mother will be with you," he assured me.

"Mommy should have told me about her fight," I said.

"Why do you want to know?"

"I want to be as tough as she is when I grow up."

Uncle Bian laughed. He pointed to the dirt road. "Follow the road. It'll lead you to the rear of the farm, where the chickens are. I'll be back in an hour. You'll need to wait for me here."

I got out of the truck and nodded, and Uncle Bian drove away.

I didn't know what to think as I walked down the dirt road toward the chicken farm. Papa didn't know I was coming because Uncle Bian had only learned of his route the day before. I said to myself, *No matter what, I mustn't cry. I'm not a boy anymore.*

The dirt road led to a barbed wire fence. On the other side of the fence were hundreds of white chickens. They were all hens! I had never seen that many hens packed together so tightly. No way I could catch enough cockroaches to feed them all. The hens jerked their heads and strutted around looking for grain on the ground. Then I saw Papa. He was wearing dirty trousers and a worn straw hat while gingerly wading through the hens, casting feed while chanting, "Guk-doc, guk-doc . . ."

When Papa saw me, he was very surprised. "How did you get here?"

"Uncle Bian gave me a ride."

"Will he come back for you?"

"Of course. In an hour," I said. "Can I feed the hens?"

"No, you cannot. You shouldn't be here. Now, you wait there. I have something for you." He went to a little shed outside the fence.

"Who's there?" A man emerged from a flat-roofed one-story building on the opposite side of the shed.

"He's my son," Papa said as he walked toward me.

"Get him away!" the man said. "You know the rules: No visitors!"

"I will." Papa walked up to me and secretly handed me a hard-boiled egg. "Don't let anybody see it. Now, go wait for Uncle Bian to pick you up."

I put the egg in my pocket and, without saying good-bye, walked back up the dirt road. I felt bad but didn't cry. The family picture from Hong Kong, with Papa looking sharp and handsome in a suit and tie, came to my mind.

Uncle Bian was right. After a year at the chicken farm, Papa was released, but was relocated to work in Zhaoqing, a small city about sixty-five miles west of Canton City. Mommy succeeded in keeping all five of her children at our old place, and we continued going to the same schools.

Then the newspapers started to attack our comrade-in-arms the Soviet Union. Our teachers told us the Soviets had become traitors to communism. The Soviets, they told us, had degraded Stalin, who was dead, and wanted a peaceful coexistence with the Western world. Mao found this hard to swallow.

Ever since Mao took over China, Stalin's portrait had been hanging on the gate of Tiananmen Square, next to those of Karl Marx, Engels, Lenin, and Mao. It was routine in some elementary schools for students to stand before the portraits of these great leaders of communism and swear to behave. Now that Stalin was dead, and we were told that his successor, Khrushchev, had betrayed him, China was alone in the pursuit of communism. For my part, I didn't understand what the big deal was if the Soviets wanted to be friends with the West.

The teachers also told us that it was the Big White Pigs who had taken away our rice, wheat, and pork, as loan payments. That was why we'd ended up with puffy faces. By then, we were numb. To hell with the bad weather! To hell with helping Vietnam! To hell with the Big White Pigs! We just wanted food.

"The Big White Pigs outsmarted us this time," Auntie declared. "To be a friend of the West was smart."

"Cover your ears," Mommy told me.

"He has to listen, my sister. The West is a thousand times better than the Soviet Union and China combined." Auntie was in a good mood, and when she was in a good mood, she wouldn't stop. "Just ask your son how good those Hong Kong cookies were, especially compared to your double-cooked rice."

I laughed, then Mommy laughed, then we all laughed.

"Mao should just let the Soviets do as they please. We have enough enemies already." Auntie concluded, "Better yet, he should at least go visit Hong Kong, to learn a thing or two."

Auntie was right. Mao should go see Hong Kong. Rumors had it Hong Kong was planning to build an undersea auto tunnel connecting the island to the Kowloon Peninsula, while we Cantonese were planning to build an overpass at a traffic intersection. Papa said that Hong Kong was worse than Canton was when we left it in 1951, but in less than a decade, capitalism had propelled Hong Kong to her true great leap forward, while Mao's Great Leap Forward had given us the Great Famine.

In April 1959, without fanfare, Comrade Liu Shaoqi replaced Mao as president of the People's Republic of China, and Comrade Deng Xiaoping became Liu's right-hand man. Mao had been forced out by a majority vote during a party meeting. Liu and Deng would now run the country while Mao ran the armed forces and the Chinese Communist Party. Liu and Deng were Mao's Long March comrades. Unlike Mao, they were pragmatists.

Under the leadership of Liu and Deng, slowly but surely, sanity crept back into our lives. Deng was known for saying, "It doesn't matter if a cat is white or black, so long as it catches mice." The colors Deng used confused me at first. I knew we used red and black colors to identify people. Who was represented by white? I wanted to believe Deng was trying to remind us that China should maintain the balance of "yin and yang," such as "black cat and white cat," or locusts and sparrows. But a peasant's labors and the free lunch he got could not be paired.

Liu and Deng's "black cat" and "white cat" indeed tilted China slowly back toward balance. Experts and intellectuals again ran the country, from central to local governments and from industries to institutes, including universities. The public market started to have some produce to sell. Rationed rice was available by coupon, and the ration coupons became very valuable again. Papa's puffy face went away; the same for others. We were allowed to run in school. Tai chi was gone for good.

Rumor had it that Liu and Deng had given some land to the peasants to manage. "Free Big Wok Meal? Dog fart," the Cantonese declared. "People are selfish!" Northerners would never have said things like that. They had never had the exposure to capitalism that their southern countrymen had. The Cantonese continued: "People in Peking only know politics. Those in Shanghai just want to dress pretty. But you can't fill your stomach with politics or dresses, stupid!" To be precise, the Cantonese didn't stop at the word *stupid*; they always added the word for the male sex organ.

President Liu gained popularity by bringing us documentaries of his visits to the Third World, always with his wife by his side. The two were avid travelers, and the documentaries of their state visits were far more interesting than what I was used to seeing. Films showing people of different races in colorful and strange outfits in gorgeous landscapes, without the familiar Communist propaganda, fascinated me. *I want to travel there someday*, I'd say to myself. For about one U.S. cent, I could buy a ticket at the roofless theater not far from home and escape into a different world.

People started to talk more and more about the Lius, especially what Madam Liu was wearing. As for Mao, he was seldom seen on-screen, and his wife Jiang Qing was hardly recognized by the public.

"Mao has only himself to blame," Auntie said. "Why doesn't he go around the globe holding hands with his wife?"

"But she isn't as pretty as President Liu's wife," I said.

Auntie said, "You have good taste in women. Keep it up."

"I'm not going to talk to you," I said. I was embarrassed and ready to leave.

"Wait. Can you see the problem here?" Auntie asked.

"What problem?"

"Jealousy," Auntie said. "Jealousy can drive a person mad." She was reading *Othello* and very much into it, but I found it hard to follow, and gave up after a few pages. I preferred a simple story like *Romeo and Juliet*, but that made me cry.

"How do you know Mao doesn't resent Liu and his wife?" Auntie asked.

"How do you know he does?" I asked.

In its long history, China had never been ruled by two leaders. "A mountain can't hold two tigers," Mommy used to say. Being the president of the country meant being the ruler of hundreds of millions of people. The combined head counts of the party members and the armed forces were only a fraction of that. So, President Liu and Madam Liu's gorgeous dresses got all the people's attention.

"I'm a woman, so of course I know. Madam Mao is driven mad by jealousy," Auntie declared. "If you don't believe me, ask your mother."

Finally, Mommy told me that Papa was the victim of resentment by the young assistant in his department, a man of ambition and envy from a revolutionary family. After Papa criticized the department's inefficiency, the man accused him of using the Hundred Flowers Campaign to attack the party leadership. Once Papa was taken away, he took over Papa's position.

"How do you know, Mommy? Did Papa tell you?" I asked.

"No. But I know someone."

"Perhaps I should try to read *Othello* again, and this time finish it," I told Auntie.

CHAPTER 4

RED VERSUS BLACK

IT WAS 1961 WHEN I started junior high. Beginning in junior high, one's family's political classification started to dictate one's life. This information was kept in a secret personal file called *dang'an* in Chinese, "dossier" in English. One's *dang'an* was a collection of personal information, including one's own words and writing and others' words and writing about you. It also recorded one's parents' and even grandparents' political backgrounds. The party secretary of the school set up the file, and it would follow each student until the day he died. Our *dang'an* dictated whether we'd attend senior high and university, receive a job promotion, marry the person we loved, or be punished during a political campaign.

Every *dang'an* had one thing in common: It identified the person's revolutionary class. There were two classes, "Red" and "Black," and each class had five categories. The Red class included revolutionary cadres and soldiers, factory workers, and poor peasants. The students from the Red class were the political elites. The Black class included landlords, rich peasants, counterrevolutionaries, criminals such as thieves and rapists, and capitalist rightists.

"Red" and "Black" classmates in harmony before the Cultural
Revolution, Canton City, 1965. Front row: Hay is the last one
from the left; back row: I am the fifth from the left.

Because Papa had been labeled a capitalist rightist during the Great
Leap Forward, I was a member of the Black class. A member of
the Black class, even if qualified scholastically, was always denied
admittance to senior high and university. He or she had to accept
this quietly, without fuss.

Most Chinese did not have access to their *dang'an*, including
me. Not knowing what was in mine was perhaps a good thing for
me psychologically. By the end of my last year of junior high, I had
at least two black marks in my *dang'an*, one being Papa's downfall, which I couldn't do anything about, and the other being an
act about which I have no regrets and would repeat if the situation
presented itself again. It was that incident that gave me my first
taste of the class discrimination that would intensify during my
remaining years in China.

Ping-Pong was as popular at my school as soccer, but the
school had a limited number of Ping-Pong tables. The unwritten

rule among the students was that whoever touched a table first would claim it. As soon as the bell rang at the end of the last class of the day, students would dash out of the classrooms and run to claim a table. One day, I was called to deal with a confrontation between some of my classmates and some students from another class. Each party was angry, and I knew I was in a no-win situation when my suggestion that the two groups play against each other was soundly rejected. In the heat of the argument, a guy from the other class threw his paddle, intending to hit the leading "fighter" from my class, but it missed. The "fighter" was not someone who would back down, and he threw the paddle back, hitting a guy on the forehead and causing him to bleed. The blood scared the injured guy's companions, and they walked away with him. I was upset about the whole thing, and left the scene to head home.

The next morning, I was called to see the head teacher of my class. She'd always liked me, but not on that day. She told me that I had failed as leader of my class and must apologize to the other class *in person*. I asked why, insisting that I had only gone there to help resolve the fight and that the guy from the other class had thrown the paddle at us, and my classmate had only responded in kind. She told me that the father of the injured student had demanded that the school severely punish us, and the school authorities had decided to punish not only the offender in my class but also me because I was the head of the class. Finally, she told me that the injured kid's father was a high-ranking army leader, and that she had no choice but to strip me of my position as head of the class. The incident ended with an announcement during a school assembly. The president of the school gave me an open warning, and the classmate who threw the paddle in retaliation almost got kicked out of school. Later, I learned that the injured student was the only one who came to school in a chauffeur-driven car. This was my first encounter with the untouchable princelings.

If there was any consolation in my downfall, it was that the head teacher named me head of the study committee. I was thrilled. Being assigned any leadership position in school always made me feel better. Also, she didn't tell Mommy about the incident.

One day, Teacher Lee showed up in our classical literature class. We were delighted. He was substituting for our regular teacher. As usual, he immediately did his favorite thing, reading a poem from the dynastic era: "Luring winds bellow angrily, / Tumultuous waves hurl against the sky, / Sun and stars hide their light, / Hills and mountains lose their sight . . ."

As he reached the climax, he slowed down and bobbed his head to emphasize the lines: ". . . I admire the men of old who possessed true humanity . . . / When would they enjoy themselves in life? / They cared about others before anyone else / and enjoyed themselves after the others . . ."

Then he looked up at us and asked, "When do you enjoy yourselves in life?"

We looked at one another. No one said a word.

"I want you to remember this line: 'They cared about others before anyone else and enjoyed themselves after the others.' This is the last time I'll be reading poems to you. From now on, we will learn Chairman Mao's poems. I'll be asking you to read them aloud."

"Why?" several students replied. We wanted to continue hearing him read the classical Chinese poetry to us.

With a sad face, Teacher Lee announced that the school had implemented Mao's order that we must speak only Mandarin. "My Mandarin is bad, and it will ruin the beautiful writing," he said. "That's why I'll be asking you to read instead." His tone was depressed, and we felt it. Teacher Lee had told us that only the Cantonese dialect, with its nine tones, could fully express the feeling of classical writing. But Mao wanted all Chinese, regardless of their dialect or race, to speak only Mandarin. Even though Mandarin had only four tones, our "sophisticated" Cantonese tongues had a hard time simplifying their movements. The older we got, the stiffer our tongues became.

So, we read Mao's poems while struggling with our Mandarin: "The mountains dance like silver snakes / and the highlands charge like wax elephants, / vying with heaven in stature . . ." When we reached the climax, someone shouted out, "All are past and gone!" We looked at one another and laughed.

Mao had written good poems, and a good poem, no matter who wrote it, always stirred my soul. I asked myself, *What if Mao just sits down and keeps writing his poems instead of running the country?* I stared at the clouds through the classroom windows. *What kind of life would we have then?*

During the three years of junior high (1961–64), when Mao was not president of the country, the Red and Black classmates got along well, and I had a "peaceful" life just like everyone else. I realized I liked a quiet life more than a chaotic one.

My peaceful school life did not last long, though. In 1964, despite Papa's being a capitalist rightist and despite the punishment I'd received for the fight over the Ping-Pong table, I was admitted to senior high. But my classmate Mellow Shrimp was rejected. This was a shock to everyone. Mellow Shrimp was shy and an excellent student, and he had never made any trouble in school. He told me his father had had something to do with his not getting in. Before the liberation, his father, a businessman, had fled to Taiwan along with Chiang Kai-shek, leaving his family behind. So, rather than attending senior high, Mellow Shrimp was sent to a tea farm in the mountains hundreds of miles north of Canton. He left us quietly and before I had a chance to say good-bye. Years later, I learned that his *dang'an* had been stamped "Unsuitable for Admission."

Why was I an exception? Was being a capitalist rightist less a crime than fleeing to Taiwan with Chiang? I didn't think so. It was a puzzle I had to solve before I applied to university. I had a bad feeling that the exception they'd made for me would not be repeated. I went through several scenarios in my head until a moment of clarity came. The only person who had the power to ignore the rule was the party secretary of the school.

The party secretary was a serious young man from a very poor family. Before being promoted to his current position, he had been the head teacher of my sister Jing's class. Because I didn't pay much attention to my sisters at the time, I didn't know how he'd met Mommy, but apparently he liked her. (People usually liked Mommy after their first encounter with her.) Mommy explained to me that his only son had had some behavioral problems in kindergarten. So, he asked Mommy to babysit, hoping she could influence the boy to grow into a nice person like my sister and me. Mommy turned out to be the right person for the job. She built a good *guanxi* (personal relationship) with the boy. He soon became calmer and behaved better, and I was admitted to the senior high. It was a win-win!

My satisfaction upon finding the answer was short-lived. I started to worry that any university I applied to would not listen to what some high school party secretary said. *What more can I do?* I asked myself. The answer turned out to be completely unexpected: No high school student, Red or Black, would be going to university! I would get only two years of high school under my belt, just like my classmates, and that would be the end of my education in China.

The political organization for senior high students was the Communist Youth League. Joining it would pave one's way to becoming a Communist Party member. Being a member of the party would guarantee a good future, whether that meant landing a good job or marrying a good-looking wife. Some of my classmates from Red families were asked to join the Communist Youth League. League members were the "elites." They held regular exclusive meetings and liked doing things in secret. Though they didn't bother their non-elite classmates, their mere existence cast a dark shadow of self-doubt over me.

The split between China and the Soviet Union brought English as a Second Language to high school, replacing Russian. Our first English-language lesson consisted of two sentences: "Chairman Mao loves us," and "We love Chairman Mao." The English teacher was a soft-spoken lady with many relatives in Hong Kong. She spent a good amount of time explaining the uses of and differences between *we* and *us* and *love* and *loves*. Because we were among the first Chinese students to learn English in high school, the Canton City newspaper came to school to take our picture. The English teacher chose only me to be in the photo with her. She probably didn't know I was carrying around Papa's political baggage. I was worried she would be criticized for her lack of political awareness, but the young party secretary didn't say a thing.

Every year, beginning in senior high, we'd spend a month in a poor village to labor side by side with the peasants, to learn their revolutionary spirit. Also, the school's party secretary would hold a yearly gathering at school known as "Recall the Suffering of the Past and Treasure the Happiness of Today." He'd always invite a peasant from a poor family to come to the school to tell a story glorifying the greatness of Communist China. To prepare, we students would cook a Revolutionary Meal of wild grasses and eat them while listening to the speaker. The idea was for us not only to hear about the sad past but to taste it, too. As we walked around the school playground collecting these wild grasses, we non-elites signaled one another not to pick the kinds that were too tough to chew and hard to swallow.

On one occasion, the speaker was a very old woman. The party secretary had to assist her in taking a seat on the stage. But she was sharp and talkative. She started by saying that today's life was better because we were starting to have more rice to eat. It was an odd opening—in particular, the phrase "starting to have." The liberation had happened more than fifteen years before.

When he heard this, the party secretary interrupted the woman and said, "Our revolutionary grandmother, the students would like to hear how bad your life was under the Kuomintang government, *before* the liberation."

She said, "I know. The Kuomintang was bad, but the worst was the Great Leap Forward, after the forming of the people's communes . . ."

Like thunder appearing suddenly in a sunny blue sky, the party secretary dashed onstage again and announced, "Our revolutionary grandma is tired and needs to take a break. Let's give her a round of applause!"

We clapped as the party secretary led her backstage—but she still wanted to talk. For fear of laughing, I bowed my head and concentrated on eating. Many others were doing the same. Then I realized that bending my neck made the wild grasses even harder to swallow.

That incident was a spark that interrupted the dullness of my high school education. What followed in the months ahead would be a blazing inferno that burned down the country.

It was May 1966, two months before summer break after my second year of high school, seven years after Liu had replaced Mao as president of the country, and five years after the end of the Great Famine. I was eighteen years old. The United States and the Soviet

Union were racing to send the first man to the moon. In China, Mao struck back and reclaimed his throne with another grandiose political campaign, his Act III, to purify the party and culture. The full name of the campaign was the Great Proletarian Cultural Revolution. The Cultural Revolution ended all high school education, and after two years, in 1968, all high school students were sent to the countryside to be reeducated by the peasants. This campaign would last for ten years, ending only when Mao died in 1976.

∞∞

THE CULTURAL REVOLUTION BEGAN WITH the creation of a "big-character poster" by a young philosophy lecturer, Nie Yuanzi. A big-character poster was a wall-mounted poster that employed large Chinese characters as a means of protest. Nie posted hers in Beijing University, the cradle of the student political movements. A hard-core Marxist and Maoist, Nie was angry at the pragmatism of President Liu and Deng and with the direction the country was heading. President Liu and Deng had steered the country away from Mao's ideas such as the "Free Big Wok Meal." They had promoted intellectuals, such as professors and capable educators, to run the universities, regardless of whether they were "white cats" or "black cats." To Nie, this was Chinese revisionism akin to that of the Soviets, and against Mao's teaching. In her big-character poster, she accused the president of Beijing University of running the school in a bourgeois manner. She implied that leaders higher up in the central government were the culprits. Her complaint fell on deaf ears, and this angered Mao.

On August 5, 1966, Mao wrote a blistering short piece in support of Nie Yuanzi's poster. Called MY FIRST BIG-CHARACTER POSTER—BOMBARD THE HEADQUARTERS, it was published in every newspaper. In it, Mao stated that "some leading comrades from the central down to the local levels are adopting the reactionary stand of the bourgeoisie." I was shocked by his words, and his use of phrases such as "bourgeois dictatorship" and "white terror" to describe the forces that had struck down "the surging movement of the great Cultural Revolution of the Proletariat." Who were these bourgeois dictators? It was obvious to many that Mao meant none other than President Liu and Deng.

After Mao's article ran, the front pages of all newspapers published a full-page shot of Mao standing on the Gate of Heavenly Peace waving to jubilant students in Tiananmen Square. Mao and the students wore army uniforms and the same red armband with the words RED GUARD in Mao's handwriting. The Great Proletarian Cultural Revolution was launched, and China would never be the same.

Within days, Red Guards, identified by their red armbands, were organized in many cities. Newspapers printed images of them marching in the streets shouting angrily. The graffiti SAFEGUARD CHAIRMAN MAO WITH OUR FRESH RED BLOOD! was posted everywhere. The university students who were part of the Red Guards took the lead. Within days, Red Guard groups from every high school, cultural institute, and the performing arts were organized. Soon, young workers joined the movement. The only people absent were peasants, soldiers, policemen, kids, and old folks.

Then the newspapers reported that Mao had ordered the Red Guards to "light the fire and fan the flame" all over the country by traveling around and spreading his words. This was called the "Big Link-up." All travel by train would be free for Red Guards, but because they had no identity cards, everyone could claim to be part of the Red Guards and get a free ride. No conductor dared question anyone's Red Guard status, so they let everyone board for free.

The Big Link-up brought the first Red Guards from Beijing's 101st High School to my school. My elite classmates must have known something was coming. They moved quickly to put on army outfits and armbands and called themselves the East Wind Red Guards. They then selected those from other Red families to join them.

My sister Jing was a third-year medical student by then, and Lily and Ning were in junior high; they had never been interested in politics. Bun was in elementary school and therefore too young for politics. Mommy told me I was the only one she worried about.

"I don't want you to join the Red Guards!" She warned me.

"I can't. Red Guards are for those from the Red families. I'm from a Black!"

The East Wind Red Guards took over the school. I didn't know where the teachers, the principal, or the party secretary had gone. Where were they hiding? The East Winds quickly found them and ransacked the party secretary's office, exposing all students' *dang'an*. Papa's past was finally revealed.

Using the *dang'an*, the East Winds prepared a blacklist of teachers to be punished. Their "crimes" ranged from political to nonpolitical, such as extramarital affairs. Then all students, Red and Black, were expected to write big-character posters against them. We wrote day and night, covering every wall in the school.

Meanwhile, the East Winds set up a Cowshed in our school—in this case, a classroom guarded by East Winds twenty-four hours a day. The windows and door were blocked with desks and chairs. One by one, the teachers whose names appeared on the blacklist were jailed in the Cowshed. They were told to write out confessions to their crimes, which had been announced on the big-character posters all over the school.

What happened outside our school was even more frightening. The newspapers revealed the shocking news that Red Guards had placed President Liu and his "running dog" (accomplice) Deng under house arrest in Beijing. Many leaders of the central government in Beijing were taken down, and in Canton, Red Guards arrested the governor and party secretary. In universities, schools, factories, and institutes, the enemies were always the managers and administrators and professors and teachers from Black families. They were the capitalists, revisionists, and any other -ists, and their "running dogs"—the Red Guards succeeded in jailing them in Cowsheds without firing a shot.

I read the big-character posters written by my classmates. They all used the same technique, called *shang-gang shang-xian*—giving a person's innocuous words or actions such political significance that nothing short of a beating or torture will suffice to calm the public's hatred and anger. One of our teachers had relatives in Hong Kong who bought him a British BSA three-speed bicycle that the Chinese called a "Three Guns" bicycle. It was an elegant bike, and we all envied him. He loved it dearly and polished it daily. Then a big-character poster denounced him as a capitalist because he loved this British product. If he loved his British bicycle, he must love the British, the thinking went, and he must not love China. Therefore, he was a capitalist and a traitor. That was definitely *shang-gang shang-xian*. To the Cowshed he went!

The rumor mill was working overtime during this period. Neighbors spoke about the downfall of the famous, local and nationwide. Mommy was more aware of what was happening in the city than I was.

During lunchtime, the kids came in droves to read the posters. They read only those that exposed extramarital affairs, chatting and giggling as they read. And when a new poster appeared, they didn't miss a beat. They'd go home and tell their friends and parents, and their friends and parents in turn would tell others. Watching them, I recalled the kids stomping on those sparrows while shouting, "Down with the counterrevolutionaries!" We, the most intelligent and the fittest of all living creatures, always seemed to find joy in others' misery.

The teachers in the Cowshed were not allowed to go home, and they were interrogated whenever their captors felt the urge. There was really nothing to ask them; their "crimes" had already been detailed in the big-character posters on the walls. But to keep the revolution going, it was important to offer the interrogators some fun.

The East Winds might not have been the smartest students in school, but they were certainly the most creative at torture. Beating the teachers with sticks and leather belts was boring. Forcing them to crawl and bark like a dog in order to receive food and water was fun. Also, riding our teacher's precious "Three Guns" bicycle up and down the stairs until it broke into pieces was a special treat, available only at our school. (Savagely cutting a teacher's hair was considered "mild" and boring; this punishment was usually reserved for the female "monsters and demons.")

Monsters and *demons* quickly became the most popular criminal designations during the Cultural Revolution for any counter-revolutionary or capitalist or revisionist or feudalist or whatever other criminal lurked in the minds of the Red Guards at a given moment. The term was effective—instantly conjuring up a visual of evil that could scare the kids, an efficient, one-size-fits-all no-brainer. So, I will use this term from now on for the same reasons.

Compared to other places, the East Winds at my school were "gentler"; no one died in our Cowshed. Rumor had it that Red Guards elsewhere forced their monsters and demons to kneel on the still-burning ashes of books and other offending objects, such as violins. One famous Cantonese opera singer was hit on the back repeatedly with hardcover books while forced to kneel in hot ashes. The books were thrown at him from a balcony several stories above. Every blow brought loud cheers and laughter from the East Winds. Apparently, the singer was guilty of performing an opera that glorified the feudalism of the old dynasties, and he had therefore not followed Mao's speech given at the Yan'an Forum on Literature and Art in 1942 that demanded that all art serve the workers, peasants, and soldiers.

After the interrogation came the sentencing, which was always quick. A person's crimes would always be one of the list of crimes—counterrevolutionary, capitalist, revisionist, imperialist, or feudalist—and would have appeared numerous times on the big-character posters against him or her.

Finally, came the climax. For this, a loud, hysterical crowd was required, so everyone, Red and Black, was expected to attend. The bound "monsters and demons" were then lined up to face the crowd. Each one of them wore a large board around his neck, with a red X written over his or her name. The X symbolized a death sentence for the offender's nonphysical being: his thoughts and beliefs—Mao had not given the Red Guards the order to put to death anyone's physical being. Of course, physical death was quite acceptable if the "monster and demon" committed suicide or died in the Cowshed "mysteriously."

Every time a person's name and crime were announced, the crowd erupted in thunderous shouting of either "Down with . . ." statements, with enemies of all kinds mentioned, or statements glorifying Chairman Mao; with the latter, only the best words and phrases would be used. The louder and angrier one's voice, the more revolutionary he or she was considered. After this public spectacle, the "monsters and demons" were then sent back to their Cowshed, and the torture routine resumed.

Participating in such events made me worry about Papa. In my mind, he could not escape such punishment. I could only pray to Heaven to make him suffer less. For myself, I thought of only two things I could be punished for: Papa's being a capitalist rightist and the many pictures of me taken in Hong Kong. But I couldn't do a damn thing about either. What good would it do to worry? I scratched my head and started to feel uneasy about the English word *Mommy*. My good friends in my class also called my mother "Mommy," and she didn't mind. For them, the word was different, fashionable, and had a ring of Britishness to it.

If I'm accused of being unpatriotic, so be it. I can't deal with all my worries, I told myself, and stopped worrying about using the word *Mommy*.

"Mommy, have you heard anything from Papa?" I asked her one day.

"He's safe, so far," she said. "Heaven blesses his small city. He's lucky he's not working in Canton."

"A small city is better? Why?"

"In a small city, things could go to either extreme."

"I don't know what you mean."

"Go find out for yourself." Mommy had been impatient lately.

ooooo

ALL TEACHERS NOT IN THE Cowshed were separated from us. I learned that they were studying Mao's teachings and writing big-character posters against their colleagues. Now in control of the school and the class, the elite East Wind Red Guards turned their attention to their classmates. Overnight, I became one of the "little bastards," the term they used for those of us from Black families. The expression was based on a tenet of Chinese "wisdom" that said that who your parents were determined who you would become. In the eyes of the East Winds, they were the natural heroes because their parents were considered heroes. Conversely, those from the Black families were little bastards because they had been bred by their bastard parents.

The East Winds told us little bastards that we must align with Chairman Mao and disgrace our parents. As a little bastard, I was expected to criticize Papa's crimes in front of the class and give personal examples of how Papa had influenced me in the wrong way. All little bastards had to tell the class how they would redeem themselves by applying Mao's teachings from his "Three Constantly Read Articles."

I had expected the day would come when everybody in my class would learn of Papa's downfall. But for my good friend Hay, he didn't expect his family secret to be exposed. It was a sad story. When Hay was a baby, his father was executed during the liberation and his mother committed suicide. Hay grew up under the care of his "uncle," a family friend. Hay's *dang'an* didn't mention his biological parents, but a classmate dug out Hay's uncle's history and by chance found out Hay's secret. When Mommy heard about it, she asked me to invite Hay to the house. We learned that his biological father had been educated in Paris. Some of his father's schoolmates later became high-level Communist Party leaders in China. But Hay's father chose civil engineering in school, and returned to China to build dams for the Chiang government during the Chinese Civil War. Hay's parents didn't flee to Taiwan with Chiang before the liberation and were arrested by Communist soldiers. Hay's father was forced to design and build a dam before being executed; his mother hanged herself afterward. Hay's parents had sent him away to the family friend before they were arrested by Communist soldiers.

Mommy took Hay in with love, and soon became his god-mother. Hay would become the pioneer freedom swimmer and would inspire me during the darkest years of my life.

The Cultural Revolution revealed the darker side of humanity. The worst were the children who reported their parents' private so-called counterrevolutionary conversations and deeds to the Red Guards and cheered when they were dragged away to be punished. These children shouted revolutionary slogans when the Red Guards roughed their parents up in public. This display of ugliness by my own kind affected me, and I realized that the world was much worse than I had once believed, or wanted to believe, it to be. An animal would not hurt its own parents. How could humans behave worse than an animal?

Students' love for Mao was so intense that simply shouting "Long live Chairman Mao" was not enough. I don't know who started it, but my school soon adopted a new, more expressive form of worship: Every morning before the class, we sang and performed the "Loyalty Dance" to glorify Mao. We'd sing about Mao being the sun and we being the sunflowers that followed him; about Mao being the helmsman and we being the sailors guided by him. And we'd dance along to the song, to accentuate the lyrics. My dancing was so clumsy that I wondered if Mommy would be disgusted if she happened to drop by. Or would she be amused to see that her son, with zero talent in dancing, was not the worst among his classmates? She might even think the Cultural Revolution was not all bad—at least it made her son dance and sing first thing in the morning.

Symbols were a way to organize the masses. The red scarf worn by the Young Pioneers symbolized the blood of our revolutionary martyrs, and the red armband with Mao's calligraphy spelling out RED GUARD symbolized our spilling our blood to safeguard Chairman Mao. But people's love for Mao was so intense that a mere red armband was thought inadequate. Overnight, Mao badges appeared. Quickly, they exploded. Hundreds of different designs popped up everywhere. People collected and traded them. A few crazy ones (none from my school) pinned the badge *through their skin* to show others the bloodstain on their shirts. What else could show a deeper love?

"Don't you dare pin it through your skin!" Mommy watched as I put on the Mao badge I'd gotten for free from a classmate. I needed one, since everybody was wearing them.

"I'm not stupid!" I shouted. "I wear it so I'm no different from my classmates. I also need it because of Papa."

The East Wind Red Guards had nothing to teach. They were usually not the very smart ones in the class. They demanded that we study Mao's *Little Red Book*. Soon, we'd memorized everything. I had never thought a political movement could train a bunch of liars, but our Cultural Revolution did. I was one of the trainees. Every day, I needed to make up a new story that "logically" tied two things together: Papa's crime with Mao's teachings. Under the pretext of the Hundred Flowers Campaign, Papa had been accused of attacking the party leadership at his workplace. I didn't dare say to the class that Papa'd only criticized the poor management. No, I had to turn his downfall into some sort of crime against *the spirit* of Mao's "Three Constantly Read Articles." The challenge for the Black students was that the spirit of the three articles had nothing remotely to do with what our parents were accused of. "No one can mate horses with cattle." What I could do was make up lies using my imagination.

Mao's first article was a tribute to a Canadian physician and member of the Communist Party of Canada who had come to China to help him in his guerrilla war against the Japanese invaders; the man had died during World War II.

The second article was a Chinese folktale about a foolish old man who tries to move a mountain. Mao's intention in writing the article was to have the Chinese people apply the spirit of the story to the fight against the Japanese invaders. In the story, the old man moves the mountain by an unconventional method: shovel after shovel and generation after generation. In the same vein, we could defeat the Japanese invaders with small-scale guerrilla warfare and never-ending attacks. (We all knew Mao's guerrilla tactics: "The enemy advances, we retreat; the enemy camps, we harass; the enemy tires, we attack; the enemy retreats, we pursue.")

The third article was about serving the people and not being afraid of criticism or sacrifice. This article turned out to be the best for my purposes. For example, I could say, "I saw an old woman crossing the street, but I didn't hold her hand to make sure she crossed safely. And when I told my dad about it, he didn't criticize me. So, my dad failed to follow our great leader Chairman Mao's teaching, and this had a bad influence on me." I had to draw the line from my actions back to my father and then do self-criticism. But there weren't enough old ladies on the streets of Canton to meet the demand, and we couldn't "just change the solvent without changing the solute" and claim we had a new herbal medicine. You see, making up a lie to fit the narratives in China was not so easy.

Intuitively, every little bastard knew there was a line he should never cross, that he should never overdo the lying and create a bigger problem for himself and his parents. This wasn't easy. And with each passing day, it became progressively more difficult to come up with a new, workable lie. In the end, when you kept lying, it became second nature. This was just a snippet of how the Cultural Revolution was changing Chinese culture.

In any case, the East Winds were never satisfied with a little bastard's self-criticism, and they would scold their erstwhile playmates bitterly and loudly. Soon, they grew tired of their futile dealings with us and abandoned Mao's *Little Red Book* and the "criticism and self-criticism." Around the same time, they also grew tired of "jailing" the teachers in the Cowshed. They abandoned the "Cowshed" and let the jailed teachers go home.

Gone, at last, was the "Loyalty Dance" to glorify Mao; gone were the lies to criticize Papa and the "climax" of punishment for the monsters and demons that tore my vocal cords and shattered my eardrums. I was free, mentally and physically!

CHAPTER 5

THE BIG LINK-UP

IT WAS THE SUMMER OF 1966. With no more school for me, a heavy weight was lifted from my chest. I needed to get out of the city for the Big Link-up. I wanted to go to Zhaoqing to see Papa. He had been working there for six years since the chicken farm, but I had never been to visit. Even though he had written us "so far so good," I was still worried about him.

With three classmates, I hit the road. My classmates wanted to see the beautiful Star Lake, and we all wanted to climb the limestone hillocks that made Zhaoqing famous. It would be a sixty-five-mile walk from Canton City. A piece of cake, we thought.

We planned to drop by some villages along the way to pass out leaflets bearing Mao's quotations—and get food and a place to sleep if needed. The leaders of people's communes all over the country had instructed villagers to welcome any Red Guards who arrived and to provide them with food and a place to sleep if asked. Mommy was skeptical that we would complete the journey on foot. She said it was a dumb idea given that transportation was free.

Family photo during the Cultural Revolution, 1967.
Back row from left to right: Bun, Jing, Lily, and Ning.

"Peasants have no time for your preaching," she said.

"Mommy, I'm not going to preach Mao's doctrine. We'll just hand them some leaflets." I added, "I want to see Papa." My mind had been made up.

The villagers were friendly but not particularly excited to see us—except the kids. They knew all about the Cultural Revolution. Many homes bore Chinese antithetical couplets on the front door, LONG LIVE CHAIRMAN MAO and LONG LIVE THE CULTURAL REVO-LUTION. They knew the Big Link-up would bring Red Guards to them, and they were prepared.

I was disappointed to see some kids using our flyers to make origami, but I couldn't blame them. They were bored. While their parents were sweating in the fields, the kids, barefoot and with snot dripping from their noses, chased the paper airplanes and birds they made and tossed up into the air.

"I bet they'll use the flyers to wipe their butts," I joked to my companions. "Would that be counterrevolutionary?"

No peasants stopped to listen or talk to us. They were practical people who probably knew deep down that the Big Link-up was nonsense. But I wouldn't have dared ask what they really thought about it. I recalled that old peasant woman who spoke at our school while we were eating that revolutionary grasses meal. She had been candid and dared to tell the truth. What if a peasant told me straight to my face that I was wasting his time? I wouldn't know how to answer. Better to leave them alone.

After three days on the road, we were bored. We told ourselves we had done our part for the Big Link-up and Chairman Mao. We took the sensible way out and took a riverboat the rest of the way. The boat would run upstream westward on the Xijiang River to reach Papa's city of Zhaoqing.

The boat labored against the currents, and the wind was harsh and chilly. The river was murky and engorged from a recent rainfall. The sun was blocked as we passed Antelope Gorge. The river resembled a black snake. I looked up at the slope. Its face was rocky and rigid, with no resemblance to a kind and innocent antelope. I stood by the stern, letting the coldness seep deep into my bones. I couldn't imagine then that I would be seeing this river and this gorge again in two years, but when that happened, the Xijiang River would give me joyous and peaceful moments during the most dreadful years of my life.

The boat docked in the center of Zhaoqing. We split up. My classmates went to Star Lake Park, and I went to see Papa. He had been working in the city's import/export department. The city was small and calm. As in Canton City, there were graffiti and posters on every wall I passed. Unlike in Canton, where many shops were closed because of frequent looting by Red Guards, all the shops here were open. By asking locals, I found out that the city hall complex where Papa worked was a twenty-minute walk from the boat's terminal.

The receptionist was a middle-aged woman. She asked me who I was and why I was there. I told her my name and that I wanted to see my father.

"Why do you want to see him?" She seemed suspicious.

"I'm his son." I said, perplexed by her question.

"Follow me."

We walked past a couple of one-story buildings to reach the last one on the far side of the city hall enclosure. She knocked on a door.

"Who's there?" It was Papa's voice.

"Your son has come from Canton to see you," the receptionist said.

Papa opened the door. He looked surprised. I hadn't written to say I was coming.

"How did you get here?" he asked.

"Didn't you know your son was coming?" The receptionist was surprised, too. "You need to keep it quiet."

"I will," Papa said respectfully as she turned and left.

"Papa, are you safe?" This was my first and most important question.

"Yes, of course." Papa seemed happy to hear my concern.

He explained to me that he had a good *guanxi* (personal connection) with the mayor. The mayor wanted to protect Papa because he needed him to do the work of the whole department, so the others could leave the office to participate in the Cultural Revolution. Coming from a big city, I was surprised the mayor was not yet in a Cowshed. The small city had not been overtaken by violence yet. Mommy was right. In a small place, the political movement could go to either extreme. Heaven must have been watching over Papa.

Still, I didn't like his appearance. He was unshaven and looked dejected. I was reminded of that unpleasant visit to the chicken farm. I thought back to when he was neat and confident in his three-piece suit, his large round forehead shining. Being alone and in constant fear in a small city for too long had taken its toll on him.

"I'm fine," he insisted. "How about you?"

"I'm good." I decided not to tell him about all the nonsense at school. "My classmates and I went on the Big Link-up but gave up. We took a riverboat here instead."

"That's smart. Are you hungry? Do you have money for food?"

"Yes," I said. "Can we go out to eat something? It's stuffy here."

"I need to stay at work; I can't take you out to eat."

I got straight to the point: "Papa, will the Red Guards come here to get you?"

"So far, so good. Let's not worry about what'll happen tomorrow. If things happen, they happen."

"Can I help?" I asked, even though I had no idea what I could do.

Papa looked touched. He stood and walked to the window, but he didn't pull the drape aside. The material was old and torn and let in threads of sunlight. Below the window was the desk. A little electric fan on it made a light grinding sound.

"I couldn't have known what was waiting for me in China when I joined the insurrection," Papa said. He seemed to be talking to himself as he faced the window. He took out his handkerchief to wipe his eyes. Being alone and confined must have forced him to reflect on the past a lot. He had suffered enough. What was the point of beating oneself up?

A Chinese proverb came to my mind: "Papa," I said, "remember? 'One who knows what'll happen in the next three days will be prosperous for ten thousand years.'"

There was a long and uncomfortable silence. Finally, Papa said, "You shouldn't stay too long. You must be hungry, but I can't take you to a restaurant."

"I know. You don't need to explain."

"Go get some food. There's an eatery, a local favorite, by the ship terminal selling tasty Shaoxing zongzi, a tasty sticky rice wrap. You'll like it."

"I will." But I didn't feel like eating by myself. "You want me to bring you some?"

"I have enough leftovers."

Before we parted, Papa gave me a hug. "Tell Mommy I'm fine. Promise me you'll be careful. You need to control your temper. Endurance is a character trait you need to build."

Like my visit to the chicken farm, my visit to city hall was short. At the farm, the official had not let me stay, but I didn't know why. Here, Papa didn't want me to stay, and I knew why. As I walked out of the city hall complex, the big rat came to my mind, the one that hid inside the kitchen drain during the day and roamed our house freely at night. Unlike that rat, Papa had to hide in his small room all the time. If that was the life one had to endure, what was the point of living? Was the inability to endure such things what was driving many in the Cowsheds to commit suicide? The more I thought about it, the sadder I got. It sickened me.

As I walked toward Star Lake Park to meet up with my classmates, I kept thinking about endurance. Papa knew I didn't have that character trait. He no doubt believed I had his gene for impatience, but like most Chinese fathers, he never would have admitted to a shortcoming in front of his children. Still, he was right: If I wanted to survive in China, endurance would be a must. He had learned this the hard way. But what could I do to acquire it? How could I overcome my impatience?

Mommy was happy to see me home, but my sisters didn't care much; nor were they interested in Big Link-up in the countryside. I told them about my visit with Papa. No one had anything to say, but I could tell Mommy was relieved.

∞∞∞∞

BY THE END OF THE summer of 1966, things in Canton City became much worse. The second group of Red Guards was formed. Most of them were once little bastards of the Black class. In Canton, this group of Red Guards gave themselves the name "Red Flag." Red Flags and East Winds were at odds from the beginning, and they quickly turned into enemies of war, armed with clubs, knives, and guns. Guns? In China? Yes! Guns that had once belonged to the soldiers were now in the hands of the East Winds and Red Flags.

Dead bodies started to appear in unexpected places, and they were not accompanied by the scraping trumpets and popping firecrackers of a funeral service.

But strangely, I wasn't scared anymore. I was too numb.

"Have you seen that dead man hanging from the tree?" Mommy asked.

"No, I haven't," I said matter-of-factly. "Do you want me to?"

"You're no longer a boy. Do what you want."

I had seen and heard about enough torture and people jumping out of windows to end their suffering that I had started to believe that favorite saying of old people, "Death was a relief." What could I gain from seeing a few more dead bodies? If Mao ordered the physical punishment of little bastards like me, I would have a chance to join the dead.

Wood Win and Curly didn't see things as I did. Wood Win had been making money as a handyman, helping his dad. He had been kicked out of school for leading kids to beg for cookies at the station. The school said this degraded our great Motherland. I was lucky I had quit before I got caught. Wood Win brought Curly and me to the spot on the river where we once dove for scrap metal for the Great Leap Forward. A woman's naked body bobbed in the waves. The dead woman was facedown with her hands tied behind her back. Numerous deep slashes exposed whitish raw tissue, but there was no blood in the wounds. We flipped the body over with tree branches and saw that the woman's nipples were gone. It was horrifying.

"Why? Why nipples?" Curly asked. "Now I don't want to hide my Bible near that spot."

"What are you saying?" I was lost.

Wood Win explained that he had suggested that Curly hide his Bible under the rubble there. Red Guards had punished Curly's parents because they were Christians. So, Curly was a little bastard just like me. I suddenly felt more sympathy for him. I had learned that the Seventh-day Adventist pastor and my grandpa were good friends, and the pastor had taught Papa English. Papa hadn't kept his Bible, so I didn't know what it said, but I knew I had to help Curly hide his copy.

What an excellent idea, I thought, *to hide the "dangerous" books underwater.*

Using a branch, we pushed the dead body away from the bank. It caught the current and slowly floated off.

"Now the kids can't throw rocks at her or spit on her." I felt better.

As the body slowly drifted away, Curly prayed for her.

Wood Wind said: "This is our hiding place. Don't tell anybody."

The next day, I helped Curly hide his Bible at the bottom of the Pearl River. Before we did, he wrapped it in several plastic bags and tied the bundle up well. Thanks to him, that spot became our secret place for valuables, among them my copy of *The Count of Monte Cristo.* (In 1972, six years into the ten-year Cultural Revolution, when I was preparing for my first escape attempt, many hand-copied banned books appeared in Canton City, secretly passed from hand to hand among friends. *The Count of Monte Cristo* was one of the most sought after.)

On our way home, we saw a crowd forming in the street. We ran over and pushed our way through. Another dead body! A man, perhaps in his fifties, was hanging from a large banyan tree by a rope wrapped around his wrists. Blood covered his swollen, badly beaten face and was still dripping from his wounds. A large piece of cardboard bearing the word COUNTERREVOLUTIONARY hung from his neck, but there was no name, only a large red X. This time, the X meant physical death *in addition to* the death of one's thoughts. The spectators had no doubt that the Red Guards and the angry mob were the executioners. A kid spat on the dead man and was scolded by an old man in the crowd. Nobody else spoke. Everybody wore a wooden expression, except the old man, who shook his head.

Curly and I walked away, neither of us saying a word. When I got home, the sun was down and the large room was not lit. Mommy sat quietly on the edge of the bed.

"Mommy, why haven't you turned on the light? What's wrong?" I asked.

She didn't say a word. Finally, she spoke: "Pick up all the blueprints and throw them in the garbage can."

"Why? They're for Uncle Chang."

Mommy raised her voice: "Do as I say!"

"What did I do wrong?" I asked.

"He's gone!" Mommy's eyes started to tear up.

Uncle Chang was a manufacturing manager. He had set up a blueprint shop in our neighborhood, to offer housewives an opportunity to earn money by making blueprints of his company's engineering drawings. Mommy was among the women he hired. She needed the extra money to support the family after Papa's salary was cut. Before Uncle Chang came along, Mommy had had to borrow money from the few remaining friends who had not distanced themselves from us.

Uncle Chang had said that Mommy had "the best hand." I believed him. It took a pair of steady, delicate hands to make the perfect contact between the large light-sensitive paper and the transparent engineering drawing placed over it, and Mommy had a pair of hands adept enough to knit colorful flowers on a sweater. Working in the shade, Mommy would sandwich these two sheets between a glass plate and a flat board. After the two sheets were exposed to sunlight, the white paper was put in a container full of pungent vapor, which would turn the paper blue except where the sunlight had been blocked by the words and lines in the drawing. These would remain white against the blue background—hence the name "blueprint." I hated that vapor. It made my eyes tear and smelled much worse than the public toilet.

Mommy was smart, too. She varied the sun exposure time by judging the darkness of the shadows. "The darker the shadow," she told me, "the stronger the sunlight and the less time needed under the sun." She continued: "A good blueprint is blue enough but not too blue, so the white lines and words are still vivid." How did she know this? She told me she had been merely an okay student in high school, and she had never set foot in a college, but she had intuition. School had taught me the speed of light and its spectrum, but it couldn't teach me intuition. I realized it was a good thing if I learned something outside school.

Mommy and the other housewives always prepared treats for Uncle Chang when he showed up. And he always made the same humble remark before eating them: "Don't thank me. It's the party's policy to develop light industry in the neighborhood. I'm just doing my job." Uncle Chang loved food, and it showed. He was big, very big—at least by Chinese standards back then. He said he was fat when he was little, and he just loved food. He could talk nonstop for hours about food without catching his breath once. He had been a lot of places, and he fascinated me with tales of Inner Mongolia.

"Mommy! What happened to Uncle Chang?"

She didn't say a word, but she had stopped crying.

"Tell me, Mommy," I insisted.

"He climbed up the ladder of the water tower and let go." She wiped away her tears. "He landed on his face."

Next to Uncle Chang's factory was the tower that stored water for the area. It would take a lot of effort for anyone to climb to the top, fifty feet above ground. I couldn't imagine the tremendous determination it must have taken for Uncle Chang to haul his more than two hundred pounds up that high to end his life! What was in his mind as he climbed that ladder, step by step? The thought frightened me, and I couldn't fall asleep that night. When I finally did, I was terrified by a dream of a club-wielding gang chasing me into a dark alley, where my feet got stuck in mud. I couldn't move. The harder I tried, the harder it was to lift my feet. In a panic, I woke up sweating. I had the same nightmare again and again for months.

I learned that Uncle Chang had been put in a Cowshed and been beaten badly. Finally, he gave up on life. He arrived in Heaven with a smashed, unrecognizable face. The blueprints he left behind were turned into many beautiful origamis by the small hands of the kids in the neighborhood. The neighborhood's light industry died, washed away by the tears of the now-unemployed housewives. Mommy returned to knocking on the doors of our family's few remaining friends. She'd watch their faces for hints of their willingness to help before opening her mouth to ask for money.

People say that time heals all wounds. This puzzles me. How? Time is not a doctor. In order to heal a wound, one first must find out the cause and extent of the wound. But the Chinese government will never allow this to happen. The reason is rather simple: Any revelation would shame Mao and the Communist Party; it would challenge their legitimacy. That is why the Communist Party must censor the true number of deaths from the Great Famine, even though that number could easily be determined through the government's strict population control and Household Registration system. The same applies to the Ten-Year Calamity.

When China was poor, the weapons of censorship were labor camps, imprisonment without trial, bullets and tanks, public executions. Now that China is advanced, individuals and institutions in the Western democracies have benefited financially, so they immerse themselves in the make-believe notion that a richer China is a more democratic China. But in that richer China, the weapons of censorship have continued and advanced—reform camps, kangaroo courts, false imprisonment, rubber bullets, water cannons, financial ruin. When the internet came along, these same Westerners dreamed of democracy spreading all over the world like wildfire, including in China. But China has succeeded in turning the internet into three weapons in one—a tool of surveillance, censorship, and propaganda—to control the country's 1.4 billion citizens. An army of writers floods China's closed internet with lies to foment and grow strong nationalistic sentiment. And in a country of extreme nationalism, it is taboo to talk about, write about, or even remember the causes and extent of the wounds of the past political movements. At the same time, those who were misled by the Communist Party of China and did harm to their countrymen during those past political campaigns will never express remorse. Redemption has never been a virtue in Chinese culture, but saving face has been and always will be. Adding to that is greed, which has been a driving force behind the self-censorship of those Chinese and foreigners who benefit from China's behavior and bow to the "emperors" of the new China.

Government censorship and the lack of personal courage will bury the wounds of the Cultural Revolution and all the other political campaigns since the founding of Communist China. The pain of those wounded will ease only with the natural aging process, as they forget the painful memories of the past. (Is this what is meant by "Time heals all wounds"?) And when the wounded finally die, they will carry their unhealed wounds to their graves and leave behind many blank pages in the history of China.

Who will fill in those blank pages?

Papa's downfall had trained Mommy to deal with the stresses and pain of the Cultural Revolution. Yet, even for a tough woman like her, it was a struggle to make sense of the madness of Uncle Chang's suicide.

"Why didn't Chairman Mao send the police to arrest all the 'monsters and demons'?" Mommy asked me. "How could he rely on students and ordinary folks? If the police had arrested Uncle Chang, he would have ended up in jail instead of dead."

"You think jail would have been a better place for him?" I asked.

"A bullet to the chest would have been better than dying with a meat-patty face."

"Easier for the family? Or for the funeral service?" I was frustrated that she was comparing forms of death. "Mommy, a death is a death."

She didn't respond, but she'd given me a puzzle to solve: Why *hadn't* Mao used the police or the army to arrest and punish his enemies? China had so many enforcers. If Mao needed more, he could have called on the militia—they numbered in the millions. Fortunately, Chinese loved to discuss politics in private, especially government infighting. By eavesdropping and poking around, I eventually arrived at an answer that satisfied me.

To begin with, unlike the Soviet Union's Lenin, Mao had been merely one of several prominent leaders of different Communist guerrilla forces in different regions of China during the Chinese Civil War against Chiang. During the Long March in the middle of the civil war, he became the supreme leader by consent, and most top leaders became generals of the armed forces during the final years of the civil war. After the liberation, he became the supreme leader of the People's Republic of China, while those generals held top positions in the central government. Like Mao, they were also considered the founding fathers, and they had their own ideas about how China should be ruled. Mao's failed Great Leap Forward led many of them to vote him out of the presidency to protect Communist Party interests.

To regain his presidency and carry out his vision for China, Mao had had to get rid of those founding fathers of a different mind-set than his and their followers at all levels of the government apparatus. Mao was shrewd. He knew he couldn't rely on the armed forces for such a monumental task—what if the soldiers listened to their ex-generals instead of him? So, he had to create his own force, the Red Guards, who would round up all his enemies no matter how high placed they were. Mao further created the Big Link-up—the internet hadn't been invented yet—giving his Red Guards free transportation and room and board so they could reach all corners of the country to "fan the wind and light the fire."

Mao's Red Guards were made up of high-minded, energetic students who were crazily in love with him after being brainwashed for seventeen years (1949–66). When Mao put on his army uniform and Red Guard armband to greet the student Red Guards in Tiananmen Square, it was a declaration of war and a signal of his need for their protection. He further stressed this need by declaring that enemies from within had taken over the headquarters—hence "Bombard the Headquarters" became the title of his first big-character poster.

But Mao miscalculated. His long-standing "class-struggle" doctrine had divided the Chinese into two political classes: Red and Black. He failed to see that his Cultural Revolution would drastically deepen this class division into personal hatred. In Canton City, the young people of the undesirable, Black class formed the "Red

Flag Red Guards," calling themselves the "Rebels." The Rebels saw themselves as the true revolutionaries and defenders of Mao.

Mao also failed to see that many in the first group of Red Guards, the so-called "pure" revolutionary class (the Reds), would choose to protect their parents when they became targets of the Cultural Revolution. In Canton City, these were the East Winds, and they were accused by the Rebels of being "Loyalists." Rebels and Loyalists could not coexist under the same sky.

Lastly, Mao failed to see the unintended consequences of his decision to prohibit the soldiers from resisting the Red Guards when they came to take their guns. The Loyalists had the upper hand in taking the weapons from the soldiers merely because they had good *guanxi* with the soldiers. (Some Loyalists' fathers or relatives were in the army.) Rumor had it that some soldiers were tipping off the Loyalists as to where the weapons were stored. As for the Rebels, they had to rob soldiers of their guns or take them from the Loyalists in battle. Armed with deadly weapons, Loyalists and Rebels went to war. In Canton City, the weapons used were rifles, handguns, knives, and clubs. (I didn't hear any explosives being used or buildings being blown up.) The hospitals were open, and the doctors treated both wounded Rebels and Loyalists without discrimination. The policemen and the traffic cops were not seen in public. The streets were empty, frequented by warring Rebels and Loyalists, who had seized any trucks they could find. Both gangs identified themselves by red flags flown above the truck cabs. I call this chaos the "Red Guard War," a term not used in the history books. The Red Guard War became widespread in Canton City in the late fall of 1966. Meanwhile, both warring groups continued to hunt down and punish monsters and demons.

There was a third group of young people during the Cultural Revolution who have gotten no mention in the history books. I call this group the "Idlers." The Idlers were students from both political classes. They did not join either the Loyalists or the Rebels, and they did not have the blood of monsters and demons on their hands. They simply stayed home. I was happy to be one of them, and the same was true for Hay and my sisters and all those who visited our home. There were a lot of Idlers in Canton whom history would forget because they were not Red Guards.

ooooo

AS THE FIGHT BETWEEN THE Rebels and the Loyalists intensified in late summer 1966, our neighbors built a ten-foot-high barricade of broken furniture, tree branches, and old pieces of wood and steel at the entrance to our alley to shield the neighborhood from the Red Guard War outside. People took turns guarding it, but I was not involved because I was a student. It was at this point that I realized how many adults were homebound. They became the "old" Idlers. Their factories or companies must have been as paralyzed by the Cultural Revolution as my school.

The first sound of gunfire came to us when the fight at the East Train Station broke out. I didn't know if it was the Rebels attacking the Loyalists or vice versa. Our small bedroom was adjacent to the station's repair shop. I saw some workers running past the window holding rifles. Mommy shouted at us to duck under the window. The fighting finally stopped after midnight. I was surprised none of my sisters was scared.

ooooo

IT WAS THE WORST OF times for most people, but it was the best of times for Big Fluffy. The Big Link-up had given him a free train ride to Canton to visit us. He had grown bigger, and he had made himself look more mature by growing a thick mustache, which he groomed with his thumb and index finger from time to time. This always irritated Mommy.

"That ugly mustache won't get you a nice girl," Mommy said, sounding like Auntie.

Big Fluffy smirked, "Auntie, tell me the truth. You want me to be your son-in-law, don't you? If we weren't related by blood." My sisters—with the exception of the youngest, Bun, who was only twelve—had grown into beautiful teenagers and were getting a lot of attention from young men.

Mommy grinned. "You ran into a ghost just like your mother did. Tell me the truth. Have you done something bad today?"

Big Fluffy laughed. "Nothing, Big Auntie! I'm a good citizen, always."

I made a retching sound.

But Big Fluffy said, "Big Auntie, your son agrees with me."

Big Fluffy was always busy. He was gone during the day, every day. One day, he sneaked into my room carrying a large bag, which he kicked under the bed.

"What's that?" I asked.

"Don't tell your mother, promise?"

"I promise." I raised my three fingers, the sign for a serious promise.

"Electrical wire," he said. "But I need to find a place to burn off the insulation."

"What for?"

"Money," he said. "I can sell the copper for good money."

Big Fluffy opened my eyes to a different perspective: how to make the most of things when the world was collapsing around you. When I asked where he'd gotten the wire, he told me he'd gone to a park and climbed the lampposts to cut it down.

"The police will arrest you." I was worried.

"Where are they? The Red Guards are robbing the stores for cigarettes and cold drinks everywhere every day! I'm doing my share for the Cultural Revolution. You should do something, something rewarding, but don't let Mommy know. Old people don't get it."

I didn't feel it was right to do illegal things. Perhaps I was indeed a "bookworm," but I didn't see myself as a coward. *Someday, I'll show people I'm brave!* I said to myself.

I kept Big Fluffy's secret, but he didn't show me any tangible appreciation after he sold the wire. He didn't even tell me how he found the underground buyers for it, or how much he sold it for.

ooooo

IT DIDN'T TAKE LONG BEFORE ours became the home with the most visitors in our neighborhood. All our visitors were Idlers, who talked about many things except politics and the Cultural Revolution. It was at this point when I realized how many Idlers we knew who were smart and full of life and who had interesting things to say even as the world outside crumbled around us. *Life is full and fun without politics!* I said to myself. Mommy welcomed all visitors with open arms, and they all respected her and called her "Mommy." She always treated them well, often better than she treated us! But my sisters and I were never jealous. Soon, I noticed that people were coming to our house specifically because of

Mommy, all through word of mouth. Still, I sensed that the young men were coming because of Lily and Ning. I had no pretty girl to come see me. *Life is still fair,* I comforted myself. *No one should have all the goodies.* But I still wondered when a good-looking girl would come to see me.

One day, Jing brought a friend of her boyfriend's family home for a visit. She was a student at the provincial dance school. I'd never met a girl with such an attractive face and figure. When I was introduced to her, I was unable to move my tongue to utter a word! I didn't even know how to sit comfortably in her presence. I didn't want to stare at her—that would have been too obvious, and impolite—so, I just sat there, hoping her group would stay longer so I could listen to her talk. But she never initiated a conversation, and spoke only when asked a question. I was unable to muster the courage to ask her a single thing, and she seemed not to notice my presence. I had never felt so small and insignificant.

After they left, I started to blame myself for not being good at dancing or singing or even conversation. I promised myself that while I was home doing nothing, I would get good at the Chinese flute, which I had played haphazardly for years prior to that. Then I started to worry: What if I play poorly in front of her?

The boyfriend Jing had fallen in love with was a postdoc in the same medical school. He was boring, but Papa was excited because the young man's father was the principal of the Canton Chinese Traditional Medical College.

Mommy would never have cared about such a thing. "The most important thing for a girl is to choose a good man," she said. "His family is second."

My sisters' beauty brought good things to the family. For example, it was Lily and Ning's job to buy groceries at the public market. Meat, fish, and some fresh vegetables, like Chinese broccoli, were always in short supply; the Red Guard War had disrupted the supply chain. People would show up to the market quite early to wait in line before it opened. Yet, somehow, Lily and Ning were always able to return with a bit of pork or a piece of fish or hard-to-find vegetables, even though they went to the market at five in the morning. Their secret? Our neighbor, a young man, was desperately in love with Ning, so he'd go to the market at three in the morning with an extra stepstool to hold a spot in line for her, just for a chance to talk with her! Otherwise, we would likely have ended up eating water spinach every day, and I hated water spinach—it grew like a weed and often hid leeches. (In today's Chinatowns, water spinach is popular. The Chinese say it's a health food because of all its fiber. Even I've grown to like it.)

Among the young men who came to our house were two ethnic Chinese Indonesians, Ah Hua and Ah Fu. If they came because of my sisters, then I have to say they were subtle about it, unlike the others. Back then, Indonesians of Chinese descent were always in the news for being harmed by the Indonesian government, which was anticommunist and not a friend to China. Most of these young people ended up in Canton City: Our governor had set up a university specifically to teach overseas ethnic Chinese. Ah Hua and Ah Fu were two of its students. But now the Cultural Revolution had interrupted their studies, and many of their teachers had been jailed in Cowsheds. They had no classes to attend and no place to go for fun. They were bored and homesick and lonely.

Mommy felt sorry for them, and they became our frequent visitors. They often brought a guitar with them and were not shy about playing and singing their native songs for us. Guitars had been banned in China, for they could not serve the spirit of the revolution. But we didn't care. Ah Hua's deep voice melted into the soul-touching sound of the guitar. I saw his eyes turn red as

I pictured his song floating along the silvery moonlit beach and through the shadows of the palm trees and into the ears of a beautiful girl waiting for his return. Ah Hua was obviously homesick, to say the least.

To end the night, we'd take a long walk under the old banyan trees lining the street, to the little rice noodle shop. A bowl of plain rice noodles cost about one U.S. cent, and paying 20 percent more would get you a few pieces of pork intestine. On the way home one night, Mommy complained that the intestine wasn't clean.

Ah Fu said, "It's the way it is meant to be. Without the taste of the pig feces, how do you know you're getting the real thing?"

We were laughing at this when Ah Hua suddenly jumped and stepped aside. We didn't know why. Then he jumped again and complained, "What's wrong with the frogs tonight? Always get under my shoes." Then we heard him fart. I laughed.

"Too many frogs for you to step on?" Mommy said. "Or is the 'tasty' pork intestine fighting your intestine?"

I laughed again. Even in the darkest times, life could be fun with just a little imagination.

Soon, the worst of times came when Ah Hua was put in jail. Ah Fu told us he had been accused of being a spy. Ah Fu knew nothing about any spying. He knew only that Ah Hua had sent many letters to his parents in Indonesia begging them to send him money to return home. In one letter, apparently, he'd told his parents that his classes had been canceled because the teachers were being punished and the students were fighting among themselves.

"How could the police know what he wrote in his letters?" I asked Ah Fu.

"You don't know? The police read every letter sent out of the country."

"How do they do that?"

"They steam the envelopes to loosen the glue," he explained. Several months later, Ah Fu told us that Ah Hua had been executed in jail. Everybody was silent and sad. After Uncle Chang, Ah Hua was the second person I cared about who was gone.

∞∞∞∞

TWO OTHER VISITORS OPENED MY eyes to a different world. One was in his sixties, and the other was middle-aged. The older man was a retired physician. He had heard about Mommy through his daughter, who was Jing's classmate. We called him Dr. Lou. The younger man, a teacher, told Mommy that he'd run away from his home because the Red Guards were about to put him in a Cowshed. He immediately gained our sympathy, as did anyone who ran away from the Red Guards or came from a Black family like ours.

The younger man, whom we called Teacher Fong, knew how to read faces. Since ancient times, most Chinese were superstitious and believed in fortune-telling. I thought, *Given that I have no say in my own life, I should pay attention to some fortune-telling.* There were two schools of fortune-telling in China. One determined your fortune by your birth hour and date according to the Chinese calendar, similar to Western astrology. The other did it by reading your face.

Mommy was excited about the face reading. "You must read my face, Teacher Fong. I'm worried every day."

"Why haven't you told *me* that, Mommy?" I wasn't happy she was confiding this to a stranger rather than to me.

Teacher Fong laughed. Then he stared at Mommy's face. He even stood up to look at it from different angles. His forehead tightened, and three deep furrows appeared above his eyes. When the furrows subsided, he told Mommy, "You'll be fine. Don't worry."

Mommy asked him to read my face. He glanced over at me and smiled. "When mother is fine, her children are fine, too." I was disappointed. What kind of face reading was that?

Before they said good-bye, Teacher Fong told Mommy, "You'll meet a noble man, relax."

Mommy replied, "Indeed, I've met a noble man, and he says I'll be fine." The two laughed.

"No wonder people like to come visit us," I told Mommy after the two men had left.

Dr. Lou and Teacher Fong became frequent visitors. They both called my mother "Mommy" without asking her first. *They were too old to do that!* It turned out Dr. Lou also read faces. I didn't like what either of them had to say about my face. They both said the space between my eyes was not "full." I looked in the mirror and, for the first time, noticed the indentation there. According to them, this was one of the very important areas of one's face. Its width, fullness, color, and light reflectiveness dictated one's fortune and success. When the space between one's eyes was concave, it meant one had to go through a lot to succeed.

"My life will be miserable. Is that what you want me to believe?" I asked unhappily.

"Not miserable. It'll be good, but not easy. It'll take a lot for you to achieve your goal."

"When will the best years of my life be?" I wanted to end the conversation.

"In your late sixties," Teacher Fong said.

"Late *sixties*? Why not after I die?" I sniffed. "I don't believe you."

"Maybe in your early seventies," Dr. Lou added. "And your fortune lies far away from home."

"There is no scientific evidence for fortune-telling." I was firm. "If you're right, it's just a blind cat tripping over a dead mouse."

Teacher Fong chuckled, "You see that an apple falls from a tree, and you believe in gravity. That you can't see the science behind fortune-telling doesn't mean there is none."

"It's witchcraft—a clever kind at best." I walked out of the room, but deep inside I was torn. *Could anyone predict the will of Heaven?*

CHAPTER 6

"NO NOBLE MEN"

IN THE FALL OF 1966, the Cultural Revolution finally hit home.
It started with a few bangs on the door followed by a harsh voice:
"Open the door!"

Mommy opened the door. Two men wearing East Wind armbands were standing there. "We're from Canton Steel and in charge
of your neighborhood. Where's your husband?" No doubt they
knew something about us.

"He is in Zhaoqing City," Mommy answered.

"Search them!" the older man commanded the younger man,
who was about my age. Then he walked away.

"My name is Yong Wei," the young man said. He asked
Mommy, "What's your name?"

"Yong Yin Ling."

"Oh good. We have the same family name," Yong Wei said.

"Just do what you need to do," I told him. I wanted it over with.

"I'm just an apprentice and have to follow orders." Yong Wei
looked around and started with the dresser. He didn't really search,
just opened a drawer and glanced in.

Hay and I in Canton City, 1967.

"Are you a Red Flag?" he asked me.

"No," I said.

"My son stays home," Mommy interjected. "I don't let him go out to fight."

Yong Wei nodded and looked at me. "You should listen to your mother."

This irritated me. "That's none of your business," I said.

"He doesn't have a good temper," Mommy said.

How could she not take my side?

"I wish I had a mother like yours." Yong Wei seemed too naïve to know when to stop.

What's wrong with the world? I thought. *Do I give a rat's ass about your mother? Just do your job and go away!*

But Mommy was caring and sensitive with him: "What happened to your mother?" she asked.

"She dropped me in front of an orphanage when I was little. That was the end of it."

"I'm so sorry to hear that. Come visit us if you want someone to talk to."

I could see Yong Wei was touched. Lily and Ning didn't say a word, and Bun was nowhere to be seen.

The older man rushed back in, but before he'd opened his mouth, Yong Wei told him, "They're clean. Nothing here."

"Bring them to the alley," the older man said. "We have something big!"

As we followed Yong Wei outside, Mommy whispered in my ear, "Teacher Fong was right. Heaven sends us a noble man tonight."

"There's no noble man in the East Winds." I intentionally said it loud enough for Yong Wei to hear, and he did, but he pretended otherwise. I felt a moral victory.

Out in the alley, our neighbors had already gathered in the dim moonlight. I found Uncle Bian, and we stood by his side. Several East Winds had pushed and dragged a family of four to face the crowd. They looked miserable, shaken and frightened. I knew the son and the daughter; they lived in the building where Uncle Bian lived. They were younger than me, and well behaved. The girl always smiled when she passed by me. She had a long ponytail that flopped in the air when she ran.

The East Wind head man announced that they had discovered evidence that the family had committed the ultimate crime against Mao. He unfolded a wrinkled and dirty sheet of newspaper featuring a full-page photo of Chairman Mao waving to students in Tiananmen Square, a typical front page for every Chinese paper— Mao had been repeating such gatherings many times within the past few months.

"These villains wrapped Chairman Mao's face around a salty fish!" the head man announced. "They're from a landlord's family!"

Chinese are very frugal, and old newspapers were the best resource for when one needed a large piece of paper. Still, the verdict had been reached: The members of this family were counter-revolutionaries for they had intentionally used salty fish to insult and degrade Mao. Violently, East Wind clubs and leather belts landed on the parents and son. Blood sprayed everywhere. Yong Wei stood to the side, not participating. No one beat the small girl. Perhaps they still had a little humanity left in their hearts.

The girl was crying hysterically. She covered her eyes with her small hands. I was angry, and when I got angry, I ground my teeth. Mommy noticed this and grasped one of my fisted hands tight.

The head man became angry at his comrades' inaction with regard to the girl. He pulled out a pair of scissors and chopped off her ponytail in chunks and threw the chunks in the air. The girl cried louder.

"Stop!" I shouted.

Mommy was shocked. She pulled me back. Uncle Bian and Lily stepped in front of me to shield me from the eyes of the East Winds.

"Who said that?" the head man yelled. "Who?"

Nobody said a word.

He gave up. An East Wind brought over a bucket of the wheat paste that was used to stick posters to walls. He poured the hot, steamy paste over the parents' heads. They screamed. This elated the East Winds but brought tears to some women in the crowd. The head man warned us that he knew who the Black families in our neighborhood were and said that we must report all counter-revolutionary acts to them.

When we got back inside, I let my anger out by kicking the door.

"Stop it! Leave the door alone!" Mommy said. "You almost got yourself beaten!"

"I must take revenge!" I yelled.

"You must do nothing!" She was as firm as she could be.

The next morning, Uncle Bian dropped by to tell us he had seen the family of four who were punished the night before. They were sitting on the floor of the train platform the whole night, guarded by Red Guards, waiting to be sent back to their home village to be punished. Uncle Bian shook his head, "I can't even recognize them. They looked very bad. I gave them some water and food. They were so hungry and thirsty."

The Red Guards didn't stop Uncle Bian after he told them he was the conductor on a passenger train between Canton and Beijing.

I thought about the horrific scene we'd witnessed the night before, about the family of four, their faces bloodied. *I had to do something!* I said to myself. *Someone had to do something, and that someone should be me.* I'd pick a fight with the East Winds. I figured the best way to do it would be to join the Red Flags.

I headed to school, where I knew some junior students had formed into a group of Red Flags. On my way there, I met up with Curly; he was an Idler like me and was bored at home, so he decided to join me. The school comprised two four-story buildings of classrooms separated by the playground. I had heard that Red Flags occupied the White Building and the East Winds the Red Building.

The school was dead quiet when we arrived; we didn't see anyone outdoors.

"Where are the Red Guards?" I said.

"Must be fighting elsewhere," Curly said. He knew more about the Red Guard War than I did. He told me that high school Red Guards usually left school to follow and help out their older Red Guard comrades in the universities and factories.

I had not been to the school for about three months, not since the East Winds abandoned the Cowsheds and let the students free.

On our way to school, we saw that many stores were closed, but some had stayed open. There was damage to some storefronts. Curly told me that some stores were repeatedly robbed by both Loyalists and Rebels for cold drinks, cigarettes, dry goods, and first aid kits. No store dared stop Red Guards from looting, and the Red Guards of both camps had been emboldened by Mao's two popular quotations: "Revolution has no sin and to rebel is justified" and "Political power grows out of the barrel of a gun."

The stairs to the White Building were blocked with a pile of desks and chairs. We pushed our way through slowly. On the top floor landing were buckets of caustic, foul-smelling liquids. We assumed these were there to be poured down onto any East Wind head if they tried to break in. Three guys stood on the landing, one of them peering through a pair of binoculars to monitor the Red Building. The leader of the group was in the final grade of junior high, so two years younger than us. He seemed indifferent to us and our intentions.

"Forget it," I said to Curly, disappointed at the sight of the leader and the setting. "He's just a kid."

As we turned around to leave, the young leader said, "Come join me to grab the guns from the East Winds."

Take guns from the East Winds' hands? The idea was both frightening and exciting. I'd heard that some Red Guards had died during the fighting, but nothing so bad had happened to my schoolmates yet.

The leader liked to blab and seemed full of himself. How could he not be? A kid smoking a cigarette holding the only handgun in a group of other young boys holding only clubs?

It turned out the kid had inside information on some rifles being stored in a factory. Its building served as the headquarters of the East Winds from the factory. Before the East Winds went out to fight, they would come to the factory to get the rifles. When they were not fighting, they stored the rifles in the headquarters. When the others were off fighting or at home, the building was guarded by only a couple of East Winds. The kid's plan was to surprise and overwhelm the couple of guards stationed there and take their rifles. This sounded reasonable to Curly and me.

"Where is the place?" I asked.

"You'll know it. But I can't tell you the details, just in case they leak out," the kid said.

Besides his revolver, the kid had as weapons only some boxes of stun grenades. He said the grenades were useless other than for making a big sound and thick smoke. They'd thrown one at a rat, but the rat had survived. As for the revolver, it had become a toy for the kid, and he was proud of it.

"Haven't killed anyone yet, but it's ready."

"Don't blow away your nose," I said as he sniffed the barrel.

"One guy accidentally shot his butt, not his head," he said casually.

The next morning, the kid picked us up in a dirty old truck with an East Wind flag swaying above the cab—we would be masquerading as East Wind Red Guards. Curly and I joined several Red Flags in the truck's bed, each of us holding two stun grenades. When we reached the factory building, the kid sped up and ran over the metal gate. The truck made a screeching stop in front of the two-story building. I threw my first grenade toward the front door. A loud sound and thick smoke followed. The other Red Flags did the same. As I ran to the door, following the kid, I heard a loud explosion coming from behind me. Smoke was billowing out of the truck bed, and I couldn't see Curly anywhere. Suddenly, gunshots erupted from the building's second-floor window, and I heard Curly cry out from the truck, "I'm hit!"

I dashed back to the truck. Through the smoke, I saw him sitting on the truck bed. As I climbed up onto it, I heard bullets hitting the truck's steel side panel. I pushed Curly down, hoping the panel would shield us from the bullets. Curly whimpered in pain, and my hands were covered in blood.

"Fuck!" I shouted toward the building, "Curly's been hit! Come back!"

The Red Flags threw their grenades at the building and rushed back to the truck. The kid was the last one to sprint back, firing his revolver at the building as he did. He continued to fire as he drove the truck away.

Almost half of Curly's T-shirt had been burned away, and I saw a large bloody spot on the right side of his chest. I smelled sulfur. Curly looked down at his hand, where a metal ring with a string attached to it dangled from his little finger. He had accidentally pulled the pin on his stun grenade! We all laughed.

"We shouldn't have come," Curly said. "Stupid! I did it to myself."

"Don't tell Mommy about it," I said.

The kid had lied to us. The stun grenade surely could kill a rat. Once we were far away from the East Wind headquarters, the kid stopped the truck and came back to check on Curly. The bleeding had stopped. It was only a superficial wound. The kid laughed and said, "Curly, you've made a big sacrifice for our great leader Chairman Mao!"

Hearing him, I realized we had joined the wrong fight! The Red Flags were not fighting the East Winds to take revenge; they were fighting for Mao. That was not what Curly and I wanted. I berated myself for being so stupid.

As soon as I got home, Mommy was all over me. *How had she found out?* Had I mentioned my plan to any of my sisters? I couldn't recall. I didn't have a chance to say a word. Mommy told me she had asked Uncle Bian to make arrangements for me to go to Beijing "to do the Big Link-up or whatever." She was angry.

∞∞

THE FREE TRANSPORTATION FOR THE Big Link-up had flooded the trains with too many freeloaders, but Uncle Bian, as the train conductor, brought us to the train before the gate opened to the public, so we were able to grab seats. All my sisters were going, Jing's boyfriend too, and Big Fluffy would never have missed anything free. My classmate Hay joined the group, as did an Indonesian Chinese student called "Little Bird"—even though he had plenty of money to buy a ticket. He was in love with Ning.

I was excited. Heck! Why not? It would be fun: free sightseeing in the capital city and a free place to sleep at some university.

The train was jammed with people. The car was so crowded I could barely make it to the toilet, which smelled so bad that I almost passed out before I got the chance to puke. The train reeked of body odor, a stench only made worse when peasants boarded with their chickens. Through the window of the car I saw Uncle Bian bar passage to a peasant with a small pig on a leash.

It was a long journey of one and a half days, but we finally arrived in Beijing. There, we parted ways with Jing, her boyfriend, and Lily, Ning, and Bun. Jing's boyfriend had arranged a place for all of them to stay. I saw the disappointment on Little Bird's face, but I was relieved; Big Fluffy was, too. As usual, Hay wouldn't speak ill of others.

"Let's go with style!" Little Bird said as he waved to the driver of an auto-rickshaw, a motorized three-wheeler. Little Bird was rich because his parents were rich. He, Big Fluffy, Hay, and I squeezed in. The auto-rickshaw shook our guts as we headed to the Academy of Beijing Opera, which, according to the Red Guard information booth at the train station, had space for us to sleep.

The receptionist at the opera house asked Little Bird if we were there to see Chairman Mao. Little Bird was surprised by the question, and his face turned red as it usually did. Before he had a chance to tell the truth, I interrupted: "Yes, of course." Little Bird was not as good a liar like us natives. The woman told us where the big-character posters were located. Again, before anybody else could speak, I said, "We'll be sure to read them. Thank you." No one in our group was interested in seeing Mao or reading the posters. We were there only to sightsee.

We visited the Great Wall. I was not impressed. Perhaps, in my imagination, it was much taller and bigger. We also went to the Imperial Palace, but we were not allowed in. Prime Minister Zhou Enlai, a shrewd politician for all seasons, had arranged for soldiers to guard it from destruction by Red Guards.

In China during those years, the only politician most people openly admired without fear, other than Mao and his handpicked successor General Lin, was Prime Minister Zhou. Since becoming a Communist in 1919, he was the only top leader not tripped up or disgraced by the ensuing political campaigns. Mao's wife Jiang Qing, however, was one whom many people trashed behind closed doors. Jiang, his fourth wife, had lived in obscurity until the start of the Cultural Revolution, at which point she rose through the ranks to become deputy director of the Central Cultural Revolution Group, a promotion that made her as powerful as Prime Minister

Zhou and General Lin. Her also-ran actress past and her "empress" status apparently gave her the "legitimate" skills and the power to rid China of the "Four Olds" (Old Customs, Old Culture, Old Habits, and Old Ideas) and to create the "Four News" (New Customs, New Culture, New Habits, and New Ideas).

I've always believed that the name "the Cultural Revolution" was deceptive, its intent being to cover up the brutality of political persecution. It should have been called the "Political and Cultural Revolution." Not only did it wipe out the "Four Olds" in people's minds, replacing them with the "Four News" glorifying Mao's thoughts, but it also purged Mao's opponents, securing Mao's untouchable and unquestioned supreme power.

We were grateful for Zhou's foresight in having ordered the soldiers to guard select heritage sites from the hot-headed and violent Red Guards. Zhou was a prominent leader in the army before the founding of the People's Republic of China. The soldiers would listen to him but not to Madam Mao.

Even though we were disappointed at missing the Imperial Palace, we were happy. We loved China's past and its heritage. We were the true patriots!

Soon, Little Bird ran out of money, and we were forced to take the city bus instead of pedicabs. The bus was much cheaper, but not free, which bothered Big Fluffy.

"We're not going to waste money on bus tickets. If the much more expensive trains are free, the city bus should be, too. Old Mao just overlooked it."

We all agreed and boarded the buses without tickets. We'd sit in the back and pretend to be asleep. Infrequently, we'd come across a sharp and aggressive conductor who would repeatedly yell at us, "Comrades, buy tickets now!" As soon as the bus got to our stop, we'd all jump off and run away. I didn't feel bad at all. We'd just done our part as Mao had taught us: "Revolution has no sin, and to rebel is justified."

The weather forecast said a cold front was coming. To our hot-climate bodies, this was a serious concern, as we didn't have any warm clothes with us. My sisters wanted to stay put in Beijing, but the guys wanted to head back down south. I went to my sisters' lodging to say good-bye. When I got back to the opera house to pack up my belongings, I discovered that the guys had already left for the train station. I had to stay overnight by myself, with plans to head south by train the next morning.

That evening, some soldiers arrived and instituted a lockdown. No one was allowed in or out. We even needed the soldiers' permission to use the toilet, which was in an adjacent building. The soldiers announced that the next day, we would be going to see Chairman Mao. It would be the eighth time Mao greeted the Red Guards. For security reasons, the date of each greeting was announced only the night before. The news brought many to tears of joy, but not for me. I didn't feel like crying for the chance to see Mao.

We were woken up at four o'clock the next morning. The cold front had arrived, and each of us was handed a long, thick, musty army coat. We were split up into several groups of a dozen each. A soldier chose me to be the leader of our group because I was a senior high student and all the others were in junior high. He asked me to search every member of my group and confiscate anything sharp, such as a pocketknife. Then he searched me from top to bottom. Before we headed out, we were instructed to pee. To speed up the process, we peed on the ground in a line. The girls were led to a different area and did the same. It amazed me when my pee turned to ice as it hit the ground. How beautiful! I'd had never seen such a thing in my whole life—after all, we never had snow in Canton! The guy next to me in line told me to squeeze the urine out; otherwise, my pee would freeze inside my penis, which would be painful.

"Really?" I asked. He laughed.

The soldiers led us on a long walk. No one knew exactly where we were going, and the soldiers wouldn't answer us when we asked, but it was definitely not Tiananmen Square. For three hours we walked in the freezing cold. The others chatted, but I was not in the mood to talk. My nose was frozen, and I was afraid my tongue would freeze if I opened my mouth. I missed the heat and humidity of home and fantasized about swimming in the cool Pearl River, a luxury the northern people could only dream of. They were so excited about the Cultural Revolution and seemed so naïve and pure. I realized I was an outsider.

We arrived at an abandoned airfield on the outskirts west of Beijing. It held more people than Tiananmen Square. The sun did not come out, and the sky was laden with dark clouds. We sat on the frozen ground. I struggled to get every part of my body inside that long, foul-smelling coat, and I prayed that Mao would come soon, before I turned into an ice pop.

At around ten o'clock, the noise from the crowd increased. Then, suddenly, out of the mist, a jeep emerged bearing a large standing figure waving one arm. Following it was another jeep with a short figure who was also waving. I assumed this second man must be Mao's handpicked successor, Lin Biao, who was short and small. The larger, taller figure must be Mao.

The people around me started to cry. They were really in love with Mao, in a genuine way. I wondered if their tears would freeze on their faces, because their crying just would not stop. I felt like an outsider again and wondered why I was not moved. *What's wrong with me?*

Many jeeps followed Lin's. Then the show was over. For exactly one minute of Mao and Lin, we had spent six hours in the cold.

Our departure was chaotic, as everyone was desperate to get warm. Without soldiers to maintain order, everyone pushed, shoved, and stepped on one another's heels. Many screamed for lost shoes. Thank Heaven all my team members were tall and strong—they were from the north. Still seeing me as their leader, whom they should protect, the guy who'd joked about my pee freezing got his friend to help him lift me off the ground so no one would step on my heels. And they kept my feet off the ground until we got out of that mess. Before that event, I had deemed northerners simple, but from then on, I told myself I must respect them as much as the Cantonese.

To celebrate our great leader having greeted us, a special dinner was announced: two white wheat buns and a bowel of cabbage soup with a few pieces of pork. What a treat! We were so hungry and cold that the meal was indeed remarkable. My fellow northerners were again touched, and before they ate, they shouted, "Long Live Chairman Mao!"

I couldn't fall asleep that night. I kept thinking that something must be wrong with me. Why did I not feel the same way toward Chairman Mao as the northerners? I decided that on my way home, I would visit Mao's birthplace, in Hunan Province, where Papa's hometown was. Perhaps knowing Mao's past would change my feelings toward him. I had planned to use the Big Link-up as a chance to visit Papa's hometown and Papa's sister, Big Auntie; the Beijing-to-Canton train ran through both provinces. The problem was I had to manage my journey by myself, as there was now no way I could contact Uncle Bian for help. Fortunately, during our bus rides in Beijing, I had learned the trick of slipping onto a bus from the side rather than pushing my way through from the front.

When I arrived in Big Auntie's small town in Henan Province, it was dark and I was very hungry. There was a food stall next to the train station that sold fried noodle dishes. More than a dozen thin, dirty kids surrounded the stall. When one man finished and stood up to pay, the kids congregated around his place, grabbing the leftovers. I was shocked watching them stuff their mouths with noodles. It pained my heart even more to see the stall owner and the other patrons seem not to notice the kids' presence.

I gave my order, and the vendor dumped a couple of spoonfuls of noodles onto the plate used by the last customer and handed it to me.

"Did you wash the dish?" I asked.

"No. What for?" he said.

Being a southerner, I was used to better hygiene. But here, it was a luxury. Mommy had warned me, "When in Rome, do as the Romans do." So, I ate only the top layer of noodles, leaving the bottom layer untouched on the plate. I couldn't afford to get sick far away from home. Before I stood up, I signaled to the kids around me to take the rest.

Seeing their dirty hands, the skin stretched over their little bones, made my heart sink. I remembered reaching out my clean hand to accept cookies from visitors from Hong Kong all those years back. Mommy had not lied or exaggerated. The rumors she'd heard almost a decade ago about northern people eating corpses during the Great Famine must have been true.

I got lost looking for Big Auntie's house and asked for help from two Red Guards pasting a slogan on a wall. As they pointed me in the right direction, a kid ran up from nowhere, reached into their bucket of wheat paste, and stuffed a handful of it in his mouth. The Red Guards turned around and shouted at him and were ready to chase him down, but they stopped when I yelled, "Fuck, it's just wheat paste!" I realized I had just used too strong and offensive a word, so I added, "I'm a Red Guard from Canton City." I had a feeling that being a Red Guard from a big city would earn me respect. It worked, and they seemed to forget the little wheat-paste thief. *There was no place for a gentleman in a rough world,* I concluded.

I finally found myself in front of Big Auntie's small house of dry mud bricks. Inside, the house was sparsely furnished. Big Auntie was happy to see me and asked if I was hungry. I told her I'd already eaten.

Big Auntie was the oldest among my aunties on my father's side. (The Chinese use "big" to indicate not body size but age when addressing or referring to a relative, or to show respect when referring to a nonrelative.) Big Auntie and her husband were school-teachers, and they had two boys. That night, her husband was with the older boy, who had been hospitalized for a high fever and diar-rhea and needed hydration. The younger boy, who was preschool age, stared at me quietly.

I slept well that night. The next day, Big Auntie brought me to the farmers' market. She picked a large watermelon from a pile. She taught me how to tell if it was ripe and sweet by listening to the sound it made when you patted it with your fingers. A resonant sound was good; if the melon was "ugly," it was even better.

"A sweet thing can also be an ugly one," I said.

Big Auntie smiled and said I was smart.

We brought the watermelon to my cousin in the hospital. He was small for his age, but he had a good-size head and his sunken eyes were bright. The Great Famine had hit the family very hard, especially my cousin. Being deprived of adequate nutrition at a young age, when he needed it most, had stunted his growth. Thank Heaven, he'd been left with a good-size head, and he later became a top scientist for the U.S. Navy. (He left China after witnessing the June 4, 1989, Tiananmen Square Massacre.) He stared at me with intense curiosity from his hospital bed and didn't want to let go of my hand as I said good-bye.

That night, I asked Big Auntie why Papa loved China so much.

"You should ask your papa," Big Auntie said. "It's difficult for me to say."

"I did, but he wouldn't tell me. He didn't even say much about you and my younger aunt and uncles. I know only that Grandpa and Grandma died very young, and the pastor of the church taught him English."

"Your papa is very smart at learning new things, but he cannot let go of the old Chinese way of thinking. I think he carries a burden in his heart that's eating him." Unlike the two Fluffys' mother, Big Auntie spoke slowly and clearly, phrasing things well.

"What burden?"

"He left home early and didn't suffer as much as his six siblings."

"Six? Papa told me he had five."

"The youngest one died when he was a boy. He died under my watch. Your papa wasn't around."

"Where was Papa?"

"He had left home to work for the customs office. I was the oldest after he left, so I took care of the others. Your grandparents had long gone."

"You were the 'parent,' then," I said.

"I couldn't find enough food for my brothers and sister." Auntie looked sad, and her eyes turned red. She spoke haltingly, fighting back tears: "I lost my little brother. The roundworms in his tummy were so hungry that they crawled up to his mouth. He was too weak to cough them out. They crawled down his windpipe. He couldn't cry. He choked to death."

We were silent then. In the small, dimly lit room we could hear each other's breathing. I heard Big Auntie's soft weeping. She couldn't possibly have guessed what I was thinking: For too many people, life was harsh and unfair. It didn't give my little uncle a voice to cry with or the strength to cough up those worms to save his own life. Then I remembered Uncle Chang, who ran the blueprint shop and loved to eat. He also hadn't found peace before he died.

Calmly, Big Auntie said, "I think your papa carries around the guilt of our suffering because he was having a better life. So, he returned to China to be close to us. It makes him feel better about himself."

"If he had told me this, I would have understood," I said.

"But he must save face. You should forgive him. He's too stubborn to change."

Big Auntie and I talked late into the night. I learned about the early passing of my grandparents; the absence of the oldest son to take over the family; the protracted poverty and famine; the corrupt government under Chiang; the withdrawal of the Seventh-day Adventists from my hometown; the indiscriminate air bombing by the Japanese invaders; and the never-ending Chinese Civil War that drove Papa's siblings from home (except for Third Uncle). I had finally found the reason, a humane reason, for Papa's decision to bring us back to China from Hong Kong. He wanted to be close to his sisters and brothers. And with a sense of peace, I fell asleep.

The next morning, Big Auntie walked me to the train station. I was on my way to visit Third Uncle. As the train started to move, we waved our farewells, but Big Auntie's thin form remained on the platform until I could no longer see it. In this desolate land, I had found a shining jade.

Third Uncle was a man of few words. He and his wife lived in a place not much better than Big Auntie's. He told me he had prepared dishes for me without any hot spices. Hunan Province was known for its very spicy food. Third Uncle chuckled when I told him hot food would give me pimples and that Mommy would force me to drink "cool tea" to get rid of them.

"If you love our spicy food, you can be a politician when you grow up," Third Uncle said. "Hunan is the land of politicians."

"But I hate politics," I said.

I knew Mao had been born in Hunan, but who else? Third Uncle told me many officials and generals in Chiang's army had been born in my little hometown—per Chinese custom, we called the birthplace of our ancestors our "hometown."

Third Uncle was proud of this fact: "If they stretch their arms and hold hands to form a circle, they could surround the town center."

The next day, I said good-bye to Third Uncle and took a bus to Mao's birthplace. It was a bumpy two-hour ride to the small village where a lot of visitors, mostly Red Guards, waited in line to get in the house. The house was big, with many rooms, and faced a pond. Mao was from a rich peasant family! The more I thought about it, the angrier I became. Papa was from an extremely poor family. If China followed its own rules, it would not be punishing Papa. If China followed its own rules, I would be destined for the university instead of being a little bastard. China was so screwed up. I'd had enough of the hypocrisy. I'd had enough of the betrayal.

I'd seen enough. I needed to get out. I missed home, and I missed Mommy.

When I returned to Canton City, Mommy was relieved to have me back in one piece. Our home again resumed its role as a gathering place for our friends. Meanwhile, outside, Loyalists and Rebels were still busy fighting and killing one another, shouting, "Revolution has no sin!" and "Rebellion is justified!" as they looted the stores. There were very few monsters and demons left to punish.

Everybody except me was delighted when Teacher Fong and Dr. Lou showed up at our house. Often Teacher Fong rationalized his refusal to tell our fortunes by saying too many people were present that day. I believed he was trying to hide his reputation for fortune-telling, which was definitely one of the Four Olds that Mao wanted to get rid of.

When he learned about my visit to Papa's birthplace, Teacher Fong told me, "Your grandpa bestowed a lot of blessings on you."

I didn't want to hear his face reading. He had said nothing good about my face. I shrugged. "I can read your face, too, and say the same thing: Your grandpa bestowed a lot of blessings on you; otherwise, you would have been beaten to death in a Cowshed. Oh, and my grandpa didn't even know me. He died many years before I was born."

"That's fair," Teacher Fong said, smiling. "Your grandpa's blessing is from Heaven."

"Give me something I can verify."

"I'll tell you two things about the near future that can be verified. The political life of Mao's handpicked successor, President General Lin, will not last, and Deng, not President Liu, will make a comeback."

"I've never liked Lin Biao's face," I said. "Not trustworthy. Why can Deng make a comeback?"

"Look at his body shape," Teacher Fong said. "Like a roly-poly toy, isn't it?" Chinese called a roly-poly person "one who won't fall down and keeps lying flat."

"I'll wait and see," I said.

CHAPTER 7

ROOFTOP UNDERGROUND

THE BIG LINK-UP IN BEIJING brought Hay and me closer. One day, he came over and said, "I want to show you something. Come with me."

I followed him to his home. I believe I was the only classmate he'd invited there. His parents' tragedy had taught him not to trust others easily. It made him cautious, a young man of few words. I had never heard him comment on politics or on any one person, but I knew we shared many viewpoints.

Hay grew up and still lived with his "uncle," not a biological one. "Uncle" soon became the name even Mommy used for him, just as everyone called her "Mommy." Uncle was a skinny man with his chest tilted to one side as a result of part of his lung having been removed because of tuberculosis. No one asked how old Uncle was, but he looked much older than Hay. Uncle had more education than we did, but he was cautious and tight-lipped. During the writing of this book, I learned from Hay that Uncle's father had been the wealthiest and most powerful landlord in Big Fluffy's province,

Looking at Snake Mouth, China, from the New Territories of Hong Kong, 1993.

Guangxi, where Mommy was born, but he refused to flee to Taiwan and was executed by Mao's army during the liberation.

In today's China, both Hay's and Uncle's fathers would not have been killed; instead, they would have been the "men above all other men." Why? Three years ago, in 2018, I visited a schoolmate in Canton City and incidentally used the word *landlord* in a negative sense.

My classmate corrected me: "In today's China, we don't use 'landlord' to mean a bad person anymore."

"Why?" I asked.

"Landlords contribute to our economic development because they have money and knowledge."

Again, it was the same simple and singular truth about China: serving the national interest. Like the female fetuses under the Hero Mother and the One Child policy, landlords had to serve the national interests of the time.

Hay and Uncle lived in an addition that took up half the flat rooftop of a four-story building, a common structure in Canton. Their home consisted of a single large room that served for eating, sleeping, and studying and a separate, smaller enclosure for cooking, a toilet, and bathing. Through the windows, one could see anyone approaching across the unused part of the rooftop. A string tied to a small bell dropped down to the locked front door of the building. A visitor had only to pull the string to ring the bell. With no neighbors next to their dwelling, Hay and Uncle were able to monitor who was coming across the rooftop and who was waiting at the door of the building.

When Hay and I got there, Uncle was finishing making a transistor radio. He turned the dial and quickly located the station he wanted. A man speaking good Mandarin reported what was happening in China and elsewhere in the world. I had never heard anything like it. I hung on every word the voice said.

Hay was proud. "It's the broadcast of Voice of America from Hong Kong," he said.

"America?! How come my radio can't get it?" I asked.

"This is a shortwave radio. Yours is an AM radio." Uncle explained: "It's hard for the government to block the shortwave frequency, but it tries."

"Don't tell anybody," Hay reminded me.

"I won't. Can I come again to listen?" I was excited to hear what "our worst enemy" was saying.

The two chuckled. "You can come anytime," Uncle said.

All of a sudden, I felt I had grown up.

I became a frequent visitor to Hay and Uncle's home, and met several interesting people there. They included Hay's biological older brother, Mau, and three nonbiological "cousins," Yun and Shan (two males) and Kok (a female) related to Uncle. There were also two older guys, Lao and Yu, who were Uncle's friends. Counting me, we were a group of nine. We are all Idlers. We all shared the same political viewpoint: We all hated the Cultural Revolution. We were all of the Black class. Uncle always produced the sharpest, most insightful criticism of government policy, Mao, and Madam Mao.

We all also admired the West but knew very little about America. The others seemed to know Hong Kong more than I, and more than half of them had relatives there. We looked down on all socialist countries and admired all capitalist countries, even though we didn't know much about any of them. Uncle was the only one who had attended university, where he'd majored in literature. I respected his political analysis because no one put things the way he did. Mommy said he was the worst antirevolutionary in the group, and I laughed. I told Mommy if the group were arrested, I could see Uncle leading all of us in a line to the execution site. Mommy laughed. As time went on, I referred to our group of nine as the "Rooftop Underground."

"You get up early and you're happy," Mommy noticed. She joked: "Is something wrong?"

I was whistling a joyous tune. When I was happy, I whistled. Nothing escaped the eyes of Mommy.

"I'm going to Uncle's place," I said and headed to the door.

"If Uncle wants to adopt you, I won't mind." Mommy was in a good mood, too.

∞∞∞

IN THOSE DAYS, I WAS getting my "education" from the Voice of America and the Rooftop Underground. Yes, we wasted time ridiculing Mao's wife any chance we got—her extramarital affairs were part of the rumor mill—but I learned about the outside world, too. It was unthinkable to me that Voice of America knew as much about us as it did, but I was excited by its analysis of events in China. It just made sense. Chinese news media shaped its take on events to support the same old Communist line. It was always about the class struggle or the success of socialism or the guerrilla war in some underdeveloped country. But Voice of America varied its commentary and conclusions depending on the event. It carried me away to many places over many different continents.

I was struck by the news that America and the Soviets were ready to bury each other with nuclear bombs. Being in hell already, we Chinese would definitely not have minded having both of them join us.

I didn't need to hear about the killing of Dr. Martin Luther King Jr. from the radio. Mao had already published a piece about it in the newspapers, telling us to support the blacks in overthrowing the U.S. government in response to King's assassination. We Chinese poured out into the streets to demonstrate, carrying our old and useless World War II rifles. A month after Dr. King's death, I was shocked to learn that the brother of the president of the United States had been shot dead, too. Chinese media didn't say a word about the assassination of that white man.

Americans seemed to partake in a lot of killing among themselves, but their college students hated being drafted and sent to Vietnam to kill Communists. Meanwhile, our all-volunteer Communist Red Guards were eager to shoot other Communist Red Guards. It was all very confusing.

One of the most refreshing things I learned was that Americans seemed not to feel shame when they lost face. Indeed, I was surprised when Voice of America admitted that the North Vietnamese had beaten the Americans for the first time. All along, we had been told by the Chinese media that the North Vietnamese had been winning because the Chinese were helping them. The

American public didn't support the Vietnam War, and they dared to show it. And unlike the Chinese, they seemed to feel no shame in telling others when they'd lost face. Given that I'd never liked the Chinese custom of saving face, I found that the American style of candor suited me well.

It was eye-opening to learn what was happening in the world, and stimulating to discuss and debate the radio announcer's comments and analysis. It was even more exciting when, one day, Uncle asked me, "Can you promise not to tell anybody what we're going to tell you?"

"Absolutely," I said.

"Hay and I are planning to escape to Hong Kong," Uncle said calmly.

"To escape?" I almost jumped. "How?"

"We have some ideas but no solid plan yet," Hay said.

"I don't know anything about escaping. Do you want me to leave?" I asked.

"No. You can stay," Hay said.

"My choice is limited because of my lungs," Uncle said. "But Hay can swim or use a boat."

"You've lost me," I said.

Uncle opened a map and spread it out on the table. It was of the south half of Guangdong Province. It also showed Kowloon Peninsula and Hong Kong Island. It was a strange-looking map. Groups of irregular concentric loops resembling layers of ripples radiated out from a small spot.

"What are those lines?" I asked.

"Those are topographic lines," Uncle said. "You need to know only one thing about them: The closer the lines are stacked together, the steeper the slope."

"Oh. If there are no lines, then it's flat there?"

"Yep," Hay said.

Above the Kowloon Peninsula to the east are a lot of steep mountains and very few flat lands. To the west are some gentler hills and more flat land. A narrow river in the middle, called the Shenzhen River, separates the Mainland to the north and the Kowloon Peninsula to the south. Hong Kong Island is south of Kowloon Peninsula, separated by only a narrow harbor. Hong Kong is in the South China Sea.

"It takes no time to swim across Shenzhen River, Uncle," I said. "You could do it."

Hay said, "We can't take that route. There are soldiers, German Shepherds, and fences. Twenty-four hours a day, every day."

"When a typhoon hits, one has a better chance of success," Uncle said. "That's how the locals do it," he added.

East of the Shenzhen River is Mirs Bay, a large body of water that is part of the South China Sea. To the west of Shenzhen River is Shenzhen Bay, which opens wide where it meets the Zhujiang River Estuary.

Pearl River runs into the north end of the estuary, which in turn empties into the South China Sea to the south.

"I'd approach from the west to swim across Shenzhen Bay," Hay said.

"How far to swim across?" I asked.

"The longest distance is from Snake Mouth, at the junction of Shenzhen Bay and the Zhujiang River Estuary." Hay paused. "About six miles."

"Six miles?!" I was alarmed.

"If you miss, you'll be flushed out to the sea," Uncle said.

As for Uncle, he would try to get a boat, probably starting somewhere in the Pearl River Delta and then heading south by way of the Zhujiang River Estuary.

It was all too much for me to digest. My head was spinning. How long had they been planning this? I had always been impressed by Hay's ability to keep things to himself. Now he had impressed me even more with this thoughtful planning. He and Uncle didn't mention any dangers beyond patrols. I could see that the worst case would be if a typhoon hit.

They must be very determined, I thought. Was I as determined as they were? Yes, I wanted to go to Hong Kong—China gave me nothing but pain—but I had never even swum in the sea. And I had certainly never swum for hours at a time. Could I make it? What if soldiers caught me? How many years would I be in jail? Would they shoot me in jail the way they'd shot Ah Hau? Then I thought about Mommy and Papa. Unlike Hay, I had parents. Would they allow me to take such a risk? Would they be able to stand it if I died? I was sure that if anything bad happened to me, they would carry their sorrow and blame themselves for the rest of their lives. Was China really that bad that I had to leave now? *The Cultural Revolution has to end someday*, I thought. Wouldn't life return to "normal" then?

And what about those damn face readings? What if Teacher Fong was right? I had noticed that indentation between my eyes. What if face reading was indeed a treasure of China's long civilization, and not Teacher Fong's way to get attention? What did it mean that I had to go through a lot to succeed? Still, he had said my fortune lay far from home. That was good. Hong Kong was not that far away, but at least it was away from China.

Fortunately, Hay told me that he and Uncle were still thinking and planning. They had not set a date yet. I still had time to think.

Heaven didn't bless me with advice on escaping. If It had, it would have given me a hint through a dream, which didn't happen. Instead, a member of the Street Committee showed up at our door.

"Listen!" she told Mommy in a stern voice. "Chairman Mao has ordered all students to return to school immediately. Make sure all your children go to school tomorrow morning."

∞∞∞

IT WAS THE SUMMER OF 1968. I was twenty, Lily was eighteen, and Ning was sixteen. The Cultural Revolution had been running for two years. By then, the Rebels and Loyalists had purged all enemies of Mao. Madam Mao no longer needed the Red Guards— all the Four Olds had been destroyed, and she did not need Red Guards to create the Four News. China was in ruins and the Red Guard War had to end. So, Mao ordered all high school students to go to the countryside to be re-educated by peasants. In Guang-dong Province, hundreds of thousands of Idlers woke up. They started the massive escapes to Hong Kong. They made up the great majority of the freedom swimmers. They showed valor for freedom and opportunity. After three years working as peasants, Ning and I joined these freedom swimmers.

But what to do with the young people of junior or senior high age when the Cultural Revolution had started two years before? The schools had no teachers or textbooks. Factories and institutes needed to start back up. The only place to send the students to was the countryside. Unlike with the Great Leap Forward, the Cultural Revolution had not destroyed the countryside. Sending the students there was Mao's only option. With the addition of "to be reeducated by the peasants," the "sent-down" order was hailed as another example of Mao's political acumen in raising diehard Communist successors—but a heartbreaking decision for the others, such as Ning, Lily, and me. For everyone, it was the end of the destructive part of Cultural Revolution, but for those between the ages of sixteen and twenty-one, it was the beginning of their adulthood.

It was then that hundreds of thousands of sent-down Cantonese students, most of them Idlers during the past two years, started risking their lives to escape to Hong Kong. These were the freedom swimmers. Most, if not all, living in the twenty-two provinces outside Guangdong have never heard of us, not even today. But we were the true rebels. Ning and I were proud to be among them, and we are still proud of it. But first we had to endure years in the countryside.

In 1976, two months after Mao's death and ten years after his first big-character poster, Madam Mao and her three accomplices were arrested for being the culprits of the Cultural Revolution and put on trial. They were labeled the "Gang of Four." To calm the anger of the Chinese people, the Communist Party accepted a modicum of blame and labeled the Cultural Revolution the "Ten-Year Calamity," so that every Chinese would shut up and move on. Internally, the Communist Party's postmortem on Maoism was that it was 70 percent right, 30 percent wrong, whatever that means.

Two years after Mao's death, in 1978, Deng became the supreme leader of China and, the following year, the first president of China to visit the United States. I'll never forget watching in horror as a small group of student demonstrators on the campus of the University of Washington in Seattle, where I was a junior at the time, chanted, "Down with Deng Xiaoping!" and "Long live Chairman Mao!"

It was Deng who brought the sent-down students back home to join their "white cat" or "black cat" families and work their butts off to become "some of the first to get rich"—provided they served the interests of the Communist Party of China and did not make trouble. (Some later did, on June 4, 1989, in Tiananmen Square, where they were gunned down by the troops from the People's Liberation Army. That really pissed off the civilized world, who dubbed the incident the Tiananmen Square Massacre.)

In 1980, Deng "rehabilitated" President Liu (though he had died in confinement in 1969), other founders of the People's Republic of China, and all monsters and demons who had been purged by Mao during the Cultural Revolution and survived.

While in China, I didn't realize that I had survived two of the largest man-made disasters since World War II: Mao's Act II, the Great Leap Forward, which was designed to secure China's economic power and ended only with the Great Famine; and his Act III, the Cultural Revolution, which ended only with the Ten-Year Calamity. Should I be sad for having been on the receiving end, or proud of being one of the survivors and witnesses?

ooooo

WHEN I GOT TO SCHOOL the next morning, the soldiers had already set up a checkpoint. I saw one soldier standing on the rooftop of the White Building with a rifle. All the makeshift barricades had been cleared from the buildings. There were no teachers around, but most of my classmates had shown up. I joined my classmates in the classroom, but we didn't speak to one another, and our facial expressions were flat. A soldier with a handgun hanging from his belt walked in to announce that the Cultural Revolution was over for us. He ordered us to relinquish our weapons within twenty-four hours. "Weapons" included guns, clubs, knives, and so on. Anyone who disobeyed the order would be punished.

He then announced that Chairman Mao had ordered all students of both junior and senior high to go to the countryside to be reeducated. This caused quite a stir, and our flat expressions were replaced by looks of shock.

"Quiet!" the soldier yelled. After he'd regained control of the class, he laid out the plan for our relocation. Our school offered two choices. Students could choose to go to the rubber farm on Hainan Island, in the South China Sea, or to a village in one of two regions, one to the east of Canton City and the other to the southwest. Both villages were about one hundred miles away from Canton and in very poor regions. The school would make all the arrangements. We were also given the option of making our own arrangements with any village that would take us. (No student was being offered a place at university or in a factory or office, no matter how Red his family was.) There were exemptions for health reasons, or if one had many relatives overseas. Still, when I saw their expressions and their mute reaction to the announcement, I was sure the few princelings in my class would get an exemption.

When I got home, I found that Mommy had already heard the news. She was sitting on the edge of the bed, her eyes puffy from crying. There was nothing I could say as I sat down next to her. Then Lily and Ning came home. Lily was madly in love with a smooth-talking amateur painter and factory worker. She was the romantic type, and he was, as Mommy put it, "able to talk a bird into landing on the ground." Lily was angry; she was about to marry this young man. Ning had had only one year of junior high under her belt before the Cultural Revolution, and she didn't seem to fully understand the gravity of the situation. Bun was in the fifth grade when the Cultural Revolution started, so she would stay home to finish up elementary school. Lily and Ning had no confidence that she would be a capable helper for Mommy. As for Jing, she was deemed graduated from medical school, despite wasting two years with the Cultural Revolution, and was waiting to be sent someplace to practice medicine.

Lily, Ning, and I attended different high schools. Each school had its own offerings for relocation, and they were all different. Each of us would go someplace different. This only added to Mommy's worries. Soon, Papa learned about it, and he was sad and worried as well. He and Mommy wanted all three of us to go to the same village. The good thing was they both had a strong distaste for collective farms. For Papa, this stemmed from his bad memory of the chicken farm; for Mommy, it came from intuition. We had a couple of months to find a village and make arrangements, and Papa said he would take care of it. He told us not to worry.

One day, the annoying Street Committee member came again and announced that the residents of the city had been ordered to dig holes around their house to hide in when the Soviets drop an atomic bomb on us. She said we needed holes for only Mommy and Bun, as Ning, Lily, and I would no longer be city residents. Our names would be taken off the family Household Register, she said, and we could no longer legally remain in Canton City.

"Are you going to kick me out of my home?" I tried hard to control my anger.

"Unless you have a travel permit from your village," she said sternly.

"By the way, do you know how stupid that is? To dig a hole to shield yourself from an atomic bomb?" I wouldn't back down.

Mommy pushed me into the other room. She was scared I'd get into a fight.

The ground around our building was hard, but we were finally able to dig a shallow hole. The Street Committee members, all lazybones who didn't get their own holes dug, didn't even come by to inspect ours.

"Children, you listen and listen good," Mommy announced. "If I hide inside that hole and get buried by the tremors of a nuclear bomb, leave me in peace. I don't want you to dig me out and waste your money for my funeral just to bury me again."

We all laughed hard. Mommy was sounding exactly like Auntie at last.

Mommy badly needed that laughter. She had been crying alone at night ever since the sent-down news broke. She asked herself repeatedly what she'd done wrong that her three children were being punished like this. In her eyes, we were too young to live by ourselves. In Mommy's mind, *Who will make sure the mosquito netting is well tucked under their straw mattresses every night? Why does Heaven not punish me and leave my children alone?*

I knew that Mommy was not alone in crying in the dark for her children, but no student dared make public that his mother had been crying. Auntie's remark came back to me: Two years of the Cultural Revolution had taught us Chinese how to survive by slipping our "right" hand tightly into the pocket of our red sweater and waving our "left" hand high so everyone can see. Crying behind closed doors was mothers' (and perhaps daughters') only option to express their true feelings.

Lily cried because she didn't know what would happen to her wedding, which was set to take place soon. There wasn't an exemption for married couples; otherwise, many high school students would have lined up in front of the marriage bureau. Ning didn't cry, and that surprised me. *She's tough*, I thought. And of course, I didn't cry, for I believed the saying "Men shed blood, not tears." I had no illusions that my life would be easy or in my control. *A dog can't spit out a tusk of ivory.* All I learned from the Rooftop Underground had made me a man without any illusions about his future in China.

The newspapers were accurate in reporting people's response to Mao's order. Jubilant Red Guards were indeed beating drums, waving red flags, singing songs glorifying Mao, and shedding grateful tears for his new and brilliant direction for our generation. "The same rice nourishes a hundred types of people," the saying went. Many of the more zealous students, who had been hard-core Red Guards of both the Rebel and Loyalist camps, chose the rubber farm so they could have a communal platform from which to express their endless love for Mao and communism. More than a decade later, when I was finishing medical school in America, almost all those sent-down students had moved back to the cities after Deng took over the country. Many of these ex-Red Guards became rich from Deng's market economy, something they had vehemently hated and sought to violently destroy during the Cultural Revolution. Some of them were involved in a TV documentary glorifying their experiences during Mao's "Down to the Countryside" campaign. They credited their years in the countryside as the most valuable of their lives. I quit watching after a few minutes. What a bunch of phonies!

Whether you worked on a rubber farm, a rice farm, a tea farm, or a sheep or cattle farm, all had several things in common: a minimal salary (the equivalent of about three dollars a month), a communal kitchen, a dormitory, a set number of days off (though, one needed approval from the head of the farm to visit home), and mandatory political study. Meanwhile, village living meant you were on your own, laboring for work points just like the peasants, and taking care of all your own needs. In a village, your movements were up to you: You could stay and work, or leave and go without work points. Your absence wouldn't hurt the village, for the peasants didn't really need your participation in the first place. Indeed, some peasants were openly hostile toward the students, for they saw us as diluting the value of each work point they earned. There was no mandatory political study. Peasants had no time to engage in politics. I wouldn't need to bring along Mao's *Little Red Book*. But the most appealing thing to me about going to a village was that if I decided to escape, the villagers wouldn't care. Anyway, going to the rubber farm with my classmates had never crossed my mind.

For the first time, I realized I would need to look after my two younger sisters. Mommy and Papa were wise putting me in charge of them. I was known for doing the right thing. I'm not bragging; my school report cards every year had said so.

I thought a lot in those days. I wasn't worried about living in a village, for I was familiar with village life. Every year, the school arranged for us to work for a month in a poor village. But village life was exhausting physically and dull mentally all year long. What bothered me most, I realized, was that I was not a brave man, and I feared dying. I was certainly not as brave as Hay. He dared risk his life to escape to Hong Kong, but I hesitated. What was wrong with me? Why wasn't I brave?

Papa and Mommy, like all Chinese, would never have encouraged me to be brave—not to be afraid of the dark, yes, but not to be afraid of dying to reach a goal, no. They had warned me that being brave could be dangerous, and as all Chinese parents did with their children, they encouraged me to be smart. I didn't blame them. With the imperial examination (which has evolved into the present-day university entrance exam), the Chinese have two thousand-some years of selecting scholars—men, not women—to be "a man above other men." Mao refined this saying by adding that only offspring from a Red family could be "a man above other men." So, Mao just kept messing things up for us.

I was stuck. To escape to Hong Kong was risky and demanded bravery I lacked. To be with my sisters in the village was the moral, the logical thing to do, and an obligation I had to fulfill. After a while, I stopped worrying about being brave and I chose to accept my responsibility.

Later, at the Rooftop Underground, I told Hay that Lily and Ning needed me in the village, and he understood. It had been about a month since my last visit with him and Uncle. What a change! The intensity of their discussions, and their seriousness of purpose, had grown—and Voice of America had lost its charm. Radio broadcasts and talks of the Cultural Revolution and Madam Mao had been replaced by discussions of how to escape to Hong Kong. These Idlers had woken up with a burning desire and urgency to seek a free life in Hong Kong.

Hay's older brother, Mau, and "cousin" Yun were going to a rice and fish farm in the Pearl River Delta area. They talked quietly with Uncle about how to reach Hong Kong by way of a sampan, a flat-bottomed skiff. The journey would take a whole night of paddling from a tributary of the Pearl River to the Zhujiang River Estuary then on to Hong Kong.

"How would they get a boat?" I asked Hay.

"They plan to steal a sampan from the village where they work."

"Are you going with them?"

"No. They're still talking about it. But I need to go now."

"Anyone healthy and with a plan should go now. Don't wait," Uncle reminded everyone.

Hay's other two "cousins," Shan and Kok, were not so lucky. They were being sent to places far away from Hong Kong. Hay promised he would make arrangements for them and for me, in case I decided to escape.

"What arrangements?" I asked.

"I'll introduce you to a useful contact before I leave." He seemed to have it all figured out.

Hay had selected one of the villages offered by the school. It was in the Ma'an area, in Huiyang County, a very poor region about a hundred miles east of Canton. I remembered from the topographic map that it was directly north of Hong Kong's Mirs Bay.

"Hay, it's too far from Hong Kong."

"But I've found a very small island called Tung Ping Chau, in Mirs Bay, very close to the Mainland. It belongs to Hong Kong. We'll swim there instead."

Hay opened the map. Tung Ping Chau was a tiny bean-shaped island in Mirs Bay. It sat on the east side of Mirs Bay about two miles from the coast of China. Hong Kong's coast was many miles to its west. The Tung Ping Chau route would be the easternmost route of the East Line.

"Which route do most people take?" I asked.

"Most take the West Line, to swim across Shenzhen Bay," Hay said. "Or the East Line, crossing the mountains west of Mirs Bay."

Uncle added: "Don't tell anybody about the Tung Ping Chau route. The less people talk about it, the better."

From anti-Mao leader, Uncle had become an escape leader. "Practice your swimming," he said. "I'll arrange for a boat so all of us can practice paddling."

I was surprised by how detailed their plans were. They talked about currents, tides, and the effects of the full moon, all of which I had never paid attention to. Their talk was infectious, alive with hope and determination. I was impressed and overwhelmed.

I went home and lay in bed for hours.

"Are you sick?" Mommy asked.

"No, I'm just tired," I said.

"Where did you go?"

"Hay's place."

"Any news from the radio?" Voice of America had intrigued her as well.

"We didn't turn it on," I said.

Mommy looked at me and said, "I know. You talked about escape."

"How did you know?" I was surprised.

"Hay told me."

"Hay asked me to join him. He's going soon."

Mommy sat down and didn't say a word.

"Mommy, should I go with him?"

"I don't know. It's very dangerous. You can die in the sea, you know. But you can't waste your life in the village, either." The room was silent. We were both thinking.

Finally, Mommy broke the silence: "I can't make this decision for you. It's for you to decide. When I was your age, I was pregnant with your sister."

I saw that her eyes were red as she walked out of the room.

It was for me to decide. But I wanted her to tell me what I should do. Still, I felt relieved. If Mommy was encouraging me to go, I would have to overcome my fear of dying.

Soon, Papa found us a village to go to, and the mayor of Zhaoqing City let him take a leave to come home and make arrangements. Papa was excited about the village he'd found for us. It was about thirty minutes by bike east of Zhaoqing City, north of the Xijiang River; and close to Antelope Gorge. He said he would visit us there often to help. Mommy was happy for that. I didn't say a word, nor did Lily and Ning. What could we say? We had no choice but to go.

Papa said the village was called "White Stone," the "richest" village in the people's commune outside Zhaoqing City because it ran a small shop that carved inkstones. (Carving inkstones? How could the same pairs of hands that harnessed scary water buffalo to plow rice paddies carve the delicate stone used for painting and calligraphy?) The shop brought in more money than rice cultivation because its Japanese customers paid good money for its creations.

I found this bizarre. I had thought Japan was still our enemy. Papa had told me how horrified he was when running away from the Japanese warplanes dropping bombs on his hometown during World War II.

"Papa, you said you hated Japan," I reminded him.

"But they have money to buy China's products, and they like the inkstone made in White Stone," he said.

Mommy had her own take on Japan: "'She who has breast milk is your mother.'"

Papa frowned. "How can you say a thing like that?" He continued: "It's my job to arrange for the export of the carved inkstones." The Japanese buyers, he explained, were very picky and demanding, and the shop's peasant workers were not used to meeting their exacting requirements. Plus, the Japanese communicated in English, which Papa spoke. Uncle Lee needed Papa, so he'd gone the extra mile to get me and my sisters approved by the reluctant people's commune even though the village didn't need extra hands.

Mommy was relieved that the three of us would go to the same village, one that was close to Papa, who could help us if needed.

Unlike my sisters, I was intrigued by the thought of the inkstone shop. But White Stone's location was bad for an escape: It was hundreds of miles away from the South China Sea, and from there, only a fish could find its way to Hong Kong.

ooooo

BEFORE LEAVING FOR WHITE STONE, I went to the Rooftop Underground to say good-bye to Hay and Uncle. Before I left, Uncle said, "My little shed will always welcome you."

"I'd be much happier if no one answered the doorbell the next time I dropped by," I said. I was feeling sentimental.

Hay was upbeat: "Then you should come to Hong Kong. We'll all meet there instead!"

"Don't you die in the water, Hay! It's not allowed. Heaven has said so." I felt my throat tighten as I said it, and we hugged good-bye.

"I'll leave Mommy the name of a good contact who can help you when you're ready," Hay told me.

I cried as I walked away from their building and headed home. Would that be our final good-bye? Why did good things never last?

The dinner at home before our departure for White Stone made me cry again—not at the table, but in front of the empty chicken cage. My hen was gone; she was the last one. She had survived the Cultural Revolution but not "Down to the Countryside." Mommy had killed her for our farewell meal.

CHAPTER 8

THE CALM BEFORE THE STORM

WHEN OUR BUS ARRIVED IN White Stone, Papa, village leader Uncle Lee, and a boy of about ten were at the bus stop waiting for us. Papa was excited to make the introductions, and they all helped us unload our luggage. After the bus was gone and the dust cloud it kicked up had dissipated, I could smell a fresh breeze coming up from the paddies next to the dirt road.

Uncle Lee was a middle-aged man; the boy, Qiang, was his son, a good boy, Papa told us. Qiang was skinny, but he picked up one of the larger pieces of luggage. Uncle Lee told me with a smile that Qiang was strong enough to carry it.

The plan was to drop by Uncle Lee's home first, where his wife had prepared lunch. We followed a long, straight dirt road that cut through green fields to reach the village. On our way, we passed a large concrete slab abutting the road. Uncle Lee told us that this was where the field hands washed their bodies every evening after work. I noticed a small square hole in the middle; I figured it must be the well. What an odd place for a group of men to shower! Qiang said it was for boys, too.

With Qiang and my two boys in White Stone by Xijiang River
(with Antelope Gorge in the background), 1993.

Before the village was a pond. Qiang pointed to it and said, "We raise fish."

Uncle Lee added, "Before the New Year, half the water is pumped out, and the fish are driven to a corner by men holding a long net."

Qiang added, "The fish can jump very high."

I said to myself, *This place is better than I thought!* Lily and Ning showed no interest.

Beyond the fishpond was a huge old banyan tree with many long offshoots strangling its large trunk. It reminded me of the banyan in our neighborhood that I used to climb. Under this tree sat an old woman holding a baby who had just pooped on the ground in front of her. The old woman turned around and called to two dogs waiting nearby. They ran to her and licked the poop off the ground and the baby's butt. My heart sank, and all my good feelings about the village flew out of the window. Chinese loved to eat dogs, and in return, they fed their poop to other dogs. (Dogs were not excluded from reincarnation.) Was this our circle of life? All recycled, nothing wasted? I thought of the myth that women became ugly if they ate dog meat. I figured the women were lucky. Let the men eat that "delicacy."

The village was a collection of detached one-story houses made of brick or mud brick. Small lanes ran in front of their front doors and between their side walls. The lanes were covered with poorly laid flat stones. Open ditches ran along both sides of the lanes to drain away rain and human and animal waste. The lanes also served as open spaces for chickens, ducks, and pigs to roam freely.

The wooden gate to our new home had a rotted bottom edge and opened onto a small walled yard about five feet deep. At one corner of the yard was an old brick stove, and on it sat a large wok. Above the wok was a small hood that shielded the wok from rain. The house consisted of two side-by-side identical rooms that opened onto the front yard. The rooms were dark and had no windows; the only light was from a small glass tile on the roof.

As I stepped into the first room, I walked into a cobweb and its dead spider occupant. The moldy stench of decaying rats hit my nose. As my eyes got used to the darkness, I saw that the walls were dark and the floor was of dark, compact dirt. At the back half of the room was an open loft, and against its edge leaned a wooden ladder. Under the loft was a bed. There was a wooden table, and next to it sat a narrow wooden bench. An oil lamp sat on the dusty tabletop.

Lily and Ning stayed outside, saying nothing. Uncle Lee said to them, "You two can share a bed." They nodded.

"No way to compare it with your city living," Uncle Lee said apologetically, "but it's what I could find." He sounded sincere.

Papa said, "Thank you, Uncle Lee. It's very good. Thank you very much."

Uncle Lee glanced over the walls and said, "We used it as the public kitchen during the Great Leap Forward. The smoke darkened the walls. I should have whitewashed them."

Papa said, "We've wasted too much of your precious time. You go back to work. We'll whitewash it ourselves."

Uncle Lee left, and Qiang returned with a bucket of slaked lime and brushes. We mixed the white powder with water and started to paint. It was frustrating. After we whitewashed the walls twice, they were still dark brown—but the skin of our hands was bleached white and creased like sandpaper. We gave up.

Uncle Lee had left us two wooden buckets and a bamboo carrying pole to fetch water from the well. This was obviously my job, but I had never done it before. *A piece of cake*, I thought. The well was a typical one for Southern China: a small two-foot-square hole in the middle of a large concrete slab. The small hole led down to a much larger hole with water about ten feet below that. Holding on to the rope tied to the bucket's handle, I let go of the bucket; it hit the water below and then turned sideways. I flipped the rope every which way, but the bucket would not sink. I started to curse and heard giggling behind me. Qiang was standing there.

"What's so funny?" I was dismayed.

He didn't say a word, but took the rope from me and gave it a jerk. The rope undulated and when the undulation reached the handle, it tilted the handle and pulled the bucket into the water. *Damn! How slick was that!* It took me many tries to get the second bucket to do the same.

Qiang giggled behind me again as I carried the two buckets "home." Water sloshed over the rims every step along the way. So, once again, my boy teacher took over. Hoisting the pole with its two full buckets drooping heavily, he moved in harmony with the up and down of the buckets. No water spilled! Amazing! I liked this little fellow!

Papa, Lily, and Ning had started to prepare dinner. Papa had brought us rice, vegetables, some meat, cooking oil, salt, and soy sauce. I knew Lily and Ning saw me as worse than useless in the kitchen, so I said I would go check out the village. I walked out of the front yard. Qiang quietly followed me.

At the end of the village, we had to climb up a gentle slope to reach the top of the riverbank, about ten feet above the road. The top of the bank was flat and wide enough for the easy passage of bikes in both directions. The village was on the north side of the bank, and the south side consisted of sugarcane fields that stopped only about a hundred feet from the river. The river was the Xijiang, the one I'd traversed during my Big Link-up trip.

I pointed to the mountains downstream and asked Qiang, "Is that Antelope Gorge?"

"Yes."

"I want to climb that mountain someday," I said.

"We get the stone from there. Inside a cave."

"To make the inkstones?" I asked. Qiang nodded. "Have you climbed the mountain?" I asked him.

"Of course, with Mom, to get firewood."

The sun had lost its vigor but tried to hang on a bit longer, and the wind from the south swept the tips of the sugarcane enough to make them hum. The smell of cooking from the village chimneys reminded us it was time for dinner.

"It's beautiful!" I said.

"Not when the water buffalo fought."

"Tell me about it."

Once, two water buffaloes got into a fight by the river. According to Qiang, they trashed the sugarcane, and the dust from the fields drifted over to where we now stood. The villagers were in a panic, yelling at their kids to come home. The water buffalo fight didn't end until one of them labored for its last breath. The upside was that the villagers got a tasty meal of the dead "beast" that night. In China, beef was extremely hard to come by. The dead water buffalo was indeed a rare treat.

"I'm not scared of the water buffalo," Qiang assured me. "I know which one is nice. He lets me ride him." He looked proud.

This little guy is brave, I thought.

On our way back, we dropped by the public toilet. It was a big mistake. That's when all my good feelings from the day evaporated. The toilet comprised a straw shed covering two thirds of a large hole about eight feet in diameter dug into the ground and spanned by two long wood planks laid parallel to each other and about a foot apart. The hole was half full of human waste. Inside the shed, flies buzzed on the boards and countless maggots slithered about, waiting to be smashed by human feet. I ran away and tried to suppress the urge to puke. I had had many encounters with terrible public toilets, but I couldn't use this one. I couldn't step on maggots!

"Wait. I'll show you how," Qiang said after he'd caught up with me.

"How what? Nobody should use a toilet like this one," I said.

"Once, a little boy fell in and drowned," Qiang said.

"Don't ever mention that again!"

Finally, after a week, I surrendered, but not before Lily and Ning, and only after seeing the village women collected the human waste in buckets and spread it on the paddies before planting the rice. I realized that the public toilet would have to be a part of my life, especially in a village I couldn't leave. I had learned the worst of village living: that men ate dogs after the dogs had eaten human poop and that we ate rice fertilized by our own feces.

∞∞∞

IN CHINA, PEOPLE USED TO say women held up half the sky, and I said that in Southern China, women held up more than half the sky, but in White Stone, the women held up most of the sky. Most men in White Stone worked in the inkstone shop, earning a salary. They were respected and given a lot of slack because their salary was way more valuable than the work points the women earned. Even though the women bore the much greater burden of planting rice, and spent longer hours doing housework, caring for the kids, and raising pigs, they didn't complain. Indeed, White Stone was sought after as a place where young, unmarried women from other villages could find higher-status men to marry. That money could bring about such inequality was something I learned in White Stone that I would never forget.

∞∞∞

IT WAS OUR FIRST DAY as peasants. Our production leader was, of course, a woman, middle-aged and stocky. She assigned everyone's work each day and always took the hardest jobs for herself. I believed that's why the others respected her. Lily and Ning presented no difficulty for her: She assigned them to harvest peanuts with the old folks and the kids. But I presented a dilemma: I was both unskilled and not a woman. She looked at me and worked her brain, then asked me to wait while she assigned tasks to the others.

At last it was my turn. She said to me, "Can you go pick peanuts? I don't have any other easy work for you." She seemed to be apologizing.

"Sure. I'll go pick peanuts." From that moment on, she had my respect.

The peanut field abutted the riverbank. Lily, Ning, and I stood out among the old and the very young peasants because of our skin color. We were "white," not the healthy-looking tan of the peasants. The peasants tried to shield themselves from sunlight as much as they could, just like Mommy. She used a little parasol, but they had only their straw hats, some with pieces of cloth hung over the brim to give them more shade. Having pale skin was the foremost mark of nobility and beauty—no one of the working class had pale, smooth skin.

Lily was quiet all the time, but Ning surprised me by how talkative she was with the old and the very young. They all loved to chat with her about any trivial little detail of city life. I talked with the peasants, but they soon lost interest in listening to me; I was bad at small talk. Fortunately, I had Qiang by my side. He was not a talkative kid, so I initiated.

"How's school?" I asked. "What subject do you like the most?" It was summer break for him, and he was earning work points for his family.

"I like most subjects but math."

"Oh no! You must love math."

"Can you help me? My dad said you're a good student."

"Of course, I can. Give me a question."

He was thinking.

"How about your last assignment before the break?" I suggested.

It was a common problem. The setup was: Two cars are driving at two respective speeds, with the faster car beginning at a given distance behind the slower. The question was how long it would take the faster car to overtake the slower one.

"Have you been in a car?" I asked Qiang.

"No. The only thing I ride is water buffalo. I've told you already. You want to try?"

"No more buffalo. I'm going to give you a different but similar question, one you'll have no problem solving." I felt confident.

I rephrased the problem using something he was familiar with. "Let's say I earn seven work points a day and you earn five, but you earned ten points before I showed up. How many days until I have the same number of work points as you if we work together every day?"

It didn't take Qiang long to come up with the right answer.

"See, math's not hard, and it's useful." I was happy with my teaching.

"Who taught you this way?"

"Speed and work points? Nobody," I said, but wondered this myself.

As we worked, my body dripped with sweat under the hot sun. "I want to take a dip in that water and drink it." I pointed to the river.

"Do you know how to swim?"

"Do I know how? I can reach the other side before you finish pooping," I said. Qiang laughed.

After everyone had gone home, Qiang took off his T-shirt and shorts and waded naked into the river. With my shorts still on, I waded in, too.

Qiang shouted to me, "No one swims with shorts on! Not at this time of the day."

I shouted back, "Why?" I had never swum naked in my life.

Qiang said, "We just don't."

"Aren't you afraid your thing'll get bitten off and swallowed by a fish?" I asked as I threw my shorts on the riverbank.

What a wonderful feeling, swimming naked! Complete freedom! The river was quiet—we hardly saw a boat or a ship—and the water was clean. As I swam farther away from the bank, I drank in the water.

Qiang was not a good swimmer. Kids in the countryside didn't have the luxury of learning how to swim. There were no swimming pools, and even when there was a river, no teacher in his right mind would bring a student to a river to learn.

"Listen, I need to teach you how to swim," I told Qiang. "Your arms and legs are all wrong."

"My hands and feet, too?" He laughed.

"Everything, including your mouth." I hid my smile. "Totally no good."

ooooo

FINALLY, ONE DAY, I SET foot in Antelope Gorge. It was not because I wanted to, but because I had to. We had run out of firewood for cooking. Collecting firewood took two trips. First, I needed to cut down enough branches to set aside to air-dry—and remember where they were, because I'd then need to return to that spot to bundle them up and carry them home on a bamboo pole.

Seen from the riverbank in White Stone, Antelope Gorge was not two enormous cliffs squeezing a river, but two gentle, sloping ravines angling downward toward each other as if in a kiss, only to be thwarted near the bottom as the river inserted its hand in between them. Climbing up the gorge from the riverbank, I found the thick and tangled subtropical growth challenging. I should have spent some time looking for the trail. Perhaps it would lead me to the path of the cave, where I could see how the valuable stone was dug out. When I was done chopping down branches and setting them out to dry, I was so tired that I decided to find a place to take a nap. I climbed up the mountain and found a boulder under a tree large enough to lie down on. I glanced at the mountains across the gentle gorge and at the river far below. It was peaceful, and the breeze was soothing. I pictured how the people before me had romanticized this scene: a lonely "antelope" long, curved and pointed horns, standing on the cliff watching the disappearing sun on the other side of the river. A good imagination is always better than reality. That must be where the "antelope" and "gorge" came from. With such pleasant thoughts, I fell asleep.

I didn't know how long I slept—I didn't have a watch; nobody my age did—but when I woke, it was dark and chilly. Going downhill in the dark was hellish and frightening.

When I got back to the village, the first thing Ning said to me was "Didn't a tiger eat you?"

"Not yet," I said.

ooooo

ONE DAY, A PIGEON DROPPED from the sky and into our little front yard. Her leg was injured; I didn't know why. Qiang was excited, and we decided to keep her in my room to recover. Qiang was a marvelous caretaker. We built a large cage in the front courtyard to keep her while she rehabilitated. Soon, she attracted other pigeons, and we added a one-way door to trap them inside. I said it was our excessive feeding that had attracted the others, but Qiang insisted it was our pigeon's beauty. We were delighted when the pigeons laid eggs, creating even more pigeons. Soon, peasants wanted to buy them to go with their rice wine benders, but we yelled back, "You're out of your mind!"

The happiest moment came when we threw the pigeons up into the sky and they could all fly high, even the injured one, circling above our heads. Before sunset, they were already back inside the cage.

My workdays were not as rewarding. Most were dull or back-breaking, and made my whole body ache. Sometimes they were hell, such as the days in the sugarcane fields. Our job was to remove the outer leaves from the stems of the sugarcane and the weeds around their roots. The sugarcane was well grown, taller than people, and we'd disappear inside the field. With no air movement through the cane, the hot, stagnant air steamed us. The edges of the leaves, sharp as a handsaw, sliced my skin, and my sweat seeped into the fresh wounds, stinging painfully. I had no doubt I suffered the most because I sweated the most.

After a week, I was assigned a daily work point of seven out of ten, and Lily and Ning were both given fives, but I was doing the same amount of work as they were most of the time. I was really surprised. No peasant told me it was because I was a male, even though I knew it was. The word *sexism* was not in our vocabulary back then, or even now.

Lily, Ning, and I didn't really need work points. Papa had told us not to worry about making money. We would have been happy just to have our shares of freshly harvested, shining white rice without rat or cockroach poop. We had promised to bring some home for Mommy. She had said more than once that she could eat the rice with just soy sauce, perhaps adding a bit of pork lard, but nothing else. Like other parents whose children had been sent to the countryside, Papa and Mommy stood ready to support their suffering children while keeping hope alive that someday they'd return to the city. Hope was one of a few luxuries the Chinese were "legally" allowed.

After a while, the production leader had a better feel for our physical abilities and attitudes. Lily's mind and heart were never in the village. She had married her boyfriend, without a big dinner celebration, and all she wanted to do was go back to him in the city and stay there for good. The production leader saw this and assigned her to work beside the old people and kids. Ning was different. She worked well and communicated well with the young women, and they liked her. I was assigned to work with the other women, and they didn't talk to me much. Still, I knew they paid attention to me and would help me if they saw me having any difficulties.

My first year of village life had come and gone, and another planting season arrived to break my back. Bending over for hours on end to plant rice in the muddy soil of the paddy was grueling, and I always hated the planting. This time I had Qiang working by my side, but I had no interest in talking with him when my back was hurting—until my fingers became stuck in a sticky clump.

"Sticky! What's that?" I said.

Qiang peered over. "You've got the 'gold'!"

"Poop?! Where did it come from?"

I was pissed, but Qiang chuckled. "The public toilet."

As I rubbed my fingers repeatedly in the shallow water, trying to get rid of it. Qiang chuckled again, "Your leg!"

Three plump leeches were sucking my mud-caked leg. I jumped onto the berm, frantically trying to pull them off me, but they kept slipping from my grip. Qiang slapped them hard—so hard that I yelled, "Don't break my leg." They fell off my legs, but blood oozed from their bites. Without hesitation, Qiang spat into his palm and rubbed his saliva on my wounds.

"Did you brush your teeth this morning?" I asked.

"I forgot," he said and chuckled again.

That annoyed me. In the paddy next to us, a woman was driving a water buffalo to plow the field.

"Don't giggle, boy! Let me show you what a man can do," I said, and began walking toward the woman.

I heard Qiang shouting at me: "Don't try that one! He's bad."

I waved a hand, brushing off his warning.

The peasant woman, sensing my intention, was curious at first. Then she smiled and gave me a brief introduction to plowing. The work went smoothly at first, but then I accidentally set the plow blade too deeply into the soil, and the excessive drag upset the buffalo. It snorted loudly before exploding in anger and bolting. I held the plow aloft and ran behind the wild beast across the field as best I could. If not for the calm, strong woman who came to my rescue, it would have been a disaster. She shouted and pulled the rope hard, and the water buffalo reluctantly stopped. I was coated with mud up to my face. *The countryside is no place for a weak man like me*, I concluded.

Soon enough, my curiosity disappeared along with my body aches, and I found farming in Southern China nothing but repetitious and boring. The peasants held the dim view that "work would always outlast one's life." The kids knew that their parents had to work and that they had to be alone from dawn till dusk. The only things that moved were the chickens, ducks, and pigs in the alley, so the children watched them, sitting on the doorstep and inhaling the stench of sewage from the nearby open ditch. This really bothered me. How lucky I had been all along! The start of school would end the older kids' exposure to the foul air, but of course that's when they'd have to begin their fieldwork, to earn work points for their families. Then the work in the fields would outlast their lives.

Only three occasions gave the peasants temporary respite: the celebration of births, weddings, and deaths. The death of a peasant was mourned with a big feast, without a eulogy but with wailing that was long on decibels and short on tears. What shocked me most, though, was the bridal shower the night before a wedding, when the bride-to-be and her bridesmaids wailed, berating the groom and mother-in-law with all the meanest words they could think of.

Qiang and I eavesdropped on such a scene once, after he insisted it would be fun. Village women in China believed that marriage was a must for every woman, and that only weird, abnormal women didn't marry, even though, in her married life, a village woman was practically enslaved by her husband and mother-in-law and burdened by endless work—in the fields, in the bearing and raising of children, in caring for her never-satisfied mother-in-law, and in serving her husband. These burdens were not far-fetched; this was indeed a village bride's reality. So, the last chance for the bride-to-be to vent her anger over her impending doom was the bridal shower, where she would be backed by her loudmouthed bridesmaids and without the presence of her groom and his mother. For Qiang, listening to the colorful, over-the-top scolding of the groom and mother-in-law was his idea of fun. But not mine.

"Let's go," I said to him and walked away.

Qiang followed. "Every wedding has this," he said.

"Really?"

I believed that most marriages couldn't possibly be that bad. *Otherwise, what was the point of marriage?*

The day after the wedding, while we were washing ourselves down in the men's bathing area in the middle of the paddy, the bridegroom detailed for us his prowess in his first encounter with his bride. The other married men laughed and jeered and disputed his potency. When I interrupted them with the news that America had landed the first two men on the moon—they shrugged, and someone asked, "Do Americans also have mooncake?" All the others laughed.

I was shocked. Village life was not what I had anticipated, and not what I wanted for the remaining years of my life. There had to be more for me.

Papa would come over to spend Sundays with us, and he always brought food. Many peasants there knew him, and he always showed "excessive" humility. This irritated me at times, but it irritated Ning all the time, and she told Papa that nobody would respect him more for being excessively humble. Mommy told me Papa was not that way before the Hundred Flowers Campaign. He used to be assertive, and at times, his assertiveness even got on others' nerves. I believed that the many years of humiliation he'd suffered for being a capitalist rightist had ground away his angles. I had seen how the rude officer at the chicken farm ordered Papa to send me away, and how Papa had complied. I had seen how Papa had hidden in that small, stuffy office during the Cultural Revolution. If I wanted to survive in China, I had to not only hide my opinion but also master the skill of "patting the horse's ass"— what people in America called "bootlicking." But I was not born with that skill. Mommy always said I was too direct.

One day, we received a letter from Mommy saying she was coming to visit us and would bring us good news. The production leader heard about it and assigned me to sell sweet potatoes in the farmers' market so I could earn my work points and come home early.

When I came back to the village one day, before I had set foot in the front yard, Ning scolded me: "What did you do to make Mommy cry?" Ning was preparing food in the front yard.

"What are you talking about?" I glimpsed Mommy inside the room. "Mommy!" I ran inside, bare chested, holding my T-shirt.

Grabbing my hand, Mommy teared up. "Look at you, like a charcoal briquet," she said. "I saw you when I was still on the bus. You should wear a long-sleeved shirt."

Chinese are not expressive when showing their feelings. Hugging and kissing are not done in public, even for lovers. But I knew how heavy Mommy's heart was when she squeezed my hand, her eyes brimming with tears.

I pulled my sweat-soaked T-shirt back on. "What's the good news?"

"Hay's made it!"

I was shocked; Ning, too.

From an envelope bearing a Hong Kong stamp of the queen's head, Mommy took out a picture of Hay smiling in front of a tall building full of large round windows. He looked thin but full of spirit. His blue pants looked like a pair of long-necked trumpets with the mouths cupping his shining leather shoes, and his jacket was short, exposing a large belt buckle. Ning and I were speechless.

"Hay asks in his letter when you'll join him," Mommy told me.

"Do you want me to go, Mommy?" I asked.

"What else does he say?" Ning interrupted.

"He asks if you're surviving village life."

Papa knew about Mommy's visit and joined us later for dinner. Mommy handed him the picture. "Is this Hay?" Papa said. "He looks good."

"Your son would look the same if we'd stayed in Hong Kong," Mommy said.

Papa was silent.

After dinner, Papa and Mommy started to argue. It was clear Papa didn't want us to do what Hay had done, and his reasons were many. Any escape was dangerous. If I didn't make it, I would have no future whatsoever in China, and if I made it, Ning would be alone in the village by herself, because Lily often stayed in Canton with her husband. Papa warned Mommy: If she supported my escape attempt and I died at sea, "How could you live with yourself in good conscience?" He ended the conversation by saying that the sent-down movement would not last long. Someday, the party would bring every student back to the city. "After all, China can't afford to lose a whole generation," Papa concluded.

"How do you know?" Mommy was not happy to hear this. "When did you become Chairman Mao? During the Hundred Flowers Campaign?"

We laughed, but Papa said nothing. He only shook his head.

This ended the after-dinner conversation, and nobody was at peace. The next day, we sent Mommy to the bus stop to go back to Canton. There was no point in her witnessing our lousy existence. It would only make her cry. Our routine resumed, but my head was occupied with the thought of escaping to Hong Kong.

ooooo

ONE DAY DURING LUNCH BREAK, Uncle Lee dropped by. He started by saying that he liked us and the villagers liked us. He thanked me for helping his son with his homework. Then he said the people's commune was upset about the arrangement he'd made with Papa to bring us to the village. The party secretary of the people's commune had decided that we must relocate to another village, one that needed more laborers. Uncle Lee was obviously unhappy about the decision, but he said he couldn't do anything about it.

"Where are they going to put us?" I tried to be calm.

"The village is down the road, just before Antelope Gorge."

"When do we have to move?"

"Take your time. I'll talk to your papa."

After Uncle Lee left, Ning, Lily, and I sat quietly. I had not heard of another incident in which a sent-down student was relocated to another village more than two years after he had settled and been welcomed by the peasants. We hadn't done anything wrong! The villagers of White Stone liked us and respected Papa.

Lily said she'd stop working that day. She had been visiting her husband in Canton regularly, and was pregnant with their daughter. Ning said she'd keep working to earn work points, unless the production leader asked her not to. I decided to work, too. I couldn't sit around thinking about something I had no control over.

When Papa came over that evening, he looked dejected. He had tried so hard to keep us in a peaceful, functional place, despite the dwelling's being barely acceptable for human habitation. But once again, he had been defeated. Did Heaven have eyes? Why didn't It see the injustice done to Papa and to us?

"I'll talk to Uncle Lee and see what he can do to help," Papa said. "Don't do anything yet."

He returned an hour later and said it was no good; we had to move. He'd go to the other village to make living arrangements the next day.

Qiang was sad, and I had to cheer him up. "I'm not going to die, am I?" I said. "Save your tears for now."

This worked, and he chuckled, "Did your dad do something bad?"

I was surprised. "What do you mean?"

"I heard Pa tell my Mom he couldn't help you because of your papa."

"My dad did nothing wrong. When you grow up, you'll understand," I said.

"I wish I knew how to ride a bike," Qiang said. "Then I could visit you often."

"You can float in the river; the water'll carry you to my place," I said. The new village also abutted the river and was downstream from Qiang's village. "But don't be naked when you come."

He laughed and handed me a sleek, dark red hardwood case. "My dad made it a while ago. He asked me to give it to you."

I opened the box. In it was a dark gray inkstone featuring two small, elegant dragons, their heads and upper trunks carved in relief across the top, facing a small white column.

"A full moon chased by two dragons?" I asked.

"No, it's called 'Two Dragons Playing with a Pearl.' We called the white spot the 'eye.' The eye makes the stone more expensive."

I was touched. In a world full of "horse's-ass tappers" (boot-lickers), I had met a family who showed me genuine love and care without asking anything in return. "I'll come visit you often, Qiang. Take good care of the pigeons." I patted him on the shoulder.

In 1971, after two years in White Stone, we put our belongings on a horse cart, and Papa loaded some more on the rack of his bicycle. Qiang insisted on helping push the cart. We passed the large banyan tree. The old woman, holding the hand of the toddler, shook her head to express sorrow for us. Some of the peasants working in the field waved to us, and we waved back. It was only an hour-long walk, but I felt the road would never end.

The two years of the Cultural Revolution and the two years of village labor that ended with our being pushed out of White Stone were enough to put me on the path to rebellion. The bow was drawn, and the arrow was set. I had reached the point of no return.

CHAPTER 9

A CALL FROM HEAVEN

THE PARTY SECRETARY OF THE new village was a middle-aged man with a black patch on his right eye. Later, I learned that some villagers called him "One-Eye Dragon" behind his back. He made it very clear to us that his village didn't want us, but he had to follow the decision of the people's commune. Papa told him the people's commune had said his village needed laborers, but One-Eye Dragon said he didn't need students from the big city.

I said to myself, *The feeling is mutual; I don't want to be here.*

Later, I learned from my classmates that many villages didn't want us students, but they had to take us in because it was required of them. They saw us as "a dead cat being thrust down their throats that they had to swallow." Their antagonism toward us made sense: We had no farming skills, and our physical strength and mental toughness could not develop fast enough to meet the demands of the rapid rice-growing cycles.

The work in the new village was much harder, and the living conditions worse than those in White Stone. Ning again showed

The view from Tung Ping Chau Island—across the sea
are the mountains of China's coast, 2010.

her toughness and endurance and made friends with some village women. Lily often stayed in Canton. Papa kept visiting us every Sunday, but he was quiet. Ning and I didn't have much to talk about with him. He still refused to believe the future was dead for his daughters and son.

With every passing day, my heart sank a little more. One night, as I stared at the little square glass tile illuminated by moonlight—the common feature of the village homes—I had a moment of clarity. I had two choices: I could let China slowly but surely grind my life into dust as it had done to Papa, or I could get myself a new life in a beautiful world as Hay had done. A new life came with a risk that could end my existence, perhaps painfully, but so far, Hay and his two friends had made it, and I had not heard that anyone had died. Fear of death would follow me, but so what? I just had to suppress it and hope that my efforts and abilities reduced the risk to zero. I had the will to do it. What I needed was the calling, and a blessing from Heaven.

One night, One-Eye Dragon called an urgent meeting that everyone had to attend. The village hall was full, from the elderly to the babies. One-Eye Dragon started by saying Mao and the party had given us the opportunity to punish the last group of criminals of the Cultural Revolution, and we had to decide their punishment. This kind of people's court was a common practice back then. What could be more effective at dissuading people from considering an act than by letting them know the consequences others had faced for that act?

After yelling to the noisy crowd to shut up and listen, One-Eye Dragon pulled out a long list from his pocket and read out the names and their crimes. Most crimes were political, and almost all accused were from Black classes; they had said things critical of Mao and the Cultural Revolution. One "criminal" had said that Mao was too old and had lost his mind. Another had said that Mao was not as able as President Liu at running the country. One had said that Madam Mao had been a disaster for China.

I was uneasy. What we had discussed on Hay and Uncle's rooftop kept coming back to me. *I've committed worse crimes than them. Be calm now*, I kept reminding myself. *You need to show your active participation.* Then I asked a logical but "stupid" question: "Won't our decisions come too late if the execution is tomorrow?"

One-Eye Dragon pulled down his face and told me sternly, "Don't forget what family you're from." Some peasants heard this, but they couldn't have understood it.

The politically naïve and good-hearted peasants gave these political criminals lenient sentences—no more than ten years in prison. These irritated One-Eye Dragon. He scolded the peasants for their inability to take a political stand; the sentences he imposed were always capital punishment. There were a few non-political crimes, such as rape and theft. Almost all the peasants wanted to sentence the rapists to death, but One-Eye Dragon showed leniency toward those who had been born into Red families, saying that we should give them a chance to reform. The peasants quickly lost interest in the meeting; the kids wanted to go home; babies cried.

One-Eye Dragon announced that everyone must go to the city the next day to witness the public execution. This disturbed the peasants. Many said they had too much to do at home and didn't want to witness an execution. Then One-Eye Dragon announced that he would give everyone, except those from the families of rich peasants or landlords, the full day's work points if they attended. This really excited the crowd. They started to talk about what they would do in the city after the execution.

One-Eye Dragon read off the remaining criminals' crimes and gave the death sentence to all political prisoners. Before he was done, many villagers had left the hall.

The execution site was an open space between the county dirt road and the brick wall of Star Lake Park; it was guarded by soldiers and policemen. Big-character graffiti on the brick wall read, USE OUR FRESH BLOOD TO SAFEGUARD CHAIRMAN MAO!

Peasants from every village of the people's commune and city people had converged on the execution site. Suddenly, noise erupted as an army truck arrived carrying prisoners in its bed. The prisoners wore white T-shirts, and their heads were shorn. Each prisoner bore the now-familiar placard, rising behind and above his head, with the prisoner's name superimposed by a red X. This time the X meant physical death. A soldier standing behind each prisoner pushed the prisoner's head to face the audience while pulling him upright. When the truck passed in front of our group, I saw that their faces were a ghostly white, some with eyes closed and others staring blankly at us. One prisoner had a piece of wood jammed between his teeth; fresh blood dripped from his lips.

Then came two more trucks just like the first one. All three trucks stopped next to the execution site. Each prisoner was dragged off the truck by two soldiers, who lined them up facing the brick wall. Someone counted the total prisoners and yelled out, "Twenty-one!" The prisoners were then forced down to their knees, each with a handgun pointed at his temple and a rifle pointed at his back, behind his heart. Suddenly, all guns fired at once, and the prisoners dropped to the ground. The crowd was silent. It was a fleeting, surreal moment of death—a death of sound. The silence was broken only when a baby cried.

As I walked back to the village, I couldn't rid myself of the thought that everyone in the Rooftop Underground would qualify to be shot just like those people who'd died in front of my eyes.

It's time to go! my heart warned me. I believed the execution was my call from Heaven, even if it was an intimidating one, like "killing a chicken to frighten a monkey."

I needed to talk to Ning, but I didn't know where she was. I had heard some village girls inviting her to spend time in the city after the execution. I couldn't leave Ning behind in the village. Mommy would expect me to take care of her. But how could I persuade her to escape? I didn't need to talk to Lily. I was sure she wouldn't spend a single minute in the village once Ning and I left. Besides, she couldn't escape even if she were physically fit: She had just given birth to a beautiful daughter she named Pei.

Still, Ning could be difficult at times. She was independent, was known to be unpredictable, and liked to be different. What if she said no to escape? What if she said she wanted to stay in the village by herself? She had proven herself physically capable of doing hard work, had made friends in the village, and enjoyed earning work points. The truth was I didn't have any leverage with her, or with any of my sisters. Now you see why I hated the cultural dictate that the man be the master of the house!

"I'm going to do what Hay did," I said to Ning when she returned. "Escape to Hong Kong."

"Why has it taken you so long to decide?" she said matter-of-factly.

I was ecstatic to hear that, but I hid my emotion. "Good. But aren't you scared?" I needed to make sure she was ready.

"Why?"

"We could die in the sea."

"Too much worrying. I'll go if you take me," Ning said.

"Then we'll go together, but you must do one thing."

"What?"

"Practice swimming, every day, many hours a day, until I'm happy with it."

"When are we leaving?"

We decided to leave the village as soon as possible. I went to tell One-Eye Dragon that our mother was sick and Ning and I would go home for a while. He didn't give a damn. We decided not to tell Papa, knowing he would get upset.

I went to say good-bye to Qiang. He cried when I told him I was going to escape to Hong Kong—I trusted him not to tell anybody about my plan, not even his parents. I didn't want to hide the truth from him. He had been my good friend from the start. He asked me to bring him along. I explained to him that he and I were different, that he didn't need to take the risk, but I had to.

I wiped away his tears with my palm and told him, "I'll always remember you!"

Before we parted, Qiang drew me to the pigeon cage. "I wanted to set them free, just like you." I was so touched that it was hard to control my tears. We took them out one by one and threw them into the air, shouting for them to fly away. This time, we wired the door of the cage shut so they couldn't return. We wanted them to freely fly away.

Mommy was surprised to see us. I told her that we were done with the village and were going to escape to Hong Kong. She realized Hay's success had motivated us.

"What did your papa say?"

"We've decided not to let him know. We'll surprise him with the good news."

"It's probably better that way." She was on the brink of tears. "I knew this day would come. Your living in the village whips my heart."

"Mommy, don't cry," I said. "We'll have a new life. It'll be good for the family."

"But it'll be a broken family. How good can that be? Only Heaven knows how long before we can be together."

"You don't want us to go?" Ning asked.

"No, you must go!" Mommy said. "We can't all drown in a bitter sea. Some of us must break the curse. I can't do it. Your Papa can't do it."

"We'll do it," Ning said.

"You must listen to your brother. He'll make all the decisions."

"I know," Ning said. "I don't know a thing about the escape."

"Mommy, I'll take care of everything," I said.

"I know you will. You always do."

I was surprised by how unsurprised Mommy was. Many years later, after it was safe for escapees to visit China, I met up with my high school teacher. He said my escape shocked the school. He told me I was the last student they expected to do such a thing. In his eyes, to escape was a bad thing.

ooooo

THE YEAR 1971 BROUGHT LIFE-CHANGING hope to Ning and me. That year marked the third anniversary of the sent-down movement.

Mommy was happy. She had everybody around her except Jing. As usual, Papa was not around, but we had grown used to that. Jing had her first baby boy, Roget. But nobody had seen him. She was in a poor village up north, and told us everything was fine. Lily's daughter, Pei, was one year old and had grown bigger and taller. Lily had separated from her sweet-talking husband and was in the process of divorcing. We all, especially Mommy, were firmly behind her. Mommy had never blamed Lily for marrying the wrong man, and she took Pei in as her own. When I had time, I'd watch Pei sleep, wondering what she was dreaming. I really liked when her little fingers grabbed my big index finger; sometimes she'd do it while sleeping!

Every morning at six o'clock, Ning and I would ride a bike to the swimming pool built into the Pearl River with wood boards. Many young people would be there when we arrived. Everybody was doing the breaststroke, lap after lap. Breaststroke was the style every escapee used. We all smiled when we passed one another. It was so much fun to have camaraderie during lap swim. Normal social behavior in China didn't include smiling at strangers. Indeed, anyone doing so was seen as having a mental issue. The smiling kept the lap swimming from getting boring. Ning worked hard on her swimming and was a quick learner when I corrected her movements.

After swimming, I'd go to the Rooftop Underground to soak in all things related to escape. I learned the "secret" phrases used—even though the word *secret* had lost its meaning: Too many people had already learned these phrases, including Mommy. For example, to escape to Hong Kong was called "to adjust one's pace." To pass a checkpoint and then hide until dark to start the escape was called "to lie under a pile of dirt." Being arrested was "nailing the coffin." Why the police and their "spies" in the Street Committees did not come arrest those uttering these phrases puzzled me. The wisdom of the Rooftop Underground had a simple answer: "It's not a crime to steal cattle if it's done by a large crowd." Practically speaking, the police did not have room in jail for everyone uttering secret phrases.

Then, one day, came shocking news: an American named Kissinger had secretly met with our prime minister, Zhou Enlai, in Beijing. The news was met with skepticism. Why? Nobody had a clue. The Street Committee asked people, except for the sent down, to remove all anti-American graffiti, posters, signs, and banners from every street, wall, and building. I was amazed to see my enthusiastic neighbors, from kids to retired folks, working tirelessly from morning to dusk, all the while joking and laughing. I joined them to erase a posting on a wall.

The reason for this hasty erasure: "The American president is coming to pay respects to our great leader Chairman Mao!" a member of the Street Committee announced. She went on to say, "We Chinese are a hospitable nation. We will show respect to any friend who comes to us to pay his respects." But she didn't know when the Americans would come.

I was torn. Why would the American president come to visit China? I was not excited, since I had made up my mind to escape, and China no longer held my interest. That was the same reaction among those in the Rooftop Underground. The news brought only confusion, suspicion, and sarcastic remarks:

"Why come visit Mao? Americans have nothing better to do?"

"Who cares?"

"I'm disappointed in America!"

"Forget it. What does this have to do with our escape?"

"China will not win!"

"How do you know?"

"China is too weak to play 'Romance of Three Kingdoms' with the Soviets and the Americans—they have sent people to the moon, stupid!"

I didn't make any progress in securing a solid escape plan, and I grew restless seeing the summer fading fast. I thought I'd go crazy if I didn't come up with a plan soon. Uncle was devising a plan for everybody to practice sculling a boat. I already knew that by using a boat, we could go from a tributary in the Pearl River Delta, where Hay's brother and his "cousin" Yun had been sent down, and then head to the Zhujiang River Estuary to reach Hong Kong.

It was my turn to learn sculling. I spent a month, day and night, on a sampan with Yun. He taught me to master the *yuloh* (with an oar on a fulcrum at the stern). We slept and cooked in the boat and sculled it up and down the tributaries. We always turned around before reaching the estuary, for fear of being arrested for attempting to escape to Hong Kong. We fished from the river, cooked the rice we brought on board, and peed and defecated in the river—I knew it was bad, but Yun said everybody did it. Staring at the stars, I'd fall asleep thinking that I'd like to remember my living on the sampan when I was old. It would be a shame if I forgot. The experience was so unique. The mist of early morning always chilled me as I watched the sun's rays bouncing off it. Then the sun showed its face, killing the romantic dawn, and started to burn my already rough, dark skin—sunscreen was never a part of a Chinese fisherman's life.

After a month, I graduated. But Uncle had no plan to push the sampan out to sea yet, and I couldn't show off my skillful handling of the *yuloh* to anyone.

"Who's next?" I asked Yun.

"My brother Shan will start his training, but Mau will teach him." Mau was Hay's biological brother.

Then came shocking news. Mao's handpicked successor, President General Lin, the short guy on the second jeep after Mao's whom I'd seen five years before during the Big Link-up in Beijing, was dead. He was on his way to Mongolia to seek political asylum when the People's Liberation Army Air Force shot down his plane. I had to admit: Teacher Fong had won this round. Perhaps face reading had some merit. But even without face reading, many Chinese had gossiped that Lin's untrustworthy face did not warrant the status of "emperor" of China.

Soon after National Day, October 1, 1971, news came that the United Nations had kicked out Chiang's Taiwan government and replaced it with Mao's. Because nobody in China knew what the United Nations was all about or up to, nobody really cared.

What a year 1971 was! But for me and the Rooftop Underground, it was absolutely unmarkable. How frustrating!

The rumor mill in the neighborhood kicked back into high gear, except this time it was all about whose children had made it to Hong Kong and how much better off their families were. A successful escape to Hong Kong was seen as akin to winning the lottery. In the neighborhood, everything from Hong Kong was fashionable and admired: Lily's classmate came to visit us one day dressed in a miniskirt brought to China by her relative in Hong Kong, making everyone's jaws drop. I felt so behind the times in fashion. *I can't be a dinosaur!* Many young people became emboldened enough to sing the songs of "Golden Voice," the Taiwanese pop singer Teresa Teng, who was living in Hong Kong. People may have been reciting Madam Mao's eight model plays with their mouths, but they were singing Teng's songs with their hearts. No police or Street Committee members showed up to stop the singing, and I'll bet many of them were listening to those songs behind closed doors.

∞∞∞

Canton City was about eighty miles north of Hong Kong. To escape to Hong Kong, one needed to start somewhere closer to the coast. Starting midway between these two places would reduce the time spent crossing mountains and fields to about a week. Thanks to the sent-down movement, many students had relocated to villages closer to Hong Kong than Canton, which were ideal for "lying under a pile of dirt." Police heavily guarded the bus, ferry, and train stations in Canton City. All county roads leading to the Chinese coast north of Kowloon Peninsula were punctuated by roadblocks and checkpoints guarded by militiamen. Back then, Chinese had to have permission to travel, and passing through all checkpoints required a valid travel document. Police and militiamen were good at checking documents, asking questions, and judging one's appearance and expression. Fake travel documents were almost all used documents that had been bleached to erase the previous writing. But the bleaching left easily detectable marks on the paper, and many people were arrested on their way to "lie under a pile of dirt."

Where is the place for Ning and me to lie under a pile of dirt?
I asked myself again and again.

I yearned for the New Year, which would bring the start of
our escape. And 1972 finally came. I was twenty-four, and Ning
was twenty. This was the year! *We have to make it to Hong Kong
this year*, I kept telling myself.

But the year surprised us all with President Nixon's visit to
China on February 21, 1972. In the newspapers and on the big
screen, we were shown pictures of Mao meeting Nixon. People
commented on the strange shape of Nixon's nose. And Mao was
showing his age. But our prime minister Zhou was still looking
sharp and presentable. I was sure China would not lose face in the
world because of him.

But the Rooftop Underground stopped paying attention when
Nixon stood by Madam Mao's side to cheer her model play. For
the future freedom swimmers, only one thing got our approval.
Rumor had it that an American reporter had asked Zhou why so
many young people were risking their lives by swimming to Hong
Kong. Zhou replied that during the Cultural Revolution, China had
stopped issuing visitor visas, and the young people were impatient.
They'd taken this illegal action to visit their Hong Kong relatives.
Of course, Zhou was lying. Most escapees had no relatives in Hong
Kong. Still, the phrase "illegal visits to Hong Kong" was born. The
Rooftop Underground viewed the expression with sarcasm: "Illegal
visit, my butt!"

"But that's good: The soldiers won't shoot us on sight."

"Yeah, but the sea, sharks, and typhoons still kill us."

"Then try to escape to Taiwan or the Soviet Union. Let the
soldier shoot you without warning!"

"Are you out of your mind? The Soviet Union? Hell, no!
Taiwan, maybe."

All such discussions ended when the pragmatist said, "We escapees send Hong Kong dollars back home that the government can use." (China exchanged the incoming Hong Kong dollars for Chinese yuan, then gave the money to the recipient.)

In his letter, Hay had told Mommy about someone named Chunky, who could help me when I made up my mind to escape. Chunky had been a student at another high school in Canton before the Cultural Revolution; he was sent down to the same people's commune in Ma'an as Hay. Unlike Ning and me, Chunky and Hay didn't work a single day in the village. They had made up their minds to escape when they chose Ma'an. Unlike Hay, Chunky was caught during his first escape attempt. He had gone with his girlfriend. He didn't want to tell others how they were caught. I suspected he didn't make it far.

Chunky was tall and on the heavy side—hence his nickname. He had a pair of slanted eyes and a sharp mind for money. He liked to socialize, didn't like to be alone. Soon, everybody in my family knew him. Mommy cautioned me against dealing with him: People seemed to have a low opinion of him, saying he was stingy and full of himself. What others said about Chunky didn't bother me. I had seen enough darkness, and I didn't judge people unless they betrayed their friends or profited by harming others—I saw those who did so as human garbage.

Chunky suggested that I escape with two others and agreed to prepare three bags of food for us that would last several days. I needed to bring along the "dangerous" stuff: a compass and inflatable plastic pillows, to be used as lifesavers—considered indisputable evidence of an intended escape. Chunky would arrange for us to "lie under a pile of dirt." He said he had a perfect place for us to hide until sunset. He told me I needed to go soon, because he had to make his second attempt. He didn't tell me anything about dealing with the mountains, so I didn't ask. I didn't want to embarrass him, for I assumed that during his first attempt, he was caught before getting to them.

Chunky gave me three used travel permits and some stationery with letterhead from the people's commune. He told me a peasant had stolen the stationery for him, emphasizing how much he'd paid the man. "It wasn't cheap," he said.

I inspected the old travel permits. The stamps were quite clean and sharp.

"You know how to bleach them, right?" Chunky asked.

I needed to pay Chunky about three times what an entry-level worker made in a month for each of us. Mommy said Chunky was being greedy, but I said that helping us "lie under a pile of dirt" would be dangerous for him. I didn't know how to measure the danger to him in monetary terms. Perhaps Mommy was right about him, but I didn't have any other choice.

Crossing the mountains at night should be safe; crossing the coast, with its soldiers on patrol, would depend on the luck of the draw; and crossing the sea at night would be in the hands of Heaven; I hoped It would bless us. I could eliminate one risk by not using Chunky's bleached travel permits. I had to find a better way to prepare fake documents, but I had no idea how to do it. This bothered me day and night. I asked everyone whose path I crossed, but I came up empty.

One day, Yong Wei, the young Red Guard who'd searched our rooms, came to visit us. He said he would help. After my initial dislike and distrust of him for being an East Wind, I had grown fond of Yong Wei. And he had always been fond of our family, especially Mommy, who had taken him in immediately.

A couple of days later, he came back with good news. He brought me to see a friend of his who worked in a factory making aluminum signs for businesses and the government. The method was not too complicated: First, coat an aluminum plate with photosensitive glue in a darkroom and then place a black-and-white negative to the layer of dried glue before exposing the glue to light.

"You need to make a negative of the stamp you're going to use," Yong Wei's friend told me.

The unexposed parts of the glue (the black areas of the negative) were easily washed away. The exposed parts of the glue (the transparent areas of the negative) were not washed away, and the plate was then heat-dried to "burn" the remaining glue to a darkish brown. The burned glue prevented the aluminum underneath from being "eaten away" by the corrosive acid wash.

"I got it. Thanks," I said.

Before we left, he gave me some glue and the photosensitive chemical and showed me how to mix them. He also handed me a small bottle of acid and a small sheet of aluminum plate large enough to make several stamps.

"Good luck," he said. "Don't tell anybody!"

Yong Wei patted his shoulder. "My friend won't. I promise."

I couldn't hide my emotions as we biked home. "Yong Wei, you just don't know how happy I am, and all because of you!"

"Whatever I can do, my friend."

"This world . . . I just don't get it."

"You think too much. That's why you're not happy. I'm simple. I just go where I'm happy—like your home, especially to meet Mommy."

"You aren't simple. You're smart!"

"What would make you truly, completely, and absolutely happy?" Yong Wei asked.

"Standing on the shore of Hong Kong, closing my eyes, facing the bright blue sky, filling my lungs with the salty air, and letting my tears run wild."

"You have a one-track mind! Hong Kong, Hong Kong, Hong Kong!" Yong Wei shook his head.

"Of course! I'm running on a single track, destination Hong Kong!"

I raced ahead to the Rooftop Underground to find Hay's "cousin" Shan. He was about my age and talkative, especially when it came to things he knew something about. Everybody knew Shan had a makeshift photo enlarger and could make black-and-white negatives. He was thrilled by the idea of falsifying a stamp. Like a kid being given a new toy, he asked me to leave him the chemicals, glue, and aluminum plate.

"No way," I said. "We need them for the 'real' thing."

"How can I help, then?"

"I have the used travel permits from Chunky. The stamp looks sharp and clean. Should have no problem making a good negative."

"So, you've decided to take the Tung Ping Chau route like Hay?"

"Yes, I have no other choice. We'll follow Hay's footsteps."

Hay and many other pioneers had made the escape route to Tung Ping Chau island popular. It was the easternmost route in the East Line. By 1972, brave freedom swimmers had also pushed the West Line as far west as possible, to Snake Mouth crossing, the longest waterway (six miles) of all the swimming routes.

Chunky told me that if our fake travel documents got us to the bus stop in the people's commune where he had been sent-down, we could consider his job of helping us "lie in a pile of dirt" done. I thought he was being cocky.

"Where do we wait for you after the bus?" I asked.

"There's a roadside teahouse. Enjoy your last civilized tea before you get to Hong Kong. I'll find you there. Oh, by the way, if you get caught before the teahouse, your money is not refundable."

"Understood," I said.

Shan and I put things into high gear to make the fake stamp. It was such a success that he bragged about it often, even though I warned him not to. Using the stationery Chunky had given me, we made three perfect-looking blank travel permits, each with a sharp, clean stamp. I found a partner in Curly, and he was excited and impatient, for he had been thinking about escape longer than I had. Curly made a compass; I bought three plastic inflatable pillows and hand-copied a topographic map of the Tung Ping Chau route. Each of us would carry one plastic inflatable pillow as we got into the water. Though they were prone to leaks, the pillows were available in stores (though they had become very popular), lightweight, and therefore easy to carry. Those pillows would become our "lifesavers" in case we got tired swimming and needed a rest. Still, just like the compass and the map, the pillow was indisputable proof of an escape attempt. Any of these three items, if spotted by a policeman or militiaman, could land us in a detention center.

∞∞∞

IT TOOK THREE MONTHS FOR me to get the fake stamp made and two months to come up with a plan with Chunky. We failed to send the inflatable plastic pillows to Chunky beforehand, so we had to carry them with us. The map and the compass were easy to hide—they were small—but the plastic pillows were another story. Canton was very hot during the summer, and we wore as little as possible. So, we couldn't hide the pillows under our clothes. We had to place them in our sling bags, the only baggage we'd carry. (No sent-down student carried luggage.) Our fake travel documents had to pass inspection with flying colors, so the police would not become suspicious and search our bags.

Each of us was armed with a unique story. We were from different villages in the same people's commune—hence the same fake commune stamp. But because it was common for students from different villages in the same commune not to know one another, we would pretend we didn't know each other. That way, the police wouldn't cross-examine us.

On our fake documents, each of us put down the name of the village where we had been sent down to, so we could make up a story based on our actual lived experience. Luckily, Ning and I could use one of the two villages where we'd worked. The chances were one in a gazillion that the inspecting policeman would be familiar with each and every village.

Lastly, we bought our bus tickets at different times, so we wouldn't be seated next to one another.

One night, Teacher Fong showed up at the house unexpectedly, looking thin but in good spirits. Mommy asked him why he had not dropped by in several months, and he said he had just gotten out of detention.

"Aren't you too old to escape?" I asked.

"Am I? I saw people there older than me." Teacher Fong smiled.

Mommy brought him a cup of tea and asked about his escape attempt.

"You don't need to know. You're too old for that," he said.

"Didn't you read your face before you went?" I asked jokingly.

"It's harder than you think to read your own face. It's human nature to magnify the signs you like and downplay those you don't." His voice was subdued.

"That makes sense." Now I wanted to cheer him up. "By the way, you were right on target about President General Lin."

"Did I say something about him?" He looked somewhat surprised, or perhaps he was only pretending to be surprised.

"But you weren't right about Deng," I reminded him. "He's still nowhere."

"That roly-poly? Don't worry. His fortunes will come in due time." Teacher Fong smiled.

"Don't waste time," Mommy said. "Read my son's face."

"For escape?" Teacher Fong asked.

"No, for entering a university," I said sarcastically.

Teacher Fong was serious. He looked at my face and then stood up and moved from side to side to look at it again.

"Can't find what you want?" I asked. "Just tell Mommy I'll make it."

"Be patient," Teacher Fong said. Three deep creases again appeared in his forehead. Finally, he sat down and said, "Your time is not here yet. But you can't stop it."

I was somewhat shocked but definitely unhappy hearing this.

"Stop what?" Mommy was anxious.

"He can't stop what he sets his mind on," Teacher Fong said, shrugging. "You have a stubborn son."

"That's the only thing you've gotten right," I said and walked toward the door.

"Will he be safe?" I heard Mommy asking.

"He won't die, if that's what you want to know."

Good. I won't die, I said to myself and headed to bed.

It was a long night. I was bothered by what Teacher Fong had said. *Should I believe him? No. Should I wait for my luck to come? No.*

I was committed. The train had left the station.

In another bed, my youngest sister, Bun, was snoring. She was eighteen now and working as an apprentice in a chemical factory. She knew her brother and sister would be leaving soon, but I didn't give her any details of the escape. I saw no need to disturb her, and it might disturb her. She would prove me wrong when she finally emigrated to America twelve years later. She was bold enough to chase her big dream. Unfortunately, China had deprived her of a high school education, so she was ill prepared for the developed world. At the time, though, I thought a sense of peace was what she needed.

I had not seen Jing since I went to the village. I'd heard she was miserable, working solo as a doctor and caring for her one-year-old son by herself in a small, ill-equipped clinic in the same poor province where Big Auntie's family lived. She spent her yearly two-week break during the Chinese New Year with her husband, who was working in Beijing, 150 miles away. Such an arrangement—couples living separately during most of the year—was very common in China. I felt for her. She was smart, but there was no place for her intelligence to thrive in China. Only in America, many years later, could it blossom, in the area of medical research. We decided not to tell her of our escape plan. I sensed that if the news leaked out, she would get in trouble. Even today, for the people living in all twenty-two provinces other than Guangdong, the escapes to Hong Kong by Cantonese during the Cultural Revolution are considered a lie.

Lily and the now-two-year-old Pei spent most of their time at home with Mommy. The cracks in Lily's marriage had started to show soon after her wedding. Mommy had been right about Lily's husband. After the passion subsided, his insubstantial chatter not only grew to annoy her, but also exposed his self-absorption. Perhaps Mommy should have doubled down on her criticism of him—after all, a man who could talk a bird down to the ground could not ask the bird to dance—but Mommy had warned her, and she wouldn't listen. Lily was always driven by dreams, by romance and passion. But Mommy supported her: "Don't worry about leaving your husband. You and Pei have me." Lily needed this reassurance, especially while going through the divorce.

Ning usually didn't talk much, but she was smart and had a strong personality. She wanted to be different, something that was evident in her as early as preschool. In China, when you're a younger sister among several, being different is considered a "bad" trait—Confucianism demands conformity. Add to that a strong personality, and you were only asking to be spanked by the older men of the house, such as a father, uncle, or grandpa. All that had happened to Ning, but as she grew older, every time someone mentioned her having been "different" when she was younger, she brushed off the physical punishments she'd received. "Why do you mention that?" Besides, she turned out fine and tough. That was why she was up to the challenge of hard village work. That was why I had no doubt she was up to the challenge of an escape. If she made up her mind to do something, and indeed she had, I knew she could do it. For me, the best thing about her was her being four years younger than me: She would listen to what I said during the escape, making my life easier.

Even without telling him we were going to escape, Papa seemed to sense it. But he didn't ask me or Ning about it. When he left us to return to Zhaoqing City after the Chinese New Year, he told me, "Be careful." His voice trembled, and as he walked away, I saw him take out his handkerchief to wipe at his tears. That made me feel very bad.

Even though Mommy got the job done perfectly, bringing a baby to life every two years, I always had a hard time remembering how old my sisters were. I needed to pause to figure it out by adding or subtracting two years from my own age. Often, I even needed to pause to think about my own age first. My excuse for this shortcoming was a sound one. When I was growing up in China, there were no birthday parties whatsoever. As with most other families, celebrating one's birthday was not the thing in China. In my early years in America, I congratulated others on their birthday, but I didn't bother celebrating my own; my family had not been keen on it. Not remembering my own birthday actually gave me some peace—I wouldn't be reminded of what I had achieved in the year that had just passed, for I had nothing special or unique to show for it. For the poor or the hopeless, every day being the same, what could one hope to get out of a birthday celebration?

Without birthday parties and gifts, there was no memory to hold on to. But that night, I thought about the ages of all my sisters. I felt sad, not because of the lack of their birthday celebrations, but because of the lack of my interactions with them during all the time when we were living together, especially with Bun. I had lost my chances. I might not see Jing, Lily, and Bun again.

My thoughts were interrupted by Mommy, who had quietly walked in.

"Bothered by the face reading?" she asked.

"No, I was thinking about my sisters, and how soon my niece and nephew can sit by themselves on the chairs Ning and I once sat on during New Year's Eve dinner."

"It's good to be positive."

"I know. We must make it to Hong Kong for our family, no matter what."

"People say if you don't believe in fortune-telling, it won't come true."

I knew Mommy was trying to make me feel better, and I said, "Of course, but let's not talk about face reading anymore."

I, not a fortune-teller, should be the master of my life.

CHAPTER 10

THE ENDLESS SEA

IT WAS LATE, BUT I still couldn't fall asleep. I kept thinking that this would be my last night sleeping at home. The moon was almost full. Its light illuminated several dark red spots on my mosquito netting where I'd killed mosquitoes with my hand. We had decided to start the journey when the moon was almost reaching its fullness, so it would light our path as we crossed the mountains by night. Tomorrow evening, I'd be in the mountains. I wondered how much I'd miss my bed and the mosquito netting.

Mommy quietly walked in. "Can't fall asleep?"

"Where in Hong Kong was our home?" I asked her. "I can't remember a thing about it."

"How could you? You were little. It was in the middle of a hill in Causeway Bay."

"I want to walk along Causeway Bay before I die."

"Are you scared?" Nothing could escape Mommy's eyes.

"Mommy, does a soul feel anything?"

"I don't think so."

"If it can, mine will be envious after I die, I'm sure."

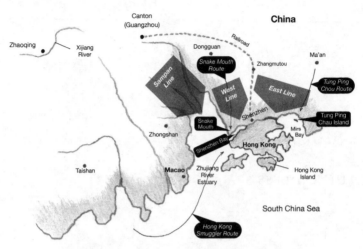

The Escape Map (or Comprehensive Escape Map)

"Envious of what?"

"Envious of others living on earth. There are so many things here on earth, Mommy. What does Heaven have? Moon, stars, sun, and clouds. Nothing else."

I could see, through the netting, that Mommy was thinking. "Let me tell you a story, your story." Mommy loosened the netting and sat on the edge of my bed. "I was lying on a gurney on my way to the delivery room when you came. You were fast. I felt two intense contractions, and there you were. What a bloody mess you made!"

"I was afraid of the dark." I chuckled. "I was impatient, too, and still am."

"I said to the nurses, 'Why such a hurry? How much this little one wants to do in the world!' They all laughed." Mommy asked, "How much have you achieved so far?"

"You should know," I said. "Not much . . . No, nothing."

"You haven't done much, and you have yet to go to university."

"I know," I said, even though I had long forgotten about university.

"You rushed into this world and haven't done much. You can't leave the world in a hurry."

I thought to myself, *Why can't I see things as she does?*

"You gave me no pain at birth and have never made me mad. You won't break my heart this time."

"Mommy, do you know what I'll miss the most?"

"How can I know? Your brain keeps spinning." This time she chuckled.

"The way you see things and explain them to me."

"Not bad for an old woman who's never set foot in university."

"You aren't old, Mommy! I don't want you to be old."

"I don't want to be old, either. It's not how many days you've lived that age you. It's the weight you carry day after day." I felt the weight her words carried.

"I'm going to take the weight off you!" I said.

"I don't need you to make money to send home. You must finish school."

"I haven't touched a book for more than five years." The Cultural Revolution had taken two years, and the village took three more.

"What has that got to do with anything? Just start it again."

"I will, I promise!"

"If you have a chance, go to America."

"America?"

"People say it's the land of opportunity."

"The Gold Mountain, Voice of America, the men on the moon . . ." I was intrigued. "I've never thought about going to America."

"You should. Go to America, and go to a university there."

"Then Mao and the party will never catch me." I could picture how safe I'd be if I were in America. "I hope America will take me. But I've nothing to offer." *Why should America want me? To chase water buffalo?* I was amused thinking about myself chasing water buffalo in America. "I don't know," I added.

Mommy said, "It's late. You need to have a good night's sleep. Tomorrow is your big day. Remember, 'Don't be scared by the dark mountains, but be afraid of the unforgiving sea.'"

She stood and tucked the mosquito netting tightly back under my mattress. A fat-bellied mosquito was hanging on the net. She clapped her hands over it, smashing it against the netting and leaving a new bright red dot. She turned off the light. The moon took over. The new red dot turned fuzzy as I fell asleep.

It was a customarily hot summer night in 1972, but in my heart, it was the first time the dead mosquito stains on my old mosquito netting were not disgusting at all.

∞∞∞∞∞

THE BUS WAS DUSTY INSIDE and out, and it was full. Before it started, two policemen came on board and two others stood outside, guarding the door.

"Take out your travel documents!" the policemen on board announced. He started inspecting the documents of each passenger. He and his partner worked from the center of the aisle to the end and quickly got their first catch. The young man looked anxious as the younger policeman examined his paperwork. The younger policeman raised the travel document against the light and showed it to the older one, "Bleached?" The older policeman took a quick look and nodded.

"Bring your belongings and follow me!" the younger policeman ordered. As soon as the young man stepped outside, the two policemen standing by the door cuffed his hands behind his back and pushed his head down, forcing him to squat on the ground.

It was my turn. "What's the name of your village leader?" the older policeman asked as he inspected my document.

"Comrade Lee, but we called him 'One-Eye Dragon,'" I said.

His eyes veered away from the paper and landed on my face. I looked him in the eye. He handed me the paper back and moved on.

The younger policeman stared at Ning, then quickly turned his head away and demanded, "Your document!" Ning obeyed. He looked it over and returned it to her, then moved to the next passenger. Once again, Ning had gotten a pass. She tended to have this kind of luck. As Mommy said, "Good looks and a nice dress go a long way." I was sure that this time Ning's looks, and not her clothes, had had something to do with it.

The older policeman gave Curly a look that made him nervous. "I was born with it," Curly said. "I mean, my hair."

"Do I care? Your document!"

Curly handed him the document. The policeman read through it and handed it back to him.

After a bumpy three-hour ride, the bus stopped at a roadside teahouse, and we got off. Soon Chunky and two young peasants arrived on their bikes. I had to admire Chunky's ability to hire peasants for illegal help. A whimsical commentary on human nature by our ancestors came to mind: "Money can make a ghost turn a millstone." On the rack of each bicycle was a large bag of food that Chunky's girlfriend had packed for us. Chunky told me he would make another escape attempt with her next month. He didn't say anything about our getting together in Hong Kong. Instead, he said that after he was gone, this escape route would be gone, too. He seemed to think he owned the route, forgetting that Hay was one of its pioneers.

The foothills of a tall mountain lay to our right, and to our left, a terraced paddy sloped gently away. There was not a single living soul other than us in sight. Chunky showed us a large, dense group of subtropical growth on the foothills. We got off the bikes, grabbed our bags, and disappeared into the greenery. Chunky and the peasants turned around and biked away.

Previous escapees had pushed the seemingly impenetrable bushes outward, so we were able to fit our bodies inside the spaces created there. The stagnant air in these voids trapped the sun's heat, steaming us. We kept motionless and speechless, and prayed for the sun to go away soon, but the sun didn't bother listening. Finally, darkness came, and we slowly crawled out.

The road was dead, and we swiftly climbed the hill. The farther up we were, the more careless we became. We started to talk to make the climb easier and more pleasant. As we got deeper into the mountains, the vegetation became denser. The moon came out to illuminate the sky, but it was concealed from us by the mountains on both sides. I realized we were traversing the valley. Little creatures that crawled or jumped or flew were eager to irritate our skin; they ignored our scolding slaps.

Our plan had been to reach the top of the mountain that first night. Like all other escapees, we planned to hide and rest during the day and cross the mountains during the night. But the darkness and the dense growth made this impossible.

"Let's call it a night," I said. "We can't see anything, and we're not making progress."

Curly and Ning agreed. We made some space in the thick vegetation, lay down, and fell asleep in no time. We were exhausted, mentally and physically.

We awoke at dawn to the annoying drone of insects and the joyful chirping of birds. The cool air of the valley and the fragrance of the flowers energized us.

"We wasted one whole night," Ning said.

"Can't continue this way," Curly said.

I took out the map and tried to decipher where we were. "We'll take the mountain ridges. They'll lead us to the sea." I was ecstatic as I visualized the ridges running more or less north to south. "I know for a fact the ridges have much less vegetation."

Ning was puzzled. "Whatever you say."

I handed the map to Curly to show him, and he got it. "How do you know so much about mountains?"

"I've left my share of footprints on Antelope Gorge."

Curly was mystified, and Ning explained: "He used to collect firewood from the mountains near our village. It was his only contribution to the cooking." Ning emphasized the word *only*.

We started to climb the hill in daylight. The cool temperature and the better visibility made all the difference, and soon we reached the top. The ridge was a strip of relatively flat ground with sparse vegetation. What a pleasant change! The strong mountain winds and full exposure to the punishing sun had driven away most of the moisture, and the insects that came with it. That was just fine with us.

Suddenly, Curly signaled us to lie down. Two peasants emerged not far below the ridge, each shouldering a large bundle of branches on the ends of a bamboo pole. We watched them disappear behind the bushes and trees.

"That's what you did to get firewood?" Curly asked me.

"Yeah."

"Damn." He shook his head.

We found a spot to rest and eat some of our food under a large tree surrounded by bushes. Unfortunately, black ants had beaten us to our meal. They had eaten through the plastic bags and buried themselves in the sea of sweet foods.

"How can we get rid of them?" I asked. "Any idea?"

"No way. They're everywhere." Curly was correct.

"Then we have to eat them," Ning said matter-of-factly.

"Just thinking about it makes me queasy." Curly was anxious.

"I heard that eating ants will enhance your manhood," I said, hoping to find some good in the bad.

"How do you know?" Ning asked.

"I read it somewhere."

We swallowed the food (fried wheat flour mixed with sugar and peanut oil), washing it down with a lot of water because it was so dry. Stingy Chunky had not put in enough peanut oil.

Occasionally, we heard from down below the muffled sound of peasants yelling at water buffaloes. As the sun disappeared on the horizon, it dappled the water in the paddies with patches of different colors and shades. It was so quiet we could hear one another breathing. We spared no time indulging in melancholy and started our walk along the ridge toward the south.

Soon, the moon showed her face to us, and sparkling stars littered the sky. The cool mountain wind rejuvenated our spirits. We picked up our pace. Occasionally, we shouted, just to hear the echoes of our voices and to claim the title of Masters of the Universe!

At one point, we ran into another group of escapees, and the camaraderie was palpable. We sat down in a circle to exchange anything worthy of mention from our short journeys. Before we parted, we wished one another the best of luck. One of them said we should meet again at the revolving restaurant on top of a sky-scraper in Kowloon someday. I had never heard of a restaurant that rotated! I was ignorant of Hong Kong's luxurious and more romantic offerings.

The mountain ridge led us downward. In the vast space below were a couple of large, silvery patches. According to the map, these were water reservoirs. Several dark patches with blurred outlines dotted the gray land, and tiny fickle lights inside the patches hinted at life in what we guessed were villages. It was too late for us to cross the open fields to reach the mountains on the other side before sunrise, so we decided to stop for our second night. The mountain winds whirred and whistled, reminding us that the dark world below was alive.

"'Where are the great men of the past? / Where are those of the future? / Sky and earth forever last. / Here and now I alone shed tears.'" Standing on the edge of the mountain, I had become sentimental. "Curly, who wrote that poem?"

"Who cares? A guy from the Tang Dynasty? Just don't shed tears. I don't have my handkerchief with me." Curly could be funny at times. But he was right: There was no sentimentality in eating ants or falling off a cliff.

"Where's Mommy?" Ning wondered.

"Over there." Curly pointed to distant mountains to the northwest. "Behind those mountains."

"She won't believe I'm thinking about her here and now," Ning said.

The following day, we carefully made our way toward the bottom of the mountains before dark. When the last ray of sun dis-appeared, we started to run across the paddies. The moon was late, and visibility was bad. We slipped often in the soggy soil, splashing through mud that coated our clothes and bodies.

Suddenly, a loud voice came from in front of us: "Who's there?"

We swiftly stopped and lay down. The shallow water was more than enough to soak our bodies thoroughly.

"I saw you! Come out!" A light appeared from a house. A dog barked, then many others followed suit.

"He can't see us," I whispered to Ning and Curly.

"I'll shoot!" the voice warned, but we kept still.

A loud gunshot echoed, bringing angrier barking from the dogs. We held our breaths and continued to lie motionless. Time seemed frozen, and at last the silence returned. We waited for a short while before resuming our run across the field.

We reached the reservoir, but were unable to tell how large it was. We decided to swim across. This was a mistake, for we should have walked around it instead. Swimming with clothes on while dragging large bags of food and other items wore us out. On the other side of the reservoir were the foothills. The cold mountain winds gusted down, making our teeth chatter.

The food got drenched, and Curly complained, "Porridge!"

"Look on the bright side: The ants are dead," I said.

The climb was dull. No one spoke; we were exhausted. The moon was nowhere to be seen. As I paused to catch my breath, I glimpsed sparkles of light in front of us; they were coming through a dark mass of vegetation.

I pointed. "What's that?"

We picked up our pace, and the sparkles grew in size and intensity. As we got closer to the ridge, the growth thinned out to reveal a lustrous grayish-white slope. Curly and Ning trudged on, but I stayed behind and watched as their silhouettes seemed to melt into the light. When we reached the ridge, we came upon a silvery halo emanating gracefully from behind the distant peak. A full moon of unimaginable scale!

"Do you believe in the Goddess of the Moon and her jade rabbit?" I asked Curly.

"You mean Chang'e, the deity of immortality?" Curly said. "No, I don't believe in folklore. But I like the Mid-Autumn Festival, especially the mooncake."

I felt love for the moon. She was never intrusive like the sun, which always tried to burn me into charcoal and flood me with my own sweat. Now her appearance calmed me as I traversed the mountains at night. Perhaps our ancestors felt the same way and did not want the shadows on her face deemed an imperfection. What could be more bittersweet than a lovely lady drinking the elixir of immortality to avoid an evil-minded pursuer here on earth, and so becoming the deity of the moon, living alone with a rabbit by her side, shown as shadows on the moon's face, to remind the mortals on earth? There she was, to watch over those of us who paid homage to her every year on the seventh day of the seventh month. *Does she know she is guiding the freedom swimmers crossing the mountains at night?*

The next day, our third, a rainstorm hit. We tried, but failed, to shield ourselves under a large plastic tarp we'd brought along. We were soaked and freezing. We sat close to one another, trying to keep warm. Occasional thunder boomed directly over our heads, seeming much louder than the thunder we were used to at home. There was no need to get out from under our covering to retrieve water; instead, we merely stuck out our tongues to catch the voluminous raindrops rolling down our hair and faces. Far below us, through the curtain of the downpour, I saw peasants planting the paddies. It reminded me of how much I hated planting in the pouring rain—with an aching back, bloodsucking leeches, and bits of human waste floating around my legs!

"Should we start to walk?" I suggested. "We're already soaked. Even if they saw us, they wouldn't want to climb up the mountain in the rain."

A sudden crash of lightning illuminated the mountains near us. How vulnerable we were! We must wait it out! Subtropical rain seldom lasts a whole day. Soon it stopped, and the sun came out, throwing two rainbows, one on top of the other, across the land. The raindrops had carried away the tiny dust particles suspended in the hot air to reveal the vivid details of the green leaves and colorful wildflowers around us. I tried to whistle to express my joyous state of mind, but I quickly gave it up, for the sound of my whistling destroyed the perfect harmony of nature.

"Good," I said. "Tomorrow will be a sunny day!"

"How do you know?" Curly asked.

"Because of the red sky late in the day."

"We learned that from the peasants," Ning explained.

We couldn't ask for a better ending to a dreadful day. We started our passage along the mountain ridges. The lingering twilight finally went away. Ahead of us was a bright light illuminating the mountain tops and radiating upward.

"What's that?" Ning exclaimed. "Can't be the moon."

"It must be the neon lights of Hong Kong." I was convinced of this. I recalled the photo from the Hong Kong magazine showing the intensely lit buildings jammed and layered up to the middle of the hills. Mommy had told me Hong Kong had a great many neon signs, and she warned, "Don't walk under those signs during a typhoon."

We were in a world of darkness, and had been yearning for a better world for so long, and now, in front of us, the New World was giving us the first hint of things to come. We were moved. What could be a more dramatic welcome than lighting up half the sky for us?

"Curly, you can throw away the compass," I said with joy.

"Yeah, here it goes!" Curly threw the compass toward the dark fields below.

"All our life, we've been the frogs living at the bottom of a well," I proclaimed. "But the end is coming!"

Excited, we jogged along the ridge toward the lit-up sky. Soon we were tired. Several days and nights in the mountains had sapped our strength. We stopped jogging and walked quietly, wondering when we would see the sea. Dawn started to knock at the door, causing the lights of Hong Kong to retreat.

Our excitement over the full moon and our first glimpse of the night sky illuminated by Hong Kong's neon were the highlights of our mountain crossing. Our anxiety grew during the following four nights. *Where is the sea? Are we on the right path?* I had heard of a group of escapees who became lost in the mountains and, after several days, were captured someplace near where they started. I laughed then. What if that happened to us?

Finally, after seven days, we saw the sea! Its blue water stretched to the far edge of a much lighter blue sky. We were speechless. How grand it was! Unlike the Pearl River, which was pushed around by mountains and crowded by unsightly human things, nothing could push or crowd this sea. It was so peaceful. But why had our ancestors warned us, "Don't bully the sea, even if you've bullied the mountains?" What did that really mean? Of course, we had never seen a picture or a movie showing an angry sea. Though we had all experienced what a typhoon could do, no one had told us what it could do to the sea. None of us had ever seen the sea, and even though I was born by the sea, and Mommy had told me she had brought me to Repulse Bay Beach in Hong Kong, I had been too young to remember it.

A little island sat closer to our side of the sea, enjoying its solitude. "That has to be the island of Tung Ping Chau," I said.

"Where is Hong Kong?" Ning asked.

"That island is a part of Hong Kong."

"Oh yeah. Hay said the Coast Guard came to pick them up there. I hope they won't forget to come tomorrow," Ning said.

"Of course they won't." I was sure.

We tried to sleep but couldn't. Dark clouds crept up behind us, followed by lightning and thunder. Then came the winds, which agitated the sea, throwing up ever-enlarging whitecaps that obscured the little island. At last the rain came, hard and furious.

"Leave us alone!" Curly shouted at the sky.

"What if we miss?" Ning asked.

"If the wind doesn't stop, we must wait another day." Intuitively, I knew it would be dangerous to swim in a sea of whitecaps.

"What if we don't make it to the island?" Ning was persistent.

I didn't like to think about death. I had always hated such thoughts and had tried to avoid the subject whenever possible. But this time I couldn't.

"We'll be washed out into the endless sea," I said.

I was horrified at the thought of what I would do as my life was slipping away. Would I still be able to think straight? Would I be sorry for choosing escape instead of living a lousy life in a village? Would I blame myself for getting Ning and Curly to come with me?

"Then we'll die," Ning said without much emotion.

I might just face death head-on. "The sea will tear our bodies into pieces if the fish don't get to us first. And if they do, we might turn into a fish of some kind in our next life."

"I'm not going to be a fish or a crab in my next life." Curly was serious.

"I don't believe in reincarnation," Ning said.

"Right. Then we'll make it together and be free by tomorrow morning."

Perhaps Heaven overheard our conversation and knew we would not back away. The final chain of lightning brought in a round of rumbling thunder—and then it and the rain went away. The land below us was quiet. We decided to descend the mountain on our way to the sea in daylight.

When we reached the foothills, it was dark. The foothills descended into a marsh, and we started across it, treading carefully to minimize the splashing sound of our footsteps. At the end of the marshland was the coast. With Curly leading and Ning in the middle, we slowly crawled toward the sea.

"Stand up!"

We froze.

"Stand up, or I'll shoot!"

The metallic sound of a bullet being chambered was followed by a flashlight beam landing on Curly.

Curly slowly stood up, but Ning and I lay still.

"Raise your hands," said the soldier whose rifle was pointing at Curly. "Walk slowly. Keep your hands up. How many are you?"

"I'm the only one," Curly said as he walked toward the soldier. Ning and I kept still and held our breaths.

Another flashlight swept across the field, to and fro, its beam approaching Ning and me. We turned our faces to the mud and waited for the inevitable.

"Two more!" a second soldier shouted. "Stand up!"

The game was over. Ning and I stood up and raised our hands. The soldiers tied our wrists using a long, thick rope and linked us together. "Sit down, and no talking!" the soldiers ordered.

In front of us, the island of Tung Ping Chau looked like a thick black disc buoyed by the silvery sparkles of the sea, but our hearts had sunk to the bottom of the ocean. It hurt, really hurt, that we were mere hours away from reaching freedom, just like poor frogs climbing up the slippery wall of a deep well and almost reaching the rim, only to be slapped all the way to the bottom by some nasty kids. Teacher Fong's prediction came back to me. How much I hated the thought that his face reading of me had been right.

The remainder of the night was quiet. The soldiers did not catch any others. We couldn't keep our eyes away from the little island, but our brains were blank and numb.

"What is so good about Hong Kong that you want to die in the sea?" one soldier asked us in Mandarin. Both were very young and came from Northern China. They had no idea about Hong Kong, other than its being a rotten capitalist colony. Northerners were ignorant in many ways, but stubborn in one thing: They would never betray their Motherland. I believe that was the reason all soldiers guarding the seashore were from the North. Otherwise, we could, perhaps, have persuaded them to join us in swimming to Hong Kong. Northerners had no knowledge of the world outside China. In their eyes, China was better than Heaven, and Mao was greater than God.

Like three helium balloons ascending to greet the arriving sun, we had been punctured and deflated, dropping to the earth, again, into the endless darkness.

CHAPTER 11

LIFE AND DEATH IN HEAVEN'S HANDS

AT DAWN, THE SOLDIERS DRAGGED us by the rope to an army truck. The truck headed west, stopping in a few places to pick up several more captured freedom swimmers, who had taken different routes on the West Line. The two soldiers held their rifles the whole time. "No talking!" They kept shouting at us.

The truck arrived at Shenzhen City, on the north bank of the Shenzhen River. The colony of Hong Kong was to the south of the river. But we could not see the Shenzhen River, nor the bridge that Hong Kong residents and Chinese holding passports and visas used to get to the other side.

The truck stopped at the Shenzhen Detention Center, which processed all freedom swimmers caught from the East and West Lines. It consisted of two one-story concrete buildings facing an open space where armed guards patrolled all day long. Each building was divided into several cells of roughly twelve square feet. Ning was put in the cell for women, and there were a lot of them. Curly

Ning at the coast of Hong Kong, where she landed after
swimming across six miles of sea, 1973.

and I ended up in the same cell. No one cared to count how many
detainees were there on any given day, but I guessed over a hundred.

An iron-barred door and a small iron-barred window let in
some fresh air, but it could barely dilute the stench of human waste
and the odor of bodies that had not been washed for many days.
A wooden bucket sat in one corner, serving as the toilet. It stank,
and many flies buzzed around it. A detainee told me that each
morning, two randomly picked detainees would carry the bucket
on a bamboo pole to a nearby open ditch to empty it; two guards
with rifles followed them. The unselected would "congratulate"
the two for winning the horse race in the Happy Valley of Hong

Kong. Horse racing in Hong Kong must have been one of the great attractions enticing the freedom swimmers to risk their lives, because it was mentioned in many creative ways and used for many different situations.

Being noisy was a hallmark of detainees in their first few days in detention: They still had the energy to speak and listen and they had interest in others' escape journeys, especially how they'd been caught. As the days passed, though, hunger depleted our energy, and lessened our interest in knowing anything other than when a meal would be served. Soon, we lost track of the date, and every newcomer became a reliable source of this knowledge for the "old-timers." Homesickness drove detainees to seek promises from one another. Whoever was released first was asked to drop by a detainee's home to inform the family members that their son or daughter was alive and "well." Very often such promises didn't work. For one, no one knew who would be released first; second, when someone was let go, he would often forget what he had promised in the detention center. Occasionally it worked when the two detainees became friends planning to escape together the next time. As the days passed, we became too hungry to talk about anything except food—the food that would be within reach once we got out, homemade food, local food, but not the food in the revolving restaurant in Kowloon.

There were so many useful things to learn from the other freedom swimmers—a mixed bag of students (mostly), peasants (a few), and factory workers (even fewer)—and I listened and learned. For example, I learned that the name "the Peak" was more popular than "Victoria Peak," simply because that was what Hongkongers called it. So, we used "the Peak" instead of "Victoria Peak." Also, the residents of Hong Kong called themselves Hongkongers, to distinguish themselves from Mainlanders. Hongkongers didn't care about Mao or his Communist Party or its political campaigns; they minded their own business, and they spoke Cantonese (all of them) and English (some of them), but not Mandarin—all music to my ear. They used English for their street names, but added the Cantonese-sounding Chinese words below the English. (I thought that was smart and good for the Cantonese.) Years later, I saw the same method of naming of streets in San Francisco's Chinatown.

Also, Hongkongers had adapted some commonly used mono-syllabic English words, such as *bus* and *lift* (*elevator*) into sound-alike Cantonese words for the sake of efficiency—because their Cantonese translations consisted of three or four words.

"Time is money!" was what Hongkongers believed, and followed. *No lazy ghosts in Hong Kong!* I thought. *I like it! Papa's a natural fit.*

But what really got to me about Hongkongers was their Cantonese food—apparently it was more refined and tastier even than ours in Canton City! Almost all the detainees said so. *Damn!* The Hongkongers were luckier than Cantonese in Canton, for they lived a hybrid life: the best parts of the British (the British governor didn't bother them) combined with the best parts of the Cantonese (more refined Cantonese cuisine). Still, history would see their good fortune being cut short in 1997, when the British handed Hong Kong back over to China and went home.

I was disappointed that none of the detainees talked about wanting to go to America. I was a weirdo for not only wanting to go there but also wanting to attend university there. It seemed the other detainees just wanted to get to Hong Kong and make money. So, I kept my mouth shut about America; it was easy to do.

With us as their prisoners, the guards and their commanding officers at the detention center were stuck with a new category of "enemy"—not the usual counterrevolutionaries, but "illegal visitors to Hong Kong." That's what Prime Minster Zhou had told the reporters accompanying President Nixon. So, the job of the detention officers was to send us illegals back to our sent-down villages to be reeducated by the peasants. But because we had come from all over the province, it must have been a logistical nightmare—too many escapees were being caught every day. Detention centers were overwhelmed, and the detainees were being kept in them for weeks and months on end—all the while lying on bare concrete floors and looking forward to be sent back to the villages.

Thanks to China's strict media control, stories of these "illegal visits" to Hong Kong did not spread to other provinces. Even though almost all of the escapees were from our province, they numbered in the hundreds of thousands. If those sent down from the other twenty provinces had joined us, we would have numbered in the millions. That would have given Hong Kong residents and their British governor nightmares.

As with the number of deaths during the Great Famine, China, for reasons of national interest, will never make public the true number of escapees. It would not be difficult to do so, though, since almost all sent-down students were brought back to their homes in the city after Mao's death and their names were put back on the Household Registers. So, all missing persons would be escapees, whether they were now alive in Hong Kong or were killed during their escapes. Only a tiny number of the sent down did not return to the city because they had married a local in their sent-down village.

Because the guards couldn't shoot the escapees, their means of punishing us was through beatings. Some local guards were "good" guys—perhaps they had friends or relatives who had escaped to Hong Kong. The repeat offenders would tell the new arrivals who the good guards were and whom one needed to watch out for.

Most of the escapees in our cell were sent-down students from Canton City. No one cared where the others had been sent down to, unless that place had value for "lying under a pile of dirt." In their young minds, the Cultural Revolution was dead, and they took pride in being escapees, even *captured* escapees.

Curly and I were respected because we had almost reached the finish line. That we had been caught on the coast of Mirs Bay, and that Tung Ping Chau island, the easternmost route of the East Line, was our destination, only added to the others' admiration for us. Many of them had never heard about this route.

Every detainee seemed to want to have another go at escaping. I might not have been brave, but I would never give up once I decided to do something. Curly was as determined as I was, and he told me in no uncertain terms that he wanted to do it as soon as possible. I hadn't had a chance to talk to Ning since we were caught, but she was tough; she had grit. She would follow me, of that I was sure. In fact, no detainees I came across wanted to back out. We now all knew what the worst outcome would be. We had all heard of people who'd died at sea—some detainees were living with the memory of dead friends—and we'd all heard of dead bodies floating to the coast of Hong Kong. The most devastating story was of a threesome, two men and a woman, all young, all dead, linked to one another by a rope tied to each one's waist. They died during a storm, determined to be free or die together.

Brushing aside the failure and the fear of death, these determined rebels made the detention center come to life. I gathered as much useful information as I could from them. In return, I gave them many details I thought would be helpful for their next attempt. The only information I held back was how to make the stamp. It could have seriously bad consequences for me if a loudmouth leaked it.

Looking back, I saw that though Mao's Cultural Revolution had taken away my university study, it had taught me about myself and others like me, in the university of the free mind. We had turned the detention center into a "college campus," a center of escape education and the exchanges of ideas: choosing a good route, successfully passing a checkpoint by deceiving police and militiamen, making a compass, procuring topographical maps and tide tables, preparing food, and so on. I'll bet the detention guards heard some of our conversations, but they didn't seem to care. They knew their hands were tied because our prime minister refused to declare us enemies of the state when speaking with the Americans.

I also learned from the repeat offenders what was ahead for us. Our interrogation there at the Shenzhen Detention Center would be an easy one, as it was a transfer point where we would stay for only a few days. We needed to tell the officials there only the name of our sent-down village. We would then be sent to the central detention center, in Zhangmutou, a town midway between Canton and Shenzhen along the train route. In Zhangmutou, we learned, the interrogator would push hard, resorting to beatings if he felt they were needed to get what he wanted.

"Who helped you escape?" would be the most important question. Of course, everyone should claim to have acted alone. Otherwise, the interrogation would not end until the name and address of one's accomplices were known and verified.

Another must-ask question would be "How many times have you tried?" The repeat offenders' advice was to stick with "once" and to expect immediate scolding and even some beating, depending on the mood of the interrogator that day.

The interrogator seldom asked why one wanted to escape, because this would have elicited many colorful lies he'd hate to hear. "My grandma in Hong Kong is in the hospital dying and cannot come to Canton to see me. I'm her only grandson. I must see her before she goes to Heaven," was one of a few I liked and planned to adopt, with some modifications of course.

From Zhangmutou Detention Center, we would be transferred to a local detention center close to the village where we'd been sent down. For Ning and me, this meant going first to Tianhe Detention Center, on the outskirts of Canton City, before being sent to Zhaoqing Detention Center, in the city where Papa worked. This gave me a headache because of One-Eye Dragon. He was a pain in the butt and hadn't liked me, no matter how hard I'd tried. The detention center could release Ning and me only to him, so he could continue to reeducate us through labor in his village, though he'd never wanted to accept us in the first place.

∞∞∞∞

It was a good day for the Shenzhen Detention Center, but a bad day for the escapees—many had been caught the night before. The cell I was in was so full that when we all sat down, no one could avoid touching the person next to him.

In the early afternoon, the food finally arrived—our first meal since being caught the night before. Each cell took turns eating. We were ordered to form a line and to squat in the open area outside the cells. Each of us was given a bowl, and discolored rice mixed with salty preserved vegetables was plopped into it. I did what the others did and ate it with my fingers rather than waiting for chopsticks. One detainee spotted a small piece of fatty pork in the food bucket, grabbed it, and stuffed it in his mouth. The guard manning the bucket swung the large wood spoon at his head, fast and hard, as he was gulping it down. "Not worthy of winning the Royal Horse Race," I heard someone comment. Chinese loved to gamble, a tradition among the "Four Olds" that Mao and his wife had wanted to get rid of but would never succeed in doing.

After our meal, the interrogations started. I was taken to an office, where I told the detention officer my name, the name and address of my sent-down village, and my home address in Canton City. That was it.

The next day, we were ordered to squat in two lines in front of the buildings while the guards handcuffed us in pairs to be transferred to Zhangmutou Detention Center. I was cuffed to someone I didn't know. I saw Ning among the female detainees at the other side of the open space. We were marched to the train station under guard. Along the way, many peasants stopped to let us pass. They didn't seem surprised to see a long line of handcuffed young men and women. I guessed they must have seen this sight many times. Still, I saw a kid pull at her mother's clothes, nudging her to look at us. She slapped his little hand and dragged him away.

After a short train ride, we arrived at Zhangmutou train station. Again, still handcuffed in pairs, we were marched under guard, this time to the detention center. The only difference in my new cell was that it contained fewer people, so there was room to lie down and sleep. The concrete floor was cold, and there was no mattress. That night was horrible. I was hungry, and in addition to the foul body odor in the cell, there were lots of mosquitoes.

The next morning, we woke at dawn to the guards shouting and rattling the iron gate of our cell. All detainees were ordered at gunpoint to haul rocks from a big pile to the site of a new detention building going up close to the existing ones. A guard saw a detainee pick up a small rock, and he swung his bat to hit the detainee's arm.

"Big like an ox, and you pick a small rock? Are you tired of living?" the guard shouted.

Curly and I saw this and quietly dropped our smaller rocks and picked up bigger ones.

After moving the rocks, we were driven like ducks into a muddy pond with our clothes on. "Clean your filthy bodies, you dirty pigs!" the guards shouted.

The interrogation came in the afternoon, and it was indeed difficult. The head guard, a fat, bald man holding a club in one hand and a cigarette in the other, asked, "How many times have you tried to escape?"

"My first time," I said.

"Lying. This is your third time! I recognize your face, the face of a loser!" he shouted at me. "I'm giving you one last chance. How many times have you tried?"

"I'm telling you the truth. It's my first time."

The head guard raised his club. I ducked and covered my head with my hands, waiting for the inevitable, but instead, I heard the loud thud of his club hitting the desk.

"Get out!" he shouted.

I was dragged back to my cell, where I saw that Curly was also unharmed. I had no idea how Ning was being treated. A detainee told me the head guard liked women and was lenient with them, especially the good-looking ones.

Life in the Zhangmutou Detention Center—meals, sleep, and chatting with other detainees—was about the same as in the one in Shenzhen, except here, many escapees were caught when they were still "lying under a pile of dirt," before they'd even gotten the chance to climb the mountains or face the amazing sea. For this reason, these "early failures" were eager to learn from us, the "advanced failures." I learned a lot about the routes of the West Line. I thought that because we had not had luck in the East Line, perhaps we would try the West Line for our next attempt.

One detainee told me he'd been caught at the checkpoint on his way to Snake Mouth. I recalled from listening to Hay that it was six miles by sea from the coast of Kowloon Peninsula. "Why Snake Mouth?" I asked. "Were you not afraid of swimming into the Zhujiang River Estuary?"

"It's a possibility, but not me. I'm a damn good swimmer," he said.

I had learned from Hay that Snake Mouth was the longest stretch of sea among all the routes of both the West and East Lines. I was glad to meet someone who had tried it.

"So?" I asked.

"So, what? Why did I choose Snake Mouth? No soldier patrols and no German Shepherds."

"How did you get caught?" I said. "That's what I meant."

"Couldn't pass the checkpoint. I took a shortcut by riding the bus to Snake Mouth, and was caught on the bus by checkpoint militiamen. Don't fuck with those militiamen at the checkpoints; they're good at what they do."

"Your plan was to 'lie under a pile of dirt' in Snake Mouth?"

"Easy to do it by myself. The place is sort of being abandoned. Many residents have gone to Hong Kong. I was planning to find a bush to hide in until sunset."

I admired the guy for doing it all by himself, and I liked what I heard: There were no soldiers patrolling the coast there. Perhaps we should consider Snake Mouth for our next attempt, after we intensified our swimming training.

I started to worry about Mommy. We had left home eleven days ago. I had told her to wait between eight and ten days for news. I'd figured on seven to eight days to cross the mountains, plus one to two days for Hay to wire fifty Hong Kong dollars to a family friend who often received money wires from Hong Kong, so no one would know the money was from Hay. The wired money would signal to Mommy that we had made it to Hong Kong safely. I was sure Mommy would start to cry when the money didn't arrive on day ten. She would know we'd failed. I worried that she would think we were gone for good. I needed to let her know we were alive but in a detention center. It would be a long shot finding a detainee to help us, but I had to try.

I spoke to select detainees by first asking where their families lived in Canton, to make sure they truly were Cantonese and knew the city well. If they agreed to visit my home after they got out, to tell Mommy that Ning and I were still alive, I promised I would do the same for them. I talked with a couple of detainees, but I was skeptical. Judging the way they spoke, perhaps they just didn't have the same bond with their mothers.

We stayed in Zhangmutou for about two weeks. Then Curly was sent to his final detention center, near his sent-down village. Each of us already knew what we would do after we got out of detention: reconnect, recuperate, and try again.

After another week, Ning and I, among many others, were sent by train to Tianhe Detention Center. I saw Ning at a distance, during the walk to the station. As usual, we were each cuffed to another inmate. We didn't wave to each other, but seeing her and noting her "normal" gait was a comfort to me.

Tianhe Detention Center was on the outskirts of Canton City. It was even more crowded than either Shenzhen or Zhangmutou. Most of the detainees there had been arrested at checkpoints: at the train station, bus station, or riverboat ferry in Canton City. These escapees, healthy and clean looking, were eager learners and quite talkative. But I was weak and tired of talking about the journey they would face. I was also homesick. I dreamed of sleeping beneath the mosquito-stained netting and having casual talks with Mommy again.

After a week, Ning and I were cuffed together and led by a guard to a bus that would take us to Zhaoqing Detention Center. On the bus, people cast curious eyes on us. I bet they were guessing what crime we had committed. If you didn't live in the Pearl River Delta area, you were not familiar with escape attempts, not to mention with how escapees looked after they were caught.

An officer at Zhaoqing Detention Center telephoned One-Eye Dragon to sign us out, but he refused to come. We were stuck. The facility was small, and guarding there was lax; men and women detainees could pass messages to one another. I learned from Ning that she had a fever but was being ignored by her guard. I shouted at the guard to let Ning go home. He and I got into a verbal fight—to no avail. At least he didn't beat me up.

A couple of weeks passed. One day, Lily showed up at the detention center. This surprised us. She signed us out and promised the detention officer to bring us back to our sent-down village at once. She lied. As soon as she saw us, she cried. We didn't. Perhaps we were too tired and weak, or too happy, to cry. She brought us nice clothes and said we looked like visitors from Hong Kong in them; she obviously wanted to cheer us up. We didn't smile. Perhaps we had forgotten how to.

Lily brought us to a restaurant to eat. We ate all the food, leaving behind shining bowls and plates. She told us she had bought return tickets for the riverboat home that evening. Later, I learned that One-Eye Dragon had dragged his feet for several days before finally telling Papa where we were. Papa then called Mommy, and Mommy immediately telegraphed Jing to tell Lily to return home at once. (Lily had gone to Jing to help her with her little boy.)

When we arrived home, Ning fell into Mommy's arms and cried, while I tried hard to hold back my tears.

"What have they done to you?" Mommy asked, tears in her eyes.

"Mommy, we're fine, still in one piece." I tried to downplay the hardship.

Mommy told me Chunky had made it to Hong Kong. "The East Line is closed for us," I said. "We need to find a new route."

"You don't need to do it again." Mommy was sincere. "We'll support you, and you can stay home." By then, many sent-down students had returned to Canton City "illegally" and become "Black households." The Street Committee didn't intervene. Rumor had it that most committee members had sent-down students in their own and in relatives' or friends' families. I believed the majority of Chinese hated Mao's sent-down policy. Of course, the minority of diehard Communist successors would continue to carry the banner right up to the shining end of communism. As the saying goes, "The same type of rice raises a hundred types of people."

"Mommy, don't worry," I said. "We'll make it the next time."

While we washed our bodies with lots of soap and water, Mommy cooked for us. We ate and ate, answering Mommy's numerous questions about how we were caught, what we'd been fed in detention, and everything in between—until our words made no sense because we were falling asleep.

More than a month of starving in detention centers had given Ning and me puffy faces. While Papa's puffy face during the Great Famine had received sympathy, ours received neighbors' admiration. It was a sign that we'd just been through a failed escape. Ning stayed home the whole time her face was puffy, but I went to visit Uncle at the Rooftop Underground. A man should not be bothered by how he looks.

Uncle was excited to see me and kept saying he wanted every-body to learn as much as possible from my experience. He turned me into a proud failure. But he was not interested in how I dealt with ants in the food, the mountains, the weather, or the moon; he wanted to know how we were treated in detention. Uncle was a very pragmatic man, and because of his poor lungs, he had set his heart and mind on using a boat for his escape.

Shan was ecstatic at my return and proudly told me how he had been using my stamp-making material. He suggested we sell fake stamps for money.

"You'd better not!" I warned him, "We'll both go to jail if you do."

He laughed. "Relax, I'm just joking."

"When are *you* going?" I asked him.

"Not yet. I need to take care of everyone's stamp first, includ-ing your next one."

I didn't like that Shan was taking all the credit for making the fake stamps, but I was even more worried that he was being a loudmouth and talking about it too much.

Ning and I returned to our early-morning swimming routine, to rebuild our strength. Strangely, being failures had given us an indomitable feeling this time around, which made the practice even more enjoyable, but we were so weak we could barely finish one lap, and had to take a long pause holding on to the edge of the pool to catch our breaths.

One day, I met Kok and her boyfriend in the swimming pool. Kok was Shan's sister. Her boyfriend, noticeably shorter than her, had a round face and looked soft, whereas Kok was a tall, strong-minded woman with an angular face that hinted at her toughness. I did my best to tell them all the useful escape details, which I thought they'd want to hear, but they didn't seem all that interested.

Then Teacher Fong showed up unexpectedly. After introducing him to them, I praised his ability at face reading. (He had earned my respect by predicting the failure of my first escape attempt.) I asked him to read their faces because they were going to escape soon. He was reluctant at first—I figured he was building himself up—then he started to work his magic by staring intently at both their faces. He even asked Kok to show him the soles of her feet. Afterward, he said he just didn't have it in him that day, and he excused himself to leave. This was unlike the man I knew, and I chased after him and pulled him aside.

"What is it? You shouldn't leave us abruptly without an explanation," I said.

"I'd rather not say it," Teacher Fong said. "If I tell them what I think, they won't believe it."

"Then tell me. I won't tell them."

"Promise?"

"Promise."

"They shouldn't go together," Teacher Fong said. "The woman is too strong for the man, and the man will not make it if they go together. But both are too headstrong to listen to any advice." He paused. "I really don't want to get involved. Sorry. I suggest you do the same." Then he walked away.

What was the right thing for me to do? Say nothing and perhaps let one of them die during their escape? Say something that neither wanted to listen to? Or say something that would make them abandon their plan, perhaps a great plan? I regretted introducing Teacher Fong to them. Perhaps he was right. Perhaps the best option was to say nothing. Still, I hated to think that someone could die because of my silence. In the end, I chose the easy way out, saying nothing and hoping that Heaven would look out for them.

Kok's boyfriend knew someone living in Macau, back then a colony of the Portuguese empire that did not want Chinese refugees. Once they got to Macau, that someone could smuggle them to Hong Kong. Macau is on the western side of the Zhujiang River Estuary, whereas Hong Kong is on the eastern side. The distance between Macau and Hong Kong Island is a hundred-some miles by sea. The escape to Macau was called the Macau Line, and the escapees started somewhere in the Zhongshan area.

Kok and her boyfriend had arranged for a sent-down student called Tong to help them "lie under a pile of dirt." Tong had been making money helping escapees because he knew the back road bypassing the checkpoint. Uncle saw him as an asset and had built the relationship so Tong would help Kok. Their plan was to bike from Canton all the way down to Zhongshan, a distance of some sixty miles. The two needed a helper in addition to Tong, and Uncle asked me if I could do it, given my escape experience. I agreed without hesitation, hoping I could help them somehow given that I hadn't warned them about Teacher Fong's bleak prediction.

It was a long bicycle journey, and I got to know Tong as we shared a bike. He was tall and strong, and pretty much did most of the pedaling and talking as I sat on the rack and listened. Kok and her boyfriend followed us on another bike. I learned from Tong that because Macau captured Chinese refugees and sent them back to the Mainland, the Macau Line was not a popular one. It required a relative or friend in Macau who could pay a smuggler fisherman from either Macau or Hong Kong to bring the escapees to Hong Kong. Tong told me that Uncle was encouraging him to get a boat locally, and Uncle would take care of the smuggling part. This was one of the reasons Uncle was encouraging us to practice paddling.

The drop-off spot was a large aboveground burial tomb about twenty feet in diameter with a round concrete perimeter wall at least two feet higher than the rim of the vault. The space between the vault and the wall was large enough to hide one person from the view of anyone standing outside the wall.

We said, "See you in Hong Kong," to one another, and quickly Kok and her boyfriend climbed over the wall, with Tong and me pushing them up from below. Then I took Kok's bike and rode back to Canton with Tong.

On our way, Tong asked me if I had ever had "beggar's chicken." It was time for dinner.

"No," I said, "but I'd like to try it."

Tong started to look for chickens, and finally spotted a few on the other side of the swale between the road and a field. While I waited with the bicycles, he ran to the field and started chasing chickens. Just as I began thinking he would come back empty-handed, he returned with a hen with her head dangling down. He'd broken her neck.

"You've just committed a violent robbery!"

"This is how the beggars do it," Tong explained.

To cook the hen, he took moist dirt from the swale and patted it all over the hen except for the head and feet. "We aren't eating those parts," he explained. Then he cut a branch, sharpened one end with his pocketknife, and pushed the pointed stick through the hen. I collected dry leaves and branches for a fire. Once the hen was cooked, we peeled off the hot mud, which pulled the feathers and some skin cleanly away, exposing the white meat. The combination of my excitement over our stealing the hen, my curiosity about the cooking method, and the emptiness of my stomach made it a memorable meal.

Tong told me he was from a poor family and just wanted to make a living in Hong Kong. His father had died as a soldier during the Korean War, when he was a baby. He lived with his mother.

"I don't need to be rich or successful. I just want to have enough to live by myself and send something to my mom." He added, "If you want to take the Macau Line, you can depend on me. And I won't charge you."

His story made me sad. I was lucky to have a caring mother and father. The world was unfair. China only made it worse. "I trust you," I said, "and I'll pay you, but I don't have any way to get from Macau to Hong Kong."

A few days after Tong and I helped Kok and her boyfriend escape, news came. Kok had made her way to Hong Kong, but her boyfriend had drowned as they swam to Macau. The news sent a chill down my spine. Teacher Fong was right again!

Several months later, Tong came across a woman escapee who needed local help to reach Macau. She promised to smuggle Tong from there to Hong Kong. As they swam from Zhongshan to Macau, Tong got tangled up in a large fishnet and drowned. The news saddened me badly.

Two deaths within a few months erased all my good feelings about our next attempt, but didn't erode my determination. I realized that death was not something any escapee could control. *If I can't control something, I shouldn't waste my time worrying about it*, I kept reminding myself. The two deaths seemed not to dampen any of the Rooftop Underground's determination, and everyone was frantically looking for an opportunity.

The Chinese New Year of 1973 arrived. I would be twenty-five in a few months, and Ning would be twenty-one when summer came. Papa came home for a week. He had changed. He no longer mentioned the government's intention to bring sent-down students back to the city. Perhaps he had realized our failed escape attempt had further stained our personal *dang'an*, which were already blemished by his downfall. He knew our chances of returning to

Canton City were reduced. By then, what most people talked about around the dinner table was "So-and-so made it to Hong Kong," and how much better off his or her family had become. Envy always won over admiration in those deprived of success. Honestly, I really didn't know what had changed Papa's mind about our escape, but I was sure he'd never blame China. We just didn't talk about China anymore at our dinner table, and that was easy for me to do.

In any case, I was happy. Papa told me if there was anything he could do to help, he would do it. I told him I was looking for a few rubber sheets, the kind used for patients who soiled their hospital beds.

"What for?" he asked.

"I want to make an inflatable rubber raft."

"You want to escape during the winter?"

"Yes. But I can't find those sheets in Canton. They're sold out."

"Let me see what I can do. I have a business trip to Shanghai City soon."

On New Year's Day, Mommy made a dish of many chicken feet, which she gave mainly to Ning and me. Papa was not aware of this, but chicken feet had become a symbol of goodwill and a blessing for soon-to-be escapees, based on the fact that chickens ran very fast and chicken feet were easily available in the farmers' market. In those days in any restaurant in Canton, one could easily spot who the departing escapee was by the chicken feet those at his table offered him with the words "Bottoms up for the chicken feet!" Yet no plainclothes police were arresting those eating the most chicken feet, for it wasn't a crime to eat them.

Papa brought back the rubber sheets from Shanghai, and I started to make the raft with the help of Curly. We used a file to clean the rubber surface, applied rubber glue used for repairing bicycle tires to make air tubes, and then glued the tubes to the bottom sheet. We added a bicycle valve to inflate the raft. When we were done, we had a large, long raft that could hold three persons—or so we thought.

On a dark and chilly night, we took the raft to the river. Ning joined us. But it didn't work. It was floppy and bent in the middle, leaving us wet and shivering. It was heartbreaking, but we recovered quickly. We realized we couldn't have arranged to "lie under a pile of dirt" with such a bulky object, even if it had worked.

Finally, spring came! A new season for freedom swimmers was near. *Where should we start our second attempt?*

One day, Lily brought home her good friend from junior high, Yun. When I heard she had been sent down to a village close to Snake Mouth, I almost jumped.

"Snake Mouth? Are you kidding me? Why are you still here?"

"I'm ashamed of myself," Yun said. "I should be in Hong Kong, but I'm not a good swimmer."

"Why didn't you learn?"

"When I finally set my mind to go, it was too late, and all my friends were gone."

"It's never too late," I said firmly.

I realized this was a golden opportunity for Ning and suggested to Yun that she needed a partner to swim across the six miles of sea. I saw her hesitation and made a proposal: "I'll help you improve your swimming if, and only if, you bring Ning along."

"Of course, I will," Yun said. "I need her experience."

I had a good feeling about the arrangement from the start.

ooooo

"SHOW ME HOW FAST CAN you swim," I told Yun. We were standing in the shallow part of the swimming pool under the bright morning sun. I moved along beside her as she did a lap, noting the common mistakes in her breaststroke.

"Stop. I see what you're doing wrong."

"How bad was it?" Yun asked.

"Your legs. We're used to squatting, and when we do that, our knee joints swing outward. That is the cardinal sin in a breaststroke. Keep the distance between your knees about the same as your shoulder width." I demonstrated how I did it. Then Yun took a turn while I watched. She was getting there.

"The critical part is the 'kick and sweep,' but before doing it, you need to fan out your legs while keeping your knee joints at shoulder width. Then kick and sweep your legs and at the same time stretch your arms forward."

Yun was confused. I asked her to hold on to the edge of the pool, and I held her feet to guide her movements. After hours of trial and error, she got it. Day after day, we practiced, and Yun made good progress.

∞∞∞

ONE DAY IN LATE APRIL, Curly came and told me that two guys had offered him everything an escapee needed, from travel documents and bus tickets to food and dangerous items such as flotation pillows—all in exchange for Curly's experience in crossing the mountains and fields to reach the coast near Tung Ping Chau. Curly accepted their offer and asked me to join him. He told me they would offer me the same.

"Curly, I'm serious. You shouldn't go," I said. "The water is too cold still. Let's wait, and I'll come up with a plan. But I need to help Ning and Yun first."

"When are they going?" he asked.

"In the summer, when the water's warmer. They need to cross six miles of sea."

"Not me. I only need to swim less than two miles. April is fine, and I can't wait any longer."

His confidence really worried me. "Curly, please listen to me. The water is too cold!"

But his mind was made up, and nothing I said could stop him. I wished him the best as we said good-bye.

Ning and Yun got into high gear, and the plan was set. Both would ride a bicycle from Canton to Yun's village. They would dress like village women. Before they passed the militiamen's roadside checkpoint to Snake Mouth, they would stop by a farmers' market and buy groceries that would make them look exactly like the other villagers returning home from the market. We would provide our family's bike, a fairly new one, and Yun would prepare a travel document for Ning. They would time their travel so they reached Snake Mouth at around sunset. Once there, they would drop everything and swim across to freedom.

"Don't worry if the moon doesn't show up," I said. "Just aim toward Mount Lau Fau. You can't miss it. It's a big, dark mass against the lit-up night sky. But I bet you'll see the lights along the Hong Kong coastline." I had learned about Mount Lau Fau from other detainees.

"Why don't you warn us that if we miss it, we'll die in the sea and the fish'll get us?" Ning was in a joking mood.

"Because I have a good feeling this time."

Then tragic news came. Curly did not make it. He had died in the water. I was very upset and blamed myself for not having made a solid plan he was willing to wait for. Mommy and Ning were speechless. Finally, Mommy said, "Life or death is decided by Heaven." It sounded hollow to me this time, for I doubted that

Heaven even paid attention to ant people like Curly and the rest of us. (Chinese called the common folk ant people because they served the emperor, just like ants serve their queen.)

Word on the street among escapees was that women outlasted men in the frigid water because they had more fat on their bodies, and that men's deaths in the water were preceded by unbearable pain in the groin, when the testes were vigorously retracted into the warmer abdominal cavity. Human evolution did not anticipate that desperate men would need to survive in cold water; it cared only about protecting their sperm for future generations.

∞∞∞

THE SUMMER OF 1973 FINALLY came, and with it, the day for Ning and Yun to go. They looked like village women with their deeply suntanned skin, straw hats, and villagers' outfits. I had cleaned and polished the bike, believing that its sparkling appearance would reduce suspicion among the militiamen at the checkpoint. After all, why would anyone use a nice-looking bicycle in an escape attempt? As Ning and Yun walked out the door, Mommy gave each a piece of ginseng. Conventional wisdom said ginseng enhanced one's endurance.

"Start to chew on it when you get into the water," Mommy told them, holding back her tears.

Ning hugged Mommy and sobbed. Mommy wept; my eyes were red. All the things we needed to say had been said, and nobody uttered a word. Then, just like that, Ning left home sitting on the rack of the bicycle, the morning sunlight bouncing off its wheels. After she left, I felt empty inside. Nobody had any desire to talk. Mommy lit an incense stick and stuck it in the small pot on the windowsill. She had burned incense sticks for Ning and me the last time, and I hoped the second time was the charm.

Evening came, and I broke the silence: "They should be in the water by now. It's good the moon is out." Before Mommy went to bed, she raised the burning incense stick, faced the window, and bowed and prayed. Her voice was so soft that I couldn't discern what she said, but I pictured two tiny bodies in the intimidating black sea drifting toward the dark mountain far ahead.

The next day, our anxiety grew, and we all became more and more short-tempered with one another. In the late afternoon, news finally arrived: fifty Hong Kong dollars! Hay wired us the money, signaling that the Hong Kong police had notified him to sign out Ning. A jubilant eruption by everyone!

"One free, one more to go!" I declared.

I wrote a short letter to Papa and went to drop it in the post office. On my way, I said to myself that my second attempt must be successful, to match Ning's. Hope was burning within me.

Hope was always alive in a freedom swimmer's heart.

CHAPTER 12

LIFE IS A STREAM OF WATER

I NEEDED TO START FROM scratch. I went to see Uncle and announced the good news about Ning. Everyone at the Rooftop Underground was impressed by their bravery in taking on six miles of sea. But no one could help me with a new plan.

My failed escape had earned me "notoriety" among my classmates, and one day, two of them knocked on my door. They were good, quiet students from my high school class, and perhaps the two best Chinese chess players. Their appearance surprised me, for I had not been that close to them in school. One of them was called Cheng. I didn't really know the other guy, Hu. Cheng said his sentdown village, where many had escaped to Hong Kong following a route on the West Line, would be a good place to "lie under a pile of dirt." Even though my first escape attempt was along the East Line, Cheng and Hu believed I could help them take the West Line because of my previous experience there.

I told them of Ning's success on the farthest route on West Line, via Snake Mouth, but Cheng hesitated, for he was not a good swimmer. Hu was aloof, and spoke even less than Cheng, but he was excited about Snake Mouth, and confident in his swimming skills and his endurance. The two had never talked much in class. I guessed their friendship was built on playing chess. That was fine with me; my first escape had taught me there wasn't much to talk about after the first day or two crossing the mountains.

I told Cheng he must improve his swimming and offered my help; he agreed. Then I promised him, "I'll stay with you the whole way. It's a promise."

Then Cheng agreed to Snake Mouth as the spot where we would get in the water; apparently the absence of a patrol on the coast was the draw. But unlike Ning and Yun, who started off from Yun's sent-down village, we would have to spend a week crossing mountains and fields.

We soon got into high gear, preparing our travel documents and gathering the usual escape supplies. Then, with the blessing of everyone, including Papa, I left home as the rain started. We easily reached the mountains, hoping all the while that the rain would stop, but it didn't. For two days, it poured down harder and harder. Finally, we decided to call it quits and try at another time.

My surprise return home gave Mommy a bad feeling about the route. "Should I ask Teacher Fong to read your face?"

"No. I don't want to hear."

"If I were younger, I'd escape with you," she said. "Then I'd insist on a face reading before we went."

After a few days the rain stopped. We said our good-byes to family again and started off right away. We had to act fast, before the moon waned into a semicircle. We wouldn't need moonlight to cross the six miles of sea, but we'd need it to make the mountain crossing easier.

The journey with my quiet classmates was boring, but I did learn from them what my other classmates had been doing. For those sent down to the rubber farm, most turned out to be just what I'd predicted: political and enthusiastic for China's Communist future. Of those who went to villages, however, many were not happy, and going home to visit their parents brought them only temporary relief. Surprisingly, no one was as brave as me, Hay, or the two newcomers next to me. Compared to other schools, our high school appeared to have produced more obedient types.

"Wish we had a chess set with us, so I could learn a couple of sophisticated moves from you," I said. Cheng and Hu smiled, but said nothing. I suddenly missed the fun of my first escape attempt with Curly and Ning, before we were caught.

After several days in the mountains, we found ourselves standing on the shore of Snake Mouth. The sky was dark—no stars, no moon, but dark clouds. The sea was black. I waded into it. Its waves gushed me back with a loud howling, then dragged me out so forcefully that I stumbled. The water chilled my skin and choked me. It was bitterly salty. I had drunk plenty of water from the Pearl, Liujiang, and Xijiang Rivers, but I wouldn't drink seawater even if you'd paid me. *What is the big deal about sea salt anyway? I don't want its higher buoyancy. I just want it to be calm as a river!*

The sea pushing me up and dropping me back down like a yo-yo was annoying. I had never swum in such violent, nasty water. The sea needed to be restrained, just like the river. It was hard to know how fast I was moving. I was sloshed back and forth and pushed up and down inside an imaginary and infinitely large bowl of water, and Heaven must have been shaking the bowl by its handles. "Don't bully the sea"—our ancestors had learned this lesson. Now it was my turn. *But the sea is bullying me!*

Next to me, Cheng was struggling. He was choking, and gasping in water instead of air, which only made him cough and choke more. Occasionally, he rested on his inflatable plastic pillow.

(Before we got in the water, each of us had blown our pillow up and tied it with a string to our waist.) After swimming for a while, Hu became impatient. I told him to go ahead, and that I would stay behind with Cheng. Hu said good-bye and swam onward.

Cheng didn't want me to stay behind with him. I told him I wouldn't leave him alone. I had told him I would stay with him the whole way. "A promise is a promise," I said. Looking at him, I knew he appreciated it. I had been a much better swimmer in the river. If I had doubts about swimming in the sea, he must have had even more.

Then I thought about Curly. Was he with someone when he drowned? Or was he alone? How long before he passed out? Such thoughts scared me. *If I have to die in the sea, Heaven, please make it quick. Just keep choking me until I pass out.*

It was at that point that I started to hate the sea. I hated that it had deceived me the first time I saw it, from a long distance, with its peacefully blue water and grandiose scale. But now that I was inside it, I found it dark, pushy, and mean. *Just like a human*, I said to myself. *To see is to be deceived. I won't swim in Repulse Bay once I get to Hong Kong.* Mommy had told me how nice it was, how loudly I had giggled when she lowered my body into it so my feet could touch the sand, and how quickly I withdrew my feet from the cool incoming waves. I had enjoyed this thought. Swimming in the darkness, sensing nothing except the sloshing noise of my strokes, I needed good thoughts. *But I still won't swim for a long time, not even in Repulse Bay.*

I had lost all sense of time. I couldn't guess how long I'd been swimming. Next to me, Cheng was moving forward slowly, his arms resting on the inflated pillow. Though the sea had calmed down quite a bit, we had no energy to spare even for talking. I signaled to Cheng not to rest on the plastic pillow too long. I didn't want him to fall asleep. In the darkness, the rhythmic, humming sounds of the sea were soothing.

What was Mommy doing at this time of night? She was probably thinking about me. I wanted to tell her, *I'm all right. I'm getting closer to Hong Kong. Tomorrow, Hay or maybe Ning will wire you the money. Go tell everybody our family is done with escapes, especially those who turned their back on you when Papa was down. I know you'll forgive them. That's all right. I just want to know what they'll say now.* I wanted people to respect Mommy again. *Could you call Papa instead of sending him a letter? Don't worry about the money. You'll never need to borrow money again, to look at another person's expression to decide if you should open your mouth.*

I felt good now. I could see more lights along the coast, and of course, the big dark mountains behind. I didn't remember when I'd ever felt this way. I deserved it. Those rains in the mountains had been hell. And I was crossing six miles of sea, the longest of all escape routes, after eight days in the mountains. I was so tired, but I would make it.

Still, my thoughts plagued me. *What am I going to do in Hong Kong? No one on the Rooftop talked about that. I'm not prepared. I'll be penniless. It'll be a shame to be poor in Hong Kong. Everyone says how good this or that is there. But who will hire me? And to do what? What can I do?*

"The sunlight!" Cheng said.

I saw it, too. To our left, the sky was lighting up. The first rays of dawn illuminated many white buildings on the Hong Kong coastline. Now the sea was calm. The Chinese coast was way behind us. We had passed the midline and were definitely now in Hong Kong waters. The white buildings became clearer and clearer. It would be a sunny and cloudless day, a beautiful day! Hong Kong, here we are!

Cheng and I slowly inched ahead. He was not an emotional type, but his voice trembled, "Finally!"

The rumble of an engine behind us drew our attention. A motorized junk was heading our way. The Hong Kong fishermen? I'd heard that Hong Kong fishermen picked up freedom swimmers from the sea, warmed them up and fed them, then arranged for their relatives to come take them to their "new" homes.

"Too late," I said out loud. "We don't need your help now." We were a few hundred feet from the coast.

Soon the junk was near us. Someone on it shouted at us, "Come on up!" A long bamboo pole almost hit our heads. "Grab the pole, or I'll shoot you!"

My heart sank. Standing at the stern were two men in peasant clothes, one holding the pole and the other holding a rifle. *Hell!* They were militarized Chinese fishermen! We were two sitting ducks waiting to be castrated! I'd learned in detention centers that Chinese fishermen "invaded" the Hong Kong water all the time and Chinese government rewarded the fishermen for each freedom swimmer they caught in the sea.

We were pulled out of the sea, tied at the wrists, and pushed into a corner of the junk's stern. The wind slapped our bare chests, making our teeth chatter, but that was nothing compared to our hearts, which had sunk to the dark bottom of the sea.

"Not a bad way to make one hundred *yuan* before breakfast!" we heard one of the fishermen say as the junk sped back toward the coast of China.

How can Hong Kong allow the invasion of Chinese fishermen in its waters? I was angry and frustrated, but powerless.

∞∞∞∞

NOTHING HAD CHANGED AT THE Shenzhen Detention Center since I was there a year before. I didn't see Hu there and believed he'd made it to Hong Kong. I told Cheng what to expect during his interrogation, "The shouting will be loud. Don't argue. Just stick to the fact that it truly was your first escape attempt and that you were with only one classmate, and that's me. Don't mention Hu."

"Hu's made it," Cheng said.

"Most likely."

"He didn't want to wait for me."

"Apparently not," I said. "But we'll make it the next time."

"I don't know about that," Cheng said.

In the afternoon, we were sent to Zhangmutou Detention Center. There I was separated from Cheng. After a quick interrogation, he was immediately sent back to his village. He left quietly; it made me sad.

Ten years ago, after my visit to Tung Ping Chau island, I went to Canton City and asked a former classmate to help me find Cheng. I wanted to explain to him why I wasn't able to bring him along when I made my final escape attempt, and that I felt bad that I hadn't said good-bye before I left. My classmate smiled. "Don't worry. Cheng has told everybody he would have died in the water if not for your waiting for him." I was so touched. When we finally met, we had a good, long conversation. He told me that after he was allowed to move back to Canton City in 1978, he got a job in a factory. He was limping, in need of a hip replacement, but his savings for the surgery had been used up on his son's wedding. "I need to save money again for my surgery." His voice was calm and without much emotion, just like before. But unlike before, I felt for him. What a good man and a good father! As for Hu, he got rich in Hong Kong, but during a trip to Canton years later, he was stabbed to death during an armed robbery on a bus.

Now I had to wait for my turn through interrogation and transfer. The other detainees saw me as a "hero" and paid me their respects simply because I had been pulled out of the water—having gone the longest distance of anyone in detention. The first night was harder than I thought it would be. I crossed my forearms tightly over my chest, curled up as much as I could, and lay on my side to minimize contact between my naked upper body and the cold concrete floor. The guy next to me was kind enough to let me push my back against his, to keep warm.

I could be wandering the streets of Hong Kong under the neon lights, if not for the damn Chinese militiamen's invasion of Hong Kong waters, I thought with self-pity.

"It makes me happy to see you, bastard," the head guard said when it was time for my interrogation. "No doubt you're smarter than most, but we scooped you up like shrimp wonton. How delicious!" He twisted his bat in his hand, and when I raised my hands to protect my head, he laughed. "You lucky bastard. I don't have time to spend on you today. We catch so many of you I need a quick discharge. But your file has my notes: 'three-time offender and recommend jail time the next round.' Now, get out!" I exhaled as I left his office, for I had prepared to be beaten.

The following afternoon, all detainees were lined up in pairs, squatting. I was paired with a tall guy; in front of him was a guy of about my height. The guy in front of me was also tall. As we waited to be cuffed, the person next to me made a suggestion: "If you don't mind changing your position with my friend in front of you, we can all walk easier being cuffed to someone of the same height." I agreed and, while still squatting, quickly switched places with the tall guy in front of me. This caught the attention of the guard who was cuffing detainees. He came over and shouted, "What the fuck are you doing?" He kicked me in the chest, knocking me over. "No moving around!" he shouted.

Every time I took a breath, the pain stopped me.

"You look pale. That's no good," my new cuff mate said.

"No talking!" The guard who'd kicked me cuffed us, then moved to the pair behind us.

"What's your name?" I started to ask the short guy next to me, but the sharp pain in my chest stopped me.

"You can call me Lee," he said. "You should do something about that pain."

"What?"

"My grandpa rubbed urine on his chest where a heavy branch fell on him. He said it would prevent blood clots."

"My urine? No way." My chuckling brought on the pain again. I tried to twist my upper body a bit, but that also produced a sharp stab and brought on a cold sweat. I started to worry that my ribs were broken.

"Cover for me," I told Lee. "I think I will do it."

I reached inside my shorts with my left hand, urinated a bit, and then rubbed the dark urine vigorously on my chest until I felt the heat. I wiped my palm back and forth on the ground to clean it. The guard ran over again and pulled me up by my hair.

"Lost your will to live, have you?" He smacked my face so hard I was thrown to the ground, pulling Lee on top of me. The guard raised his boot to kick me, but instead kicked Lee on the left side of his belly. Lee screamed and then groaned. The head guard saw this and shouted, "Enough! Squat!"

On our way to the train station, Lee could hardly walk; he leaned on me with each step. I blamed myself for having switched positions. What was the big deal being cuffed to someone of a different height? And why had I believed that stupid Chinese notion about using urine as a medicine? My urine didn't do a damn thing for my pain, and now innocent Lee was hurt. I couldn't forgive myself for my stupidity.

Lee lay in our cell in the Tianhe Detention Center with his eyes closed, not saying a word but moaning the whole time. I noticed that his belly was distended, and when I touched it, it was hard and cold.

"Are you cold?" I asked. He nodded but didn't open his eyes. "Like a pregnant belly," I said, and his mouth twitched. I sensed that something was terribly wrong with him, but I didn't know what. I told myself I'd watch over him all night long. I sat up. I don't know how many hours had passed before Lee turned his head slightly to me and said something I could barely hear. The cell was dead quiet. I leaned my head toward his mouth.

"Pray for me," he said.

I had never heard a prayer and had never prayed for anyone. I remembered hearing Curly pray to his Christian God, but I could never decipher his mumbling. I asked Lee, "You mean to God?" and he nodded. I didn't know how to pray, but I'd try. Because this was all my fault, it was the least I could do for him.

I turned to the iron-barred window, to face the sky, and said quietly, "God, I don't know how to talk to you. I don't know if you can hear me. If you can, please come help Lee. He is cold and has a lot of pain. He didn't do anything wrong . . . all because of me."

Lee closed his eyes, and the wrinkles on his forehead disappeared.

I was relieved thinking his pain had subsided and soon fell asleep. When I woke up, Lee's body was stiff and cold. He had died while I slept.

His death was shocking and heartbreaking for me, but it seemed only a nuisance to the guards. "Fuck," they grumbled as they grabbed his feet and dragged his body out. They wrapped him in a dirty sheet and put him on a cart to be taken away. I didn't say a word. I just watched, knowing it was my fault. Until now, I have not mentioned it.

∞∞∞

I DON'T REMEMBER HOW I was transferred from Tianhe Detention Center to Zhaoqing Detention Center or how many days I was there. I don't remember how many times I refused to tell the guard what village I was from. I had kept my promise to One-Eye Dragon, that I would never bother him again. The detention guard yelled that he couldn't just throw me out, unless I was dead, and he could let me out only if someone came to sign the paperwork. I didn't want to tell him Papa was working for the city government. I had to protect Papa.

Every day, the guard shouted at me, and every day, I ignored him. This must have gone on for two months, because the leaves were turning brown and I shivered every time my bare back touched the concrete floor. One day, I woke up and realized I shouldn't be wasting my life in the detention center. I still had to escape to Hong Kong. I rattled the iron-barred door, and the guard came.

"What's today's date?" I asked.

"You've been here long enough. We'll need to charge you for the cost of your food."

"What's today's date?" I persisted.

It was early October 1973. I had been in detention for more than three months. I had to get out now! I told the guard that Papa worked for the city.

"What the hell!" he shouted.

Papa came and signed the paperwork to get me released. As we walked out of the detention center, the guard scolded him for failing to educate his son properly.

The sight of my thin body and bare chest caused Papa to cry. I told him I was fine.

He said, "We all thought you were dead."

"Papa, I had no way to get a message out. I missed home. I'm fine," I said.

"Look at you. You're not fine."

"I'll bounce back. I did before."

"You don't have to do it again. Now Ning is in Hong Kong, and she'll help out with the family."

"No, Papa. I started this, and I must finish it."

Papa took off his shirt and shoes and gave them to me. "Put them on. You can't go home without clothes or shoes. I don't need them to ride the bicycle."

"I'm sorry to have dragged you into this. I hope the mayor won't punish you."

"Don't worry about me. I can take it. You need to take care of yourself. Go home, get rest, and eat good food. See how thin you are!"

He gave me money to buy a bus ticket and then, without shoes, he got on his bike and, looking shaky and awkward, rode away.

Mommy started to cry as soon as she saw me. I wiped away her tears and said, "Do I look that bad?" Lily handed me a mirror, and I held it up. I couldn't believe my eyes: long and rumpled hair on a large head; a pale, bony face; a patchy beard.

"I'll look better after I clean up, but I need to eat something first." This sent both of them into a frenzy, preparing me food. How much I had missed my home! After the food and a bath, I told them that Cheng and I had been caught within several hundred feet of Hong Kong. They kept shaking their heads.

Lily comforted me: "Each time, you make some progress."

"But I need a Great Leap Forward," I said, and she smiled.

"All you need is a blessing from Heaven!" Mommy said. "And next time, I must have Teacher Fong read your face, and you must do what he says. Now you need to go sleep."

The next day, I went to Uncle's place. I kept ringing and looking up at the rooftop, but Uncle didn't show his face. I went to find Shan, and he told me that Uncle had joined Hay's brother, Mau, and several local fishermen to steal a village sampan and then paddled it overnight to Hong Kong by way of the Zhujiang River Estuary. I felt good for them but empty inside. I asked Shan when he planned to go himself, and he said very soon. He told me he'd leave me the enlarger and the materials for making the fake stamps. He seemed to have great confidence in reaching Hong Kong on his first attempt. It seemed to me I had become a perpetual failure. *Why does Heaven always close Its eyes to me?*

Other than Shan, Uncle Lao was the only one from the Rooftop Underground whose house I knew. He liked to laugh out loud, but I was not in the mood to joke or laugh with him. I went to see Cheng. He told me Hu had indeed made it to Hong Kong, but Cheng had no desire to try again.

As fall progressed, so did my sadness. I felt sad that 1973 was slipping away so fast. How much I hated to wait for next summer! But what could I do? I couldn't swim across in the winter.

The Rooftop Underground was closed after Uncle left for Hong Kong. And I didn't have the shortwave radio to listen to Voice of America. Most of the time, I stayed at home feeling sorry for myself.

"You need to get out of the house. The sky hasn't fallen yet," Mommy said.

"I'm going to visit a temple and ask for Buddha's blessing," I said.

"That's a good idea." She smiled. "You need it."

The next day, I rode a bicycle before dawn to the Lotus Temple. I had heard from the peasants in White Stone that a waterfall near the temple fed a small pond that locals had named "Nine Dragon Pond," claiming the water brought good karma. I needed good karma for my next escape attempt.

When I arrived at the temple, it was awfully quiet; no one was in sight. I took off my shoes and walked into the shrine, where a huge statue of Buddha sat. I believed that Buddha was taking notice of my presence there; his kind eyes were looking toward me. I felt small and insignificant but also calm and warm. Seeing the gold paint peeling off his face and hands, I felt sorry for him, but at least the Red Guards had not burned or destroyed him. I kneeled in front of him and bowed my head, touching the floor three times. Each time, with tears rolling down my cheeks, I muttered, "Bless me in my escape. I need you. I don't know what more I can do."

As I stepped outside the temple, I met a monk and asked him where the other monks were. He told me they were gathered somewhere to study Chairman Mao's teaching.

"Are you kidding me?" I said in a voice of disgust.

"All composite things arise and dissolve, Mister," the Monk replied calmly.

An earthworm lay on the brick path in front of me, but I didn't notice it. The monk signaled me to stop, bent down to pick it up, and held it gently in his palm while carrying it to the moist dirt next to the path to release it.

"It's not going to make it," I said. "It's dying." I shook my head.

"Not dying, Mister. Suffering."

"What about the people I knew? One was my very good friend. They didn't even get a chance to suffer. They're dead. And I'm no better a man than they were."

"Be patient. The fruits of good karma come in time, Mister."

"When?"

"Let them go, Mister. Nothing lasts. All dissolves in the void."

"I don't know what you're talking about," I said, "but thanks. Can you tell me how to get to Nine Dragon Pond?"

"Go down the trail, Mister, and follow the stream up the hill." The monk raised his hands with his palms touching, in honor of the Buddha nature within me.

I made the same gesture to him in return. "Thanks," I said and nodded.

∞∞∞

I WALKED ALONGSIDE THE STREAM, taking my time, listening to its humming and stopping occasionally to scoop up water in my hands, splash it on my face, and taste its drops on my lips. It was cool and sweet. The stream rushed and splashed against rocks, leaving behind little stagnant puddles. The golden dead leaves on the trail rustled under my shoes with a crunchy, crackling sound. Those that landed on the stream were carried away to the river to meet the sea, but the ones trapped in the puddles slowly rotted.

I stood quietly beside the puddle where dead leaves had decomposed. For the first time, I paid attention to such a common phenomenon and wondered if nature was telling me something. A falling leaf could not choose its destiny, but I could. I could choose to be sad and sorry for those I had lost, and pity myself for the remainder of my time on earth, or I could choose to stay the course, just like the leaf in the stream on its way to the river, and let Heaven decide when I should stop.

I heard the burbling sound of the waterfall and picked up my pace. As the trees thinned out, I saw the huge boulders and, behind them, a small waterfall gushing out from a crack in the mountain face. I climbed to the top of the boulders and saw a small crystal-clear pool under the waterfall. Not a single soul was in sight, so I took off my clothes and shoes and jumped into the pool naked. I felt the coldness all the way to my bones, but I managed to dive down to touch the bottom before I got out.

I was sure my whole body had been touched by the "magical" water of the Nine Dragon Pond, and I had an overwhelming feeling of satisfaction, despite several bouts of unstoppable shivering. The sun warmed me up, and I stood at the edge of the boulder to survey the land surrounding me. My eyes chased the stream until it disappeared behind layer upon layer of green trees. But in my mind, through the leaves of the trees, the stream's waters mingled with many of its kind along the way, leaving many puddles behind, before joining the Xijiang River on its way to the endless sea. I realized that life was like a little stream, moving ahead, leaving many little puddles of memory behind, but continuing to move until it joined all its own kind.

I left the mountains and felt the urge to whistle. As I biked away from the temple, the sun disappeared. I was tired, so I decided to sneak into our old place in the village to spend the night. I had locked the door when Ning and I left a year and a half earlier, and I hoped One-Eye Dragon had left the place alone. I knew that the peasants in the village, with the exception of One-Eye Dragon, would welcome my reappearance there, but I was in no mood to tell them about my escape attempts.

At Hong Kong's Victoria Peak, 1975.

I knew my way around and was confident that no one would see me, and I was right. Inside the room, the air was putrid. I opened the door to let in fresh air, lit the oil lamp, burned several mosquito-repellent sticks, and set them around me. Then I lay down on the dusty bed. Months of sleeping bare-chested on a cold concrete floor in detention centers must have built my tolerance to adverse sleeping conditions. As I stared again at the sky through the small glass tile above me, I thought about the little stream in the mountains and the many puddles it left behind. *It is time for me to say a final good-bye*, I thought.

I set off before dawn on my bike, with renewed spirits and hope, leaving behind the sound of the roosters. And I didn't look back.

CHAPTER 13

"HEY, HONG KONG! I'M BACK!"

I SOON RESUMED MY EARLY-MORNING lap swim in the pool. I smiled at the other young people there, who shared the same dream as mine. I even swam across the Pearl River alone a couple of times, with no fear of drowning. As the weather cooled, the swimming pool closed, and the first-time escapees and failed escapees both spent more time at home.

The final month of 1973 came. In Canton City, the signs of discontent were beyond audible. In one restaurant, a young man mimicked Mao's lip movements, without his dentures, and many others followed suit. I didn't join them, but I chuckled. No police-men came to arrest the impersonators. Everyone in the eatery was talking about escape to Hong Kong, some loudly, wanting to be noticed by others.

One day, to my surprise, Mellow Shrimp showed up on my doorstep. I had not seen or heard from him since graduating from junior high nine years earlier. He had been banned from attending senior high because of his father and had been working on a tea

With villagers and my two sons in front of Qingyun Temple,
Xiaoqing City, 1993.

farm ever since. He told me he had decided to escape and came to
me with a plan.

"Why me?" I asked.

"You're famous," he said.

"'Notorious' sounds better," I said.

The plan was to steal a boat and row into international
waters in the South China Sea. There we would meet up with a
Hong Kong fishing junk that would smuggle us to freedom. Mellow Shrimp's good friend on the tea farm had arranged for his
relative, a fisherman from a fishing village in Taishan, to steal a
sampan to bring the group to where the prearranged Hong Kong
smuggler's junk would pick us up. Taishan, a very poor region of
Guangdong Province, was about a hundred linear miles west of
Hong Kong, across the South China Sea. It was the birthplace
of the first group of Chinese Americans whom the white settlers
called "coolies" and "Chinks". Today the term "coolie" is largely

forgotten, but "chink" has survived, and I've been yelled at as such a few times.

Mellow Shrimp offered me a place on the sampan if I could find fellow escapees with relatives in Hong Kong who would pay the large sum of money to the smuggler when their relatives arrived in Hong Kong. I immediately thought of Uncle Lao. I told Mellow Shrimp I'd get back to him in a few days.

Mommy was excited. "Heaven has turned Its eyes on you!"

I said, "Let's see."

After I told him of the plan, Uncle Lao declared, "It's my time! My brother has a lot of money, so you've come to the right place." Uncle Lao had received money regularly from his brother, a wealthy businessman in Hong Kong, and also colorful nylon clothes, skin cream, and cologne with a pungent but nice smell. (Even in the heyday of the Cultural Revolution, Cantonese admired their bourgeois countrymen in Hong Kong, and many Cantonese saw themselves as more civilized and enlightened simply because they possessed unique things from Hong Kong.)

Uncle Lao paid particular attention to his looks and scent, and that worried me. "You need to wear different clothes and no strange odor when we escape," I reminded him.

"Don't worry. I've got it all figured out."

Uncle Lao went to Uncle Yu, another older fellow from the Rooftop Underground. Uncle Yu's relatives in Hong Kong also had a lot of money. Both of them told me that, together, their families in Hong Kong could pay the large sum of money needed for the smuggler. I was elated. My remaining job was to bring Uncle Lao and Uncle Yu, and their significant others, to the fishing village on the day of our escape. A piece of cake, I told them.

I asked Mommy to keep this plan secret from all our family members. I sensed that a leak of this operation would result in severe punishment. Stealing a fishing boat and conspiring with human smugglers would be considered a counterrevolutionary crime. So, when Teacher Fong unexpectedly showed up one day and asked me, "What are you waiting for? Your time is now," I feigned ignorance.

"Do you want me to freeze into an ice pop?" I said.

Teacher Fong laughed. "I don't know how you'll do it, but you don't want to miss your chance. Let me just be sure. I'll come see you tomorrow morning, so wait for me, and don't wash your face."

"Not wash my face?" I was perplexed.

"Washing will take away your *chi* aura."

The next morning, I patiently waited for two hours. Teacher Fong finally showed up after ten. While Mommy stood by watching, he pulled me close to the window and looked at my face from different angles. "I was right yesterday. Go now, and go as far away as you can, and remember: For your future, you should not get involved in politics. You aren't the type."

"I know," I said. "I hate dog fights."

Teacher Fong laughed. "And don't gamble, either."

"I would only gamble if you gave me the money," I said, and we laughed.

"Teacher Fong, if your prediction comes true," Mommy said, "I am going to take you to the best restaurant in town."

"Save your money, Mommy," Teacher Fong said. "I'll be in Hong Kong by then. It'll be my eighth attempt, a lucky number— and a record, I'm sure."

"Tell me the truth. Why so many times?" I asked sincerely.

"The truth is, I've been too desperate, and there were many con artists."

"That doesn't add up. Every capture costs you time in recuperation and planning. Seven times take a few years."

"That's your experience," he said. "Many times, I 'nailed the coffin' even before leaving Canton," he added, referring to his arrests. "Going through a revolving door at a checkpoint several times could make the policemen dizzy, if not yourself." Teacher Fong laughed out loud. Then he changed the subject: "You're amazing. Get to the finish line each time."

Teacher Fong was a calculating man, the kind of person who carefully selected what to say and when. Unlike me, he was the right kind of person for politics. And he eventually made it to Hong Kong—on his eighth try. I met him there a few times over the years. He had turned out to be quite nationalistic, and he hated America. That ended our friendship.

∞∞

THE DAY OF MY THIRD escape attempt finally arrived. I woke up very early, before even the first crowing of the neighbor's rooster. It was a fine day in December, and I expected a seamless encounter with the policemen on our bus ride. Our destination was not a normal one for "lying under a pile of dirt." Moreover, it was off-season for escape attempts, and we had authentic travel passes this time, prepared by a local fisherman. We were to attend a wedding in his village.

Mommy's eyes were puffy. I knew she must have been crying all night. On my desk was a hand-knitted red sweater that was almost complete. I touched the scratches on the desktop and said to myself, *I'll remember every one.*

I turned to Mommy. "Is the sweater for Yong Wei?"

"Yes. Winter is coming. He has no sweater."

"We're lucky to have him around. A good handyman, isn't he? You don't need me here anymore."

"Right now, I need you to fly away, far away."

I wanted to cry. "Yes, Mommy. But I'll write you every week."

"I know you will," she said softly.

"I'll miss home. I'll miss everything here."

"Everything will be here and won't change, don't worry," she said. "Listen, when you get to Hong Kong, I want you to change your name."

"Why? So that China will never catch me again?"

"Yes."

"I will."

"Remember, many rocks are in your way. Some will trip you, and others are for you to break. But Heaven will watch over you." Mommy touched my face and wiped my tears with her palm.

"You sound like Teacher Fong. A long time ago, you told me Heaven would talk to me through the mouth of a fortune-teller. Now you're the fortune-teller."

"Did I say that?"

"Yes, you did. I see it now. Heaven has opened Its eyes."

Yong Wei arrived to take me to the bus station. I took a long last look at the room, trying to burn everything into my memory before I hugged Mommy, crying again.

Mommy wiped my tears again and said, "Heaven will see you all the way to your New World."

Then, sitting on the rack of Yong Wei's bike, I left home.

Yong Wei turned his head to me. "I hope I won't see you for a long, long time."

"Well, you're right. I don't know if I can ever return to China. This land doesn't need me, and China doesn't want me."

"That's China's loss, brother. Can I call you that?"

"Of course, I'd be honored."

"It's stupid to push people like you away."

"You know, I must tell you I was wrong about you when we first met. You need to forgive me. If not for Mommy seeing the goodness in you . . ."

"Nothing to forgive, brother," he said. "Without Mommy, I would never have known how much I was missing in my life. I've found my home in your family."

"It's time for me to find mine." I said it quietly. "But I have no idea what's waiting for me."

We arrived at the Long-Distance Bus Station of Canton City. We hugged with great passion before we parted, then I walked across the street to meet Uncle Lao and his girlfriend and Uncle Yu and his wife. It was my job to take them via bus to where we would meet the fisherman. Mellow Shrimp and his friend had gone to the fishing village the day before.

"Slept well last night?" I asked Uncle Lao.

"Not really," he said. "But I'm excited now."

"Is the money ready?" I asked.

"Yes, ready to pay once we arrive in Hong Kong," Uncle Lao and Uncle Yu both said one after the other.

"Nervous?" I asked.

"A little," Uncle Yu said.

"That's normal. Just keep calm when you face the policemen here, and the militiamen at the destination, and stick to your story. No downcast eyes, yeah? The village is not the usual place for an escape." I smiled at them all. "Let's get this show on the road!" And whistling a happy melody, I led the way to the bus.

Several hours later, we arrived at the bus stop near the fishing village, where a young fisherman was waiting for us. "My job is to bring you five to my uncle's house to meet him, and then we'll head to the boat." He told us that the others, including Mellow Shrimp, were waiting for us in the boat.

To reach the fishing village where his uncle lived, we needed to cross a small river. The young fisherman told us there were several small rivers running to the sea, and the stolen boat waiting for us was in the river next to the one we were going to cross.

The dock was an old wood platform extending ten feet or so into the river, and the river was a couple hundred feet wide. When we arrived, the sampan was almost full. The operator yelled at us, "Two more spaces available! Any two of you want to come?"

The young fisherman shouted back, "Can you squeeze in six?"

"Hell, no! Only two of you. Come or not. Make up your mind!"

The young fisherman made a quick decision: He would take me to his uncle's first, to let his uncle know we had arrived. Then he'd return for the remaining four.

"Is it safe for them to wait by themselves?" I was not quite at ease, even though I had done my job and the young fisherman was in charge.

"No problem," he said, and turned to the other four. "Have a tea in the teahouse, and I'll return before your tea is cold." He pointed them to the shed by the bus stop.

As the fisherman and I hopped on the sampan, Uncles Lao and Yu and their companions headed to the teahouse. I didn't have a chance to say good-bye to them.

The young fisherman dropped me off at his uncle's house and immediately went back to get Uncle Lao's group. The uncle asked me to sit down and have a cup of tea. He was a quiet, stocky man in his fifties, and his rough skin was deeply suntanned. He told me the boat we would use had been assigned to him by the production team to fish with, and he knew the sea very well, for he had fished it since he was a teenager.

Suddenly, the young fisherman rushed in and said we must leave at once. He told us that when he returned to the dock, he discovered that the militiamen had arrested Uncle Lao's group.

"They are coming for us!" he told us.

Without saying a word, the old fisherman led the young fisherman and me through the village and across some fields. In the distance, we saw several men running toward us. We started to run. I was a pretty fast runner in school, but I could barely keep up with the fisherman and his uncle. Every time I looked back, it seemed the militiamen were getting closer.

"Don't look!" the old fisherman shouted at me.

Then I heard a gun firing, causing me to pick up my pace.

Finally, we reached the riverbank and ran toward the boat, where Mellow Shrimp and several others were waiting for us. We jumped on board, and the old fisherman swiftly pushed and pulled the scull—*yuloh* in Cantonese—back and forth, while the rest of us grabbed all available paddles to row furiously.

At last, we reached the sea. The old fisherman told us to lie down under a large black tarp. Through a gap between the tarp and the rim of the boat, I glimpsed many similar-looking boats fishing on the sea. I relaxed. It would be impossible for anyone to see what was going on with our boat because all the boats looked the same, and they were separated from one another by long distances. I told Mellow Shrimp what had happened to Uncle Lao's group. He didn't say a word; all the others were silent, too. The old fisherman slowly moved our boat until it was farthest away from the coast. The sun heated up the black tarp, and I began sweating profusely.

I started to feel bad for Uncle Lao and Uncle Yu and their loved partners. Why hadn't I told the young fisherman that we would all wait for the next ferry? If the young fisherman had been with them, they would not have gotten caught. Did I really have the good luck Teacher Fong predicted? Was separating me from Uncle Lao's group a plan from Heaven? I didn't dare think so.

Then I started to worry. I had a bad feeling that Uncle Lao and Uncle Yu had told the militiamen of our escape plan and that was why the militiamen were chasing us. What if the Hong Kong smuggler refused to take us tonight because we now didn't have the moneymen with us, and left us in international waters? We would have to return to the village where the militiamen were waiting. It was a torture to think about all the what-ifs. So, I gave up and instead thought to myself, *If I make it this time, I promise I'll respect Chinese face reading and fortune-telling.*

The old fisherman let the boat drift farther away from the coast. The sun had disappeared behind the ever-thickening dark clouds, and the sea started to turn rough. We pushed the tarp to the side, and I took a deep breath of cool, salty sea wind. Everyone was anxiously waiting, and no one had the desire to speak. We could hear clearly the sloshing sea beating the sides of the boat. The old fisherman pulled and pushed the scull, sending the boat toward international waters. The sea was getting rougher, and the rain started to fall, harder and harder. Darkness finally covered the sea and the sky.

Suddenly, the old fisherman said, "Cover up!" and he dipped the scull down and pulled it hard, to turn the boat around toward the coast.

Through the gap in the tarp, I saw a bright light sweep across the sea, missing us by only a short distance. The old fisherman kept moving the boat away from the beam. Lightning struck, revealing a navy ship moving away from us. As soon as it had gained some distance, the fisherman turned the sampan around, pushing and pulling the scull as hard as he could to drive the sampan toward open sea. Soon he stopped and let the nasty sea have control of the boat.

We didn't know how long we waited in silence before, suddenly, a flashlight blinked through the darkness in three sequences of two rapid flashes each. "Here they are! Everyone, up and row!" The old fisherman flashed a light back, and our boat moved fast toward the distant light. Soon, we heard the sound of an idling engine and saw a Chinese junk, just like those we saw in Zhujiang River: sail-less, high-sterned, with a projecting bow and a central deckhouse. Two men on deck gave us a hand as we climbed up onto it. Then the engine revved as we were sent down into the hold.

I paused and looked back, trying to find the coast, but I couldn't see a thing except the abandoned boat being beaten by a merciless sea. My tears fell, mixing with the rain, so no one could tell I was crying.

"Haven't seen enough?" I heard a crewman shouting at me as he pushed me back down into the hold. The door slammed shut behind me.

The sea voyage to Hong Kong was miserable. I threw up nonstop, and toward the end, I had only a scant amount of sour, greenish-yellow bile to retch up. Finally, the junk stopped, and the door to the hold opened.

I climbed up the ladder to have a look. The sun blinded my eyes. After they adjusted to the light, I saw that the junk was anchored in the middle of a bay. There were several other junks not far from us. The coast of Hong Kong was within a few hundred feet. But we weren't free yet. The smugglers first wanted to speak to the people responsible for paying them. They were furious when they learned we didn't have the moneymen on board. They accused us of deceiving them and threatened to throw us into the sea before pushing us back down in the hold and slamming the door shut to keep us in the dark. We heard them shouting at one another above us in the deckhouse. They were arguing about whether to throw us into the sea far away from the coast.

I don't know how long they argued before they stopped. It seemed very long. Then the door opened, and we were told to climb out. We were led to the shore in a small boat. Common sense had won the smugglers over. They apparently preferred taking a monetary loss over risking being arrested for murder in addition to smuggling. On shore, we were led to a road where two mini vans were waiting. We were finally free.

Aboard one of the vans, I saw newspapers scattered over the floor. The front page of one of them was about Royal Club horse racing. As we entered the Lion Rock Tunnel, in Kowloon, the driver turned up the radio, playing a beautiful and familiar song sung by the famous "Golden Voice," Teresa Teng. When the van exited the tunnel, countless sparkling skyscrapers rose in front of my eyes under a clear blue sky.

My heart cried, *Hong Kong! I'm back!*

SO MUCH HAS CHANGED, YET
MUCH REMAINS THE SAME

IT WAS MAY 1975. THE red cotton trees were in full bloom. I walked out of the U.S. Consulate General in Hong Kong with a warm and fuzzy heart. I had been intimidated by the guard at the entrance, who was dressed in an imposing marine uniform, but the tall young white man in the office said to me, in peculiarly accented Mandarin, "Welcome to America," and shook my hand after he'd stamped "Political Refugee Conditional Entry Visa Permit" on my Hong Kong resident passport. He agreed with Mommy that going to university was "a great choice." He was the first person with authority to tell me he was "sorry" for asking me to wait a few minutes, and "thank you" for my patience as he brought me into his office. How could America have such a nice government officer? I was just a nobody, in Hong Kong or in China.

The officer was serious about making sure I was truly from Canton City, as stated in my visa application. He showed me a large, detailed map of Canton and asked me several very specific questions. Of course, I passed with flying colors. America seemed to

Escapee group in Hong Kong. From left: Hay's brother Mau, Ning, Uncle,
Lily, me, Hay's escape partner, and Mellow Shrimp.

like the refugees of China more than the citizens of Hong Kong. The
Hong Kong woman in the Blue Cross office spent hours putting my
story in English for the American consulate, without asking me to
pay a penny, but she told me she only did this for Chinese refugees.
The world had turned upside down!

Across the street from the U.S. consulate was the tram station to the Peak, a must-see sight, and the one most mentioned by
freedom swimmers. I had not been to it yet, but Ning, Hay, Uncle,
Mellow Shrimp, and Chunky all had. I decided it was time for me
to visit it. I had to see it before I left for America.

The tram ride was noisy and slow, but it gave me plenty of
time to see the gorgeous views of Hong Kong. From the Peak, the
world below was spectacular, filled with skyscrapers of all shapes
and sizes, all so tightly packed together that I couldn't identify any
street where I had "left the hairs of my feet" during my countless

"walks on the streets"—Hongkongers' name for the work I now did as a salesman.

Standing on the Peak, with Hong Kong at my feet, I was proud to have such good knowledge of this land. *I will surely miss you, Hong Kong!* Looking to the north, I knew that behind those mountains was my home, where Mommy was preparing lunch. I imagined Pei pulling at Mommy's clothes, wanting her attention. Pei was almost five, and her mother, Lily, was already in America—a Cinderella story I'll tell later. Pei could not understand why her mother, aunt, and uncle had all wanted to go to America. *Who is America?* I seemed to hear her asking.

Mommy couldn't have imagined I was thinking of her while atop the Peak when I was supposed to be working. I wanted to tell her that Ning and I had our American visas and would soon join Lily in Seattle. I wanted to tell her that I had changed my name to the one she gave me before my last escape. Armed with my new name, and living in a land thousands of miles away from China, I would never again fear being caught by Mao, even if China took back Hong Kong.

But most of all, I wanted to tell Mommy that every night, I listened to the cassette tapes I'd bought at the night market, and when the American song "Yesterday Once More" came on, I'd cry. And I wanted to share with her a line from the poem we all knew so well, "May we all be blessed with longevity, / though thousands of miles apart, / to share the moon's graceful beauty."

∞∞∞

FOR OUR FAMILY, 1974 WAS the beginning of the period when family members other than Ning and me got out of China. It started with a surprise for Lily. Nixon's 1972 China visit had opened the door for Chinese Americans to visit China. Two years later, a member of Seattle's U.S.–China People's Friendship Association, Bill Chew, came to Canton to visit his godmother. Bill had lost his parents in China many years before. He'd left China at a very young age, masquerading as someone else's son after the 1943 repeal of the 1882 Chinese Exclusion Act. His godmother was also Lily's godmother, a kind and caring woman and a longtime family friend. Before Bill arrived, Lily had divorced her husband and had had custody of Pei for five years. Bill and Lily met and fell in love. After Bill returned to Seattle, he applied for "fiancée conditional entry" for Lily and, with the help of the then state governor, quickly obtained approval. China let Lily go. She arrived in Hong Kong in the fall of 1974. Ning and I went to the train station to welcome her. It was an emotional reunion.

In February 1975, Lily left Hong Kong and arrived in Seattle. Reporters from the local newspaper and the TV crew of Channel 5 interviewed her. She was the first Red China citizen to leave China legally as a fiancée of an American citizen.

"I didn't understand all the fuss," Lily recalled, "but I remember the Chinese official warning me not to say anything bad about China before giving me the passport."

ooooo

I left the Peak and walked straight down to the Central district. I wanted to tell Papa's colleague Mr. Zeng that I was leaving Hong Kong to go to America. Mr. Zeng had once worked with Papa in the customs office in Hong Kong. He'd stayed in Hong Kong, and had warned Papa not to join the insurrection. He encouraged me to go to America and found a financial guarantor in Pennsylvania to guarantee that I would not be a public burden on the United States for my first five years there.

Zeng's office was way up in the building—the first skyscraper I'd ever visited.

Back when I first visited it, I was nervous taking the lift—it would be a first for me. Standing in front of it, next to a crowd of sharp-looking white men in three-piece suits, I hesitated when the elevator car arrived and one of them held the door for me. "Are you coming?" he asked. And once in the car, I didn't know how to get it to stop at the floor I wanted, but that was easy enough to find out—everyone touched a numbered button on a shining plate.

This time, though, I was an "old" Hongkonger and had been up and down many lifts many times. I'd dressed presentably for the consulate visit and was feeling great at the thought of soon becoming an American, just like the men next to me waiting for the lift. I held the door and signaled to them to get in before me.

In his office, Mr. Zeng congratulated me. "Your papa deserved a break. If he'd stayed in Hong Kong, his office would be higher up than mine." I'd learned that the higher one's position in the company, the higher his office. That made no sense to me. I was once on a high floor when a typhoon hit. The floor under my feet moved from side to side. Scary! *If I were the boss, I'd stay on the ground floor*, I thought.

Mr. Zeng insisted on giving me five hundred Hong Kong dollars as a farewell gift, but I promised to pay him back when I made money in America.

From the Central district, I paid twenty cents to ride the upper level (first class) of the Star Ferry for the first time across the harbor. I had always taken the lower level, to save ten cents. But I wanted to try first class once before I left Hong Kong. As a salesman, I had many dealers in Kowloon and Hong Kong, and the Star Ferry was my choice for crossing Hong Kong Harbor.

In about a year, I had built up a roster of more than one hundred dealers of our product, the Konica, an AM-FM stereo/ cassette player. It was the first one designed and built by a Hong Kong manufacturer. We had to compete against big Japanese names such as Sony, National, and Aiwa. In Tsim Sha Tsui, the tourist district, my dealers had made more money per cassette player simply because their foreign buyers didn't really know about the Japanese products, and our Konica was much cheaper. North of Tsim Sha Tsui, Konica was easy on the pocketbook for the working class, too. As a salesman, I was persistent, and never took no for an answer.

During my visit to a dealer, if the manager was busy, I'd dust his shop displays and help out with his customers. I'd also move our cassette player to a more visible spot, and the manager usually didn't mind.

Off the ferry, I walked along Nathan Road, heading north. I stopped in front of the shop of a Konica dealer. I remembered the shock on the faces of the customers there two weeks before, as they stared at the TV sets showing a helicopter evacuating Vietnamese and Americans from the rooftop of the American embassy in Saigon as that city fell to the Vietcong. The voice of one teary-eyed old woman was still fresh in my mind: "We are no longer safe," she said. I took a deep breath. I was leaving Hong Kong just in time!

From Nathan Road, I turned left onto Lai Chi Kok Road, where Uncle and Chunky had opened a tiny shop to repair TVs and cassette players. Their shop was the new gathering place for the ex–Rooftop Underground during dinner hours. We cooked and ate and joked and laughed—just like in the old days. They were happy for me, and thinking about going to America as well. A few years later, Uncle came to Seattle to become an electrical engineer, and Chunky went to Vancouver, British Columbia, when the British handed Hong Kong over to China, but he stayed in Hong Kong most of the time to make money as a capitalist. His biggest enterprise was turning a ten-thousand-dollar loan from his uncle into inexpensive Taiwanese-made radios sold by young people he hired on the cheap. Shouting, "This radio will win your horse!" they sold the devices fast to hopeful gamblers as they headed to the Happy Valley Racecourse in Causeway Bay. A few hours later, most of the radios would be slammed to the ground as the disappointed horse bidders headed to the exits.

Uncle showed me new photos of Hay. He had taken a job on a cargo ship to see the world. The pictures showed him with some local kids in South America. Hay would miss our departure for the States, but I did meet up with him before he went overseas. We took some pictures together to send to Mommy. If you remember, Mommy was his godmother.

After Lily settled down in Seattle, Bill gave Hay the financial guarantee he needed to come to Seattle, too. He would go on to earn an electrical engineering degree from the University of Washington and later worked for IBM and then Intel.

Mellow Shrimp told me he wanted to come to the airport to bid me good-bye. He had also set his heart on America. He worked in the Mayflower Restaurant on Nathan Road and thought he might need to work as a cook to support himself in the New World. In early 1976, he emigrated to New York. I met him there during my bus trip to the East Coast.

The shop of my employer, Tall Guy Zeng, was a block from Uncle's. Tall Guy Zeng and his partners ran an electronics shop and did most of their business in wholesale. I told him I was going to America, and he didn't say a word. "I'll list all my dealers and their selling capabilities and credit worthiness for you," I told him. "There are more than a hundred." I added, "And before I leave, I'll teach the two new salesmen how I run the business."

Tall Guy Zeng stared at me with his sharp hawk's eyes. "I was looking forward to making you a lot of money, making *us* a lot of money." He sighed. "But you do what your heart tells you."

I had built a good relationship with Tall Guy Zeng. When Chunky introduced me to him a year before, he was not a pleasant man to deal with. "Tell you what. Many from the Mainland are lazy," he'd said. "I'll try you out for a month without pay, but the meals in the store will be free. You'll know whether you'll stay or go in a month. I won't need to fire you." That was my crash course in Capitalism 101. Then he handed me a Konica cassette player. "I've got the sole right to wholesale this baby. You go door to door to the dealers, get their orders."

No wonder Hong Kong is so far ahead of China. One must get things done!

My experiences in detention centers had prepared me to deal with all kinds of people, in the Mainland of the past and now in Hong Kong. Plus, I was persistent and never gave up. Orders started to flow in. Tall Guy Zeng saw this, but kept it to himself. I was busy running all day, from the New Territories in the north to Repulse Bay in the south, then buying cheap dinner from a street food vendor before heading to my evening English class. During my walks, I'd take a few short breaks in the shops with good air-conditioning, to combat my sweating.

One day, Tall Guy Zeng said, "Take a break, Little Wong, and follow me." We hopped in a taxi and headed to a tailor's shop in Tsim Sha Tsui.

In the taxi, Tall Guy Zeng told me that we had opened up the market for Konica, and the manufacturer had set up an office in Wan Chai. I would need a three-piece suit because I was now to be the sales manager, with two salesmen and two secretaries beneath me. He paid the tailor five hundred dollars. This shocked me. "You need to go in style," he said. Then we took a taxi through the undersea tunnel to see the new office. The tunnel was so noisy that I was uncomfortable, and asked, "What if the water leaks into it?"

The taxi driver said lightly, "We'll all die."

I said, "I don't want to die in this stupid tunnel under the sea after I risked my life trying to cross it from the top."

They both laughed. And then I laughed. That was my only encounter with the tunnel.

I returned to my ten-cent Star Ferry crossings to the Central district and my trolley rides to the office. I put on my jeans and short-sleeve shirts, leaving the high-class three-piece suit in my tiny apartment.

I told the two new hires that there was no secret to my success, "If you spend more time walking the streets and not in chatting with the secretaries, you'll do great."

∞∞∞

FINALLY, IN 1978, WHEN I was a senior at the University of Washington, great news came. Mommy and Pei were leaving China to come to America as the relatives of Lily. By then, Lily had become a U.S. citizen. She and Ning asked me to greet Mommy in Hong Kong. (We were all poor back then, and air fare was expensive for us.) I flew to Hong Kong and paced the train station platform from morning until the last train from Shenzhen pulled in. When Mommy and Pei finally arrived, it was a moment that would stay with me forever: talk and tears and laughter until we were exhausted emotionally and physically.

Later, in the hotel, as Pei bathed for the first time in a bathtub and played with the temperature valve of the gas water heater, she said so loudly that we could hear, "This is the true happiness of my life!" She was only eight years old.

∞∞∞

SEATTLE BECAME OUR AMERICAN CHINESE neighborhood. We all stayed in the same apartment building, on Bellevue Avenue in Capital Hill. During our heyday, we were many: Mommy, Papa, Ning, Bun, Uncle, Hay, Hay's brother Mau, Mellow Shrimp, his mother and sister, Hay's escapee pal Mar, and I—a Cantonese dozen! We all went to the community college to take free ESL classes. After class, Mommy, Lily, and Ning would work for Roffe, a well-known ski apparel company. The owner, Sam Roffe, had built his company from the ground up. He was loved and respected by all the seamstresses, mostly Chinese and Spanish immigrants. They called him Ah Ba, "Father" in Cantonese. His "children" would bring food for him to try; he seemed to like everything they offered. Lily and Bill would invite him home to dine, and I'd join them. When Ning and I had saved enough money for a down payment on a car, but couldn't find a lender for the rest, Roffe said, "Follow me." He brought us to the bank next door. The people there stood up to greet him.

Roffe said, "These two young people want to buy a car. Please take care of it for me." And that was it.

When the news came that he'd finally succumbed to throat cancer, I cried.

∞∞∞

PAPA LEFT CHINA WHEN I was in medical school. He was so happy that his son had been accepted to Harvard that he wrote to tell everyone, relatives and friends. This made me uncomfortable. I asked him not to do it, to no avail. Finally, he told me that his mother, my grandma, whom I had never met, wanted him to be a doctor, but he could not fulfill her wish. "But now our family has two!" Papa said. "Besides, people will respect me more." I could only shake my head—again saving face.

Papa didn't come to Seattle right away. He stayed in Hong Kong and got a job as a manager at an import/export company trying to cash in on China's economic boom. Again, his distaste for corruption got him nowhere in the "new" China, where corruption had escalated on a grand scale.

∞∞∞

IN THE WINTER OF 1982, before I'd graduated from medical school, I went back to China for the first time. Chunky kept telling me China had changed and didn't care about our having been escapees.

"Relax. Especially for you. You're holding an American passport! It's a golden pass."

But my heart beat faster and my palms sweated as the train approached Shenzhen station. My last time there, I was in handcuffs. Now the conductor took a close look at my passport and my face, emotionlessly, and then moved on. During the trip, Jing brought me to Beijing, where I met my future wife—I still didn't want to cut my ties with China.

I like the people, I feel the people, and I should always separate the government from the people, I thought as I watched kids picking up Coca-Cola cans from a large pile of garbage across from the restaurant where I was feasting with family friends, served by several eager and exceedingly polite young waitresses.

Between 1982 and 1984, Bun, followed by Jing, her husband, and their son, Roget, arrived in Seattle. Bun met her future husband at Shoreline Community College, where she was learning English. Several years later, Jing and her husband divorced, and Jing got custody of Roget. In this, she was supported by all except Papa, who shook his head. Jing excelled in her job at a research lab in the Department of Ophthalmology at the University of Washington Medical School. She was the coauthor of many research papers published in the journal *Neuron*, with her immunocytochemistry images appearing on the cover of seven issues. She got remarried, to Dan, a nice fellow working in the same department. Mommy and Dan formed a strong bond, one that crossed the language barrier and surprised and touched me.

Thus, 1984 was the year my family finally *physically* detached from Mainland China. But the memory of our thirty-three years in China—from 1951, when we moved to Canton when I was three, to 1984, when Jing's family left China—will linger until the end of our lives. As for our children and their children and so on, when our stories fade from their memory, China will eventually become just another interesting foreign country.

ooooo

As for me, on June 26, 1975, my sister Ning and I landed in Sea-Tac International Airport. Bill and Lily welcomed us. But my New World started with a shock. Bill's good friend Alan, a well-known restaurateur in Seattle's Chinatown, offered me a job: three dollars an hour to scrub filth from the restrooms, kitchen, and oven in an abandoned restaurant he'd bought and planned to reopen. The place had been closed for several years. The work was dirty and boring. *Is this my American Dream?* I asked myself. I missed the fun of "walking the streets" in Hong Kong and the comfort of my office chair, which I could turn to face the beautiful Hong Kong Harbor way below.

During the new restaurant's grand opening, Alan patted my shoulder: "You've done a good job," he said, as I collected dirty dishes from the table of Washington's governor, Dan Evans. I had started to work as a busboy there after school.

In the summer of 1975, I started an ESL course at Seattle Central Community College. Bill gave me a piece of advice: "Listen, this is the white man's country. You must work twice as hard to get ahead." I have remembered his advice ever since. But the remark that hurt me most came from one of the ESL teachers, an immigrant from Hong Kong. When I said that I planned to study medicine, he laughed at me in front of the class.

"Even Americans have a hard time getting into a medical school. You should just forget about it."

But I didn't want to forget about it. *Shouldn't be harder than escaping China!*

I didn't fall asleep that night. Finally, I made a decision: I'd form new friendships only with those born in America, so I could learn English faster. I'd ask my friends to correct my English and tell me everything about my new country. But they seldom corrected my mistakes; Americans are not like Chinese. Still, they introduced me to things, like peanut butter and spin fishing.

In the fall of 1975, I started my studies at Shoreline Community College, north of Seattle. After my first year, I went to the Office of the Registrar at the University of Washington. After the woman in the office read my transcript, she said, "Congratulations on your four-point-oh GPA. What is your TOEFL score?"

"What's TOEFL?" I asked.

She looked at me and smiled. "Let me make a suggestion: Finish two years at Shoreline, then apply as a transfer student. But make sure you take English One-oh-one."

Once I'd made my plan to stay at Shoreline for one more year, I bought a one-month Greyhound pass to see America. This was in the summer of 1976, when America was celebrating its bicentennial. I had saved money for the trip. For $165, I could go anywhere the bus went for a full month. I had already sent Mr. Zeng $500 with a nice note, to pay him back for his loan.

The bus trip opened my eyes. It shocked me how wide open, seemingly untouched, and gorgeous the landscape was along Highways 90 and 80. After a day sitting on the bus, and before sunset, I was dozing and my back was hurting. Through the dirty window, I saw a cloud of dust. As it settled, a barefoot girl wearing a cowboy hat appeared on horseback before me. How romantic! Before I could take a good look, she turned the horse and disappeared inside the rolling cloud of dust.

Damn! What if I could change places with her? Chasing a cloud of dust on my bike on the county road back in China had been such minuscule fun compared to hers. No wonder the Marlboro commercial before the movie I saw in Hong Kong—a white horse running free and wild across the vast, gently rolling hills— had appealed to me. I carried this spirit in my genes. But only in

America could I let it blossom. (By the way, I don't smoke; it makes me cough.)

I got off the bus in Philadelphia to pay a visit to the financial guarantor who'd aided me in my visa application. He was a physics professor with a nice family. I thanked him for helping me and told him I was studying at college and working as a busboy in the evenings—and that I would not become a financial burden to him. He didn't know anything about my family, and he had never met Mr. Zeng. He had just felt that helping a stranger was something he should do. What a good man!

Later, I visited the Liberty Bell. It had a crack in it. Staring at it, I tried to picture how its sound vibrated the *hearts* of the people to come together to form a government of the people, by the people, and for the people. In China, we tore our vocal cords and cracked our eardrums to shout, declaring the government of the Communist Party, by the Communist Party, and for the Communist Party. *How many Chinese Americans have noted this difference?* I wondered at that moment.

I arrived in New York City and met Mellow Shrimp at Grand Central Terminal, which was crowded and noisy. My first words to him were "Are we in Hong Kong?" Mellow Shrimp laughed. In those days, people joked about Seattle: "Are the Indians still riding horses on the streets?"

Mellow Shrimp and I went to the Statute of Liberty. As I read the famous lines "Give me your tired, your poor, your huddled masses yearning to breathe free," my heart cried again. *Too many people around me. I must hold back my tears.* When I returned to Seattle, I typed the lines and taped them at the bottom of the photo of me standing in front of the Mother of Exiles.

Mellow Shrimp left New York after two years to join us in Seattle. He was too lonely in New York with only a tiny dog he loved dearly. He went on to graduate from the University of Washington and become a civil engineer for Boeing.

My trip across the country gave me the urge to know more about America. With my limited English, I took a full year of American history. It was more time consuming than studying math, physics, and chemistry combined—too much reading and too many new words. Unlike the Chinese history class, where we'd used one textbook approved by the Communist Party, in America many scholars wrote their take on important historical events such as the Civil War, and the reading list for the Civil War was several books long. But I'm glad I did it, and proud—all foreigners see America's surface, but its history opens the door to its soul, something visible only to humble and curious minds. I came away from my study of America happy, for I saw I had chosen the best home. I even formed a friendship with my teacher, who invited me to his house for a nice dinner, my first time dining with an American family.

I graduated with a perfect GPA, and Shoreline put me on the dean's list. I was accepted by the University of Washington without taking TOEFL because I got a 4.0 in English 101. I majored in chemistry. The thought that solid matter like my body was merely a mass of itty-bitty speeding particles spinning, hugging, bouncing, and bumping into one another fascinated me. Could I pass another body through the gaps beteen those particles if I were small enough?

I did well in chemistry, and when I graduated, the department gave me two awards and hung my name twice in the entry hall. America was like China in putting a student's name up on the wall. But in China, everyone's name was on the wall, with the best scorer listed at the top.

I applied to several top medical schools and kept their names to myself. I didn't even tell Mommy—I was afraid I couldn't get in any. I took my second trip to the East Coast for the interviews. The easiest interview was with a professor emeritus of pediatrics at Harvard. The building was stately, and the office was huge.

"Would you like a cup of coffee or tea?" he asked.

"I'm fine."

"Let me suggest tea?"

"Thanks."

"Black or green?"

"Just like yours," I answered.

"I have English tea. Milk?"

"No," I said.

"Sugar?"

"No, thanks."

He then turned to his secretary: "I would like to spend time with this young fellow alone without interruption."

She closed the door on her way out. After we sat down, he said, "Tell me everything about your escape. I don't believe you had time to do the extra curriculum."

I said, "I didn't. I tutored freshman calculus."

He smiled.

I don't remember how long we talked. It seemed long. At the end, he said, "It'll be good to have you. Take care!"

I held back my tears until I'd walked down the stone steps of the entrance. *I want to come here. They treat me like a friend,* I said to myself.

I was accepted by Harvard, Yale, U Penn, UC San Francisco, and the University of Washington, among others. I chose Harvard because they treated me like a friend. When I graduated in 1983, the Dean's Report wrote a full page of my background and included my picture with the Statue of Liberty and my reason for attending Harvard Medical School.

Mommy and Papa came to my graduation ceremony, and teared up with joy. They told me it was the proudest moment of their lives. That made me cry.

ooooo

I GOOGLED THE ESTIMATED NUMBER of freedom swimmers to Hong Kong during the Cultural Revolution. According to a source in Hong Kong, it was about 550,000. For sure, China will never disclose a more accurate number, even if it could. As for the number of those who died during their escape attempt, I couldn't find this

Mommy and Papa at my graduation from Harvard Medical School, 1983.

anywhere online. I alone knew sixteen freedom swimmers (including Ning and me); among them, three died at sea.

Today, most freedom swimmers still reside in Hong Kong. Many of them have achieved great success. Those who chose to come to America as political refugees have become naturalized American citizens. Many of them went on to excel in various professions and fields.

These political refugees contribute their hard work and talent to America, and I am one of them, and proud of it. For us, America has become our new home, our only home where we have rooted our family trees. But we still love Cantonese food more than American food, still care about our parents, and still drive our children to excel, often excessively. We just can't help it.

What a journey! So much has changed, yet much remains the same.

ACKNOWLEDGMENTS

WHERE SHOULD I BEGIN? FOR a native Chinese speaker to write
a book for English readers—is it possible?

Yes, only because I had three great individuals holding my
hand, guiding me along each step of the process—and perhaps
Heaven opening Its eyes, wanting my story to be told. Well, let's
skip the Heaven part.

Who are they?

They are my editor, Jamison Stoltz of Abrams Press; my
agent, Albert Lee of UTA; and writing consultant Corbin Lewars
of Seattle's Hugo House.

Jamison gave me the most meticulous and insightful editing
suggestions. His questions, together with his knowledge of China,
brought out the best in my writing, prompting me to tackle complex
political events, their human costs, and my personal feelings about
the China of a half century ago. He is respectful, and that made
me comfortable sharing with him my thoughts and feelings. I am
indebted to him—no exaggeration—for making me work harder.

Albert and I shared the emotions embedded in this memoir;
this brought both of us to tears—and that was how we started our
agent-client relationship. How often does one come across such an

emotional bond in our materialistic world? Add to that his vision for the book, his hard work, and quick, creative thinking—and what more could I ask for?

Corbin edited my screenplay, based on the same story. It was she who suggested, sincerely and firmly, that I write a memoir. With reluctance, I wrote the first twenty-some pages. She was elated. Thus, my writing journey began. It was emotional for both of us, and we shared laughs and tears. She guided me to keep the story tight, flowing, and following a dramatic arc. My several-month writing journey turned us into friends.

I see that the world needs different voices; its people want to hear different voices. And it contains brave people with foresight like these three individuals, who want to propagate such voices through the medium of books. For that, they must be acknowledged and thanked.